Praise for Advocating for English Learners: A Guide For Educators

"This book makes a very important contribution to the field by highlighting the importance of advocacy and, through its numerous examples of advocacy in action, showing how to achieve equitable and excellent education for ELs."

—Diane August, Principal
D. August and Associates

"Staehr Fenner delves into the many facets of school-centered advocacy that promote the educational advancement of English language learners. Her thorough treatment of the roles of many stakeholders— including teachers, school leaders, district administrators, and family members—in viewing linguistic and cultural diversity from a strength-based perspective is motivation to read this valuable resource."

—Margo Gottlieb, editor of Academic Language in Diverse Classrooms series
Director, Assessment & Evaluation, Illinois Resource Center and
Lead Developer, WIDA Consortium

"Diane Staehr Fenner coaches her readers on how to develop a much needed, decisive voice of advocacy. She makes a most compelling case for educators to share the responsibility for teaching English learners within and outside the school. A must read for all teachers, administrators, teacher educators, and policy makers!"

—Andrea Honigsfeld, Professor and Author
Molloy College, NY

"This book will equip educators with the research and the courage needed to make sure their EL students succeed. A true treasure trove of answers—whether the reader is a veteran educator of ELs, or someone who is new to the profession and the field, this book will improve practice, no doubt about it!"

—Giselle Lundy-Ponce, Associate Director
American Federation of Teachers, Washington, DC

"Just when you thought no one could hear you above the din of everyday life as an educator, Diane Staehr Fenner has written a book that demonstrates a broad understanding of the challenges we face. Advocating for English Learners *is a great opportunity to engage colleagues in the reflective and collaborative discussions critical to needs assessment and proactive program development to address the needs of some of our most vulnerable citizens and newly arrived immigrant students. This book should be part of every pre-service and in-service program for teachers and administrators who serve English learners. The challenge is not what we can do for our students. Our challenge is to create learning environments that recognize and energize the potential of each child and each family to contribute to our communities."*

—Anne Marie Foerster Luu, TESOL, International Teacher of the Year, 2013
Montgomery County Public Schools and McDaniel College, MD

education program for ELLs. And she does so with a refreshing perspective, using clear, real-life examples and providing guidance about how to implement those promising practices and tackle challenges along the way. Staehr Fenner's work will no doubt dispel the myths and encourage positive changes for ELLs in our schools."

—David G. Nieto, Division Administrator
Division of English Language Learning, Illinois State Board of Education

"It's evident from the first pages that Diane Staehr Fenner knows what it's like to be in a classroom, hallway, or meeting where English language learners and their needs are being overlooked or marginalized. In this essential new book, she gives teachers the framework and the tools we need to advocate effectively and ensure our students the seat at the table they so deserve. I would recommend this book to anyone who educates ELLs, and since today that is nearly everyone in education, it could not be more timely. These beautiful, multi-talented children are the future. Thank you, Diane, for helping to make our voices stronger on their behalf."

—Barbara Page, ESL Teacher
Meadow Park Middle School, Portland, OR

"Wow! This is the first book I have encountered which is devoted solely to the area of advocacy for English language learners (ELLs). In education, where the effects of political and judicial decisions are apparent, this is a very much needed book in guiding future educators and inservice teachers to be strong catalysts in advocating effectively for the academic success of ELLs."

—Arlene Costello, 2007 Christa McAuliffe Educator/Teacher on Special Assignment
ESOL Department, Escambia County School District, Pensacola, FL

"In this timely and utterly necessary book, Staehr Fenner explains why all educators need to advocate for English language learners, based in solid yet accessible research, and how to do so with the supporting resources and activities provided. She guides readers in understanding and implementing 'scaffolded advocacy,' including effective instruction for ELLs. Margins notes included throughout will allow teacher educators to easily use this as a training manual for pre-service and in-service teachers working with ELLs. Finally, the personal anecdotes, stories, and vignettes from the field leave the reader with the crucial message of the book: everyone can and should be an advocate."

—Heather A. Linville, TESOL Instructor and ELL Advocate
College of Arts and Sciences, American University, Washington, DC

Advocating for English Learners

A Guide for Educators

Diane Staehr Fenner

Foreword by John Segota

A Joint Publication

CORWIN
A SAGE Company

tesol
international
association

CORWIN
A SAGE Company

FOR INFORMATION:

Corwin
A SAGE Company
2455 Teller Road
Thousand Oaks, California 91320
(800) 233-9936
www.corwin.com

SAGE Publications Ltd.
1 Oliver's Yard
55 City Road
London EC1Y 1SP
United Kingdom

SAGE Publications India Pvt. Ltd.
B 1/I 1 Mohan Cooperative Industrial Area
Mathura Road, New Delhi 110 044
India

SAGE Publications Asia-Pacific Pte. Ltd.
3 Church Street
#10-04 Samsung Hub
Singapore 049483

Acquisitions Editor: Dan Alpert
Associate Editor: Kimberly Greenberg
Editorial Assistant: Heidi Arndt
Production Editor: Amy Schroller
Copy Editor: Cate Huisman
Typesetter: C&M Digitals (P) Ltd.
Proofreader: Jeff Bryant
Indexer: Judy Hunt
Cover Designer: Glenn Vogel

Copyright © 2014 by Corwin

Printed in the United States of America

A catalog record of this book is available from the Library of Congress.

ISBN 978-1-4522-5769-3

This book is printed on acid-free paper.

SUSTAINABLE FORESTRY INITIATIVE

Certified Chain of Custody
Promoting Sustainable Forestry
www.sfiprogram.org
SFI-01268

SFI label applies to text stock

14 15 16 17 10 9 8 7 6 5 4 3 2

Contents

Foreword

When Diane Staehr Fenner asked me to write the foreword to this book, I began to think about my own experience with the TESOL field and what I had come to observe over the past decade and a half of working for TESOL International Association. With a background in political science and international studies, I had come to the association with an interest in working for an international nonprofit, but I had little knowledge of the TESOL field. As I began to learn more about the rich and diverse world of TESOL, I quickly came to admire and respect the uniqueness of the academic discipline and the expertise of those working in the field.

I also saw a field that was more than language teachers and researchers. With aspects of social justice and multiculturalism embedded at its core, the TESOL field is perhaps unique among all academic disciplines. Regardless of where they are working, or the level they are working at, I saw that those in the field have a deep passion for their students, often putting the needs of their students ahead of their own.

This passion and advocacy for their students is not only important, but is vital. In countries where English is the dominant language, English learners are often the most marginalized student population. In the United States, English learners are often from disadvantaged backgrounds, so they must contend not only with the challenges that other disadvantaged students face but also with linguistic and cultural differences that can be barriers to academic achievement. Those in the TESOL field understand this perhaps better than any other group of educators, and this positions them in a way to serve as some of the most effective advocates for their students.

This is crucial, as in many cases TESOL educators may be the only people advocating for the rights and needs of English learners. Like the parents of other particular student populations, such as special needs students, the parents of English learners may be marginalized, perhaps more so than other parents. Because of linguistic and cultural barriers, unfamiliarity with school systems, or even concerns over immigration status, parents of English learners often feel they are not in a position to advocate for their children, and thus there is often no one left to speak up but the TESOL educator.

In English-dominant contexts, English learners are automatically perceived to be immigrants, and thus they may also have to contend with societal attitudes that may not be the most supportive. For example, it is well documented that the majority of English learners in U.S. schools are born in this country. In addition, the Supreme Court of the United States ruled in 1982 that immigration status has no bearing on a school-age students' right to a public education. Despite these facts, it is not uncommon in some contexts in the United States for English learners to be dismissively referred to as "illegal immigrants" and a drain on resources. Even where there is no overt hostility, English learners are often viewed as a problem that could be solved with a quick-fix solution.

Fortunately, education policy has shifted in the United States over the past 15 years to more explicitly acknowledge the needs of English learners; however, they are still quite misunderstood. They are often treated as a monolithic block in terms of education policy, despite the fact that English learners as a population are incredibly diverse in terms of culture, language, socioeconomic status, and educational background. Even though they are the fastest-growing student population in the United States, much of the policy focused on English learners is developed secondarily or as an afterthought. For example, when the Common Core State Standards (CCSS) were published in the United States in 2010, they did include some discussion on the needs of English learners, but little else. It wasn't until a year later that new initiatives were announced that sought to address the needs of English learners in the CCSS.

This lack of understanding and attention impacts not only English learners, but the TESOL field itself. The unique pedagogy of the TESOL field is often not fully understood by others in education, never mind the public at large. In fact, despite a rich history of research and other academic bone fides, the TESOL field is one that is chronically misunderstood, even among its peers in education.

There are many common misperceptions about language teaching and second language acquisition that impact the TESOL field itself. For example, one of the most common myths is that any native English speaker can teach the language, or that native English speakers make better TESOL educators. Another common myth in English-dominant contexts is that ESL (English as a Second Language) is simply a remedial activity and not a core academic subject. Misperceptions such as these have often undermined the status of the field and the many programs that serve English learners.

In the United States, resources to support ESL programs have been at best stagnant over the past decade. Federal funding for ESL primarily comes from two sources: Title III of the No Child Left Behind Act of 2001 (NCLB),[1] which serves elementary and secondary education, and Title II of the Workforce Investment Act of 1998 (WIA), which serves adult education. Despite the fact that the English learner population has increased steadily over the past 10 years, neither program has received any major increases in federal funding. The EL/Civics grant program, created through appropriations in 1999, targets adult education funding at programs that combine ESL and civics education. It remains funded at the same level now as it was then (approximately $75 million) and is still awaiting authorizing language in statute. Moreover, cuts in education funding at the state and local levels have had the effect of a net decrease in funding for ESL programs in some locations.

There are a variety of other factors that do not help the status of the TESOL field. For example, in the United States, NCLB does not include ESL as one of the core academic subjects defined by the law. In addition, the requirements for teaching K–12 ESL vary tremendously from state to state in the United States, representing a broad range of credentials and requirements. For adult ESL, there are few credentials available. These issues compound many misperceptions about the field, so much so that TESOL educators must advocate not only for their students but also for themselves.

Just as many education policies consider English learners as an afterthought, so too many policy decisions fail to consider the needs of TESOL educators or include them in policy conversations. I've heard from several educators active in the field that they grew tired of waiting for invitations to participate in policy discussions, because after a while they saw those invitations were not just going to come. Instead, they realized they needed to invite themselves.

Whether it's advocating for their students, their programs, or themselves, the need for action by TESOL educators is clear. Moreover, TESOL educators can be effective at any level. Advocacy in the classroom or in the building is just as important as advocacy within the district. Advocacy at the state level is just as important as advocacy at the national level. Where it's done, advocacy by TESOL educators is vital, so much so that advocacy is included in TESOL International Association's P–12 Professional Teaching Standards and the English as a New Language (ENL) Standards for certification by the National Board of Professional Teaching Standards.

---

1. Under federal law, funding for language instructional programs is to come from state and local education funds. Title III funds are to be supplemental only and are not to serve as the primary funding source for language instructional programs.

As a closing thought, I was leading a discussion recently at a workshop for TESOL educators being run by a local TESOL affiliated association. As part of the conversation, one local educator discussed the preservice training she received that related to advocacy. While there was some significant work in terms of understanding education policy, there was very little training in terms of how to address advocacy issues (such as unequal policies or students' rights issues) once they come up. In her experience as a TESOL educator, it wasn't a matter of *if* these issues would come up, but rather *when*. "If you aren't interested in getting involved and advocating for your students," she concluded, "then you probably might want to consider another field of education."

John Segota, CAE
Associate Executive Director for Public
Policy and Professional Relations
TESOL International Association

Preface

As a newly minted English as a Second Language (ESL) teacher in a rural school in the southeastern United States, I was asked the following question by a nervously laughing fourth grade teacher: "Could you please try to have José's mom keep him[1] home from school next week during state content testing?" While this teacher appeared to be joking, I knew there was a great shred of truth behind her request. Prior to the reauthorization of the Elementary and Secondary Act (ESEA) in 2001, commonly called No Child Left Behind (NCLB), states were beginning to phase in high-stakes content area testing.

This classroom teacher surely knew that José, an English learner (EL) born in the United States to a mother who had never received any formal education in her home country of Mexico, would not perform well on the end-of-year content assessment delivered in English. She also knew there might be consequences for her career due to his potentially low test scores. José was years behind grade level in all aspects, especially in reading and writing, and still qualified for ESL support after nearly five years in an English-only academic environment. José was a frustrated kid who was starting to act out in class, because he realized he wasn't meeting his teachers' expectations or keeping up academically with his classmates.

I knew I needed to help provide a voice for this student, because he did not know his rights, and his mother, with no proficiency in English and illiterate in her native language, Spanish, was not in a position to speak up on his behalf. I needed to advocate for him because at the time I didn't think anyone else was going to do so. I had never heard the word *advocacy* in any of my teacher education courses, nor had I known that to make a positive impact on ELs' educational experience and increase their chances for academic success, someone had to speak up for them.

Although I didn't realize it at the time, the experience I had teaching ESL in this rural community in the Southeast significantly shaped who

---

1. All student, teacher, and administrator names appearing in this publication are pseudonyms unless otherwise indicated.

I am as an educator and most of all as an advocate for ELs today. I often look back on my first years as an ESL teacher in the United States as some of the most challenging yet most rewarding years of my career. Those years helped me see the stark inequities ELs can face, develop strategies for advocating for ELs, and set the course for my present work with teachers, administrators, and researchers to ensure that ELs receive the educational opportunities they are entitled to.

Fast Forward

More than a decade later, while presenting about the revised TESOL P–12 Professional Teaching Standards at the TESOL International Association convention, I mentioned how TESOL's professional standards contained a new focus on advocacy for ELs. I explained how the standards reflected recent changes and heightened responsibilities for those who teach ELs and that advocacy for ELs is central to the role of the ESL teacher. I showed how the TESOL P–12 Professional Teaching Standards helped define this need for ESL teachers to advocate for ELs in K–12 settings.

At the end of the presentation, a professor in an ESL teacher licensure program who was in the audience asked me if there were any books on advocacy for ELs that I could recommend to her. I answered her that I did not know of any book she could use in her program that could help her teacher candidates learn about advocacy for their ELs.

Immediately after that presentation, I met some colleagues for lunch and shared the outcome of this presentation with them and how I thought the field of EL education could benefit from at least one book focused on advocacy for ELs. As I told them this, I realized that my career path had been built around my role as an advocate for ELs. I had been advocating for ELs all along and knew so many others that were also advocates for ELs. I suggested to my colleagues that I could be the person who attempted to write this book, and they wholeheartedly supported this idea. In the spirit of collaborating to best serve our ELs, I would now like to share this book.

Acknowledgments

Writing this book has been a true joy for me, but I could not have written it without the support and assistance of many colleagues. The process of writing this book has been a collaborative effort, and there are many people whom I wish to thank.

I offer my appreciation to the practitioners and experts who shared their rich experiences and perspectives on advocating for English learners in this book. These individuals include Tim Boals, Catherine Collier, Jennifer Connors, Ayanna Cooper, Paul Gorski, Laura Kuti, Susan Lafond, Esta Montano, Kate Montgomery, Margarita Pinkos, Lorraine Valdez Pierce, and Sara Waring. I wish to thank them for lending their voices. A special thank you goes out to Ayanna Cooper for sharing her experiences as well as helping me with the Ice Age lesson found in Chapter 6.

I would like to point out several colleagues who provided assistance with some aspects of the literature reviews found in this book: Linda Fink, Anthony Garces-Foley, Laura Kuti, and Sydney Snyder. Their thoughtful digging for relevant research helped ground and strengthen each chapter of the book.

I am especially thankful for Sage Publications' senior acquisitions editor Dan Alpert for believing English learner advocacy was a worthy topic when I initially suggested the idea to him. I would like to express my sincere gratitude for his patience and gentle guidance from this book's start to finish. I have learned and grown so much while working with Dan. In addition, I would like to say thank you to the Corwin team, including Megan Bedell, Kimberly Greenberg, and Heidi Arndt, for supporting my work through all aspects of the publication process, and to Cate Huisman for her attention to detail while editing the book.

I would also like to recognize those colleagues in the field of English learner education who have provided me moral support as I undertook this project. This list includes Rosa Aronson, Diane August, Lydia Breiseth, Margo Gottlieb, Giselle Lundy-Ponce, Lesli Maxwell, Luciana de Oliveira, Heather Linville, John Segota, Lynn Shafer Willner, and Debbie Zacarian.

Finally, I would like to acknowledge my mother Jean Staehr, late father August Staehr, and brother Edward Staehr for instilling in me a love of literacy (Mom), hard work ethic (Dad), and interest in my heritage language and culture (Ed) while growing up in our farm family. The combination of these factors was essential for me to be able to write this book.

Publisher's Acknowledgments

Corwin gratefully acknowledges the contributions of the following reviewers:

Margaret Adams
Director of Language and Literacy
Malden Public Schools
Malden, MA

Rene Cooper
ELL Teacher
Northgate Middle School
Kansas City, MO

Lizette D'Amico
K–12 ELL Coordinator
New Canaan Public Schools
New Canaan, CT

Jacqueline Hickey
Elementary ESL Facilitator
Westerville City Schools
Westerville, OH

Luz Jorges
Support Coach, Curriculum and Instruction
Chicago Board of Education
Chicago, IL

Esta Montano
Director, Office of English Language Acquisition and Academic Achievement
Massachusetts Department of Elementary and Secondary Education
Malden, MA

David Nieto
Research and SEI Professional Development Coordinator
Massachusetts Department of Elementary and Secondary Education
Malden, MA

Heidi Perez
ELL District Facilitator
Lawrence Public Schools
Lawrence, MA

Diane Senk
ELL Teacher
Pidgeon River School
Sheboygan, WI

Marlene Torrez-Graham
ESL Community Outreach and Parent Liaison
Westerville City Schools
Westerville, OH

About the Author

**Diane Staehr Fenner** is the president of DSF Consulting, LLC, a woman-owned small business that supports the achievement of English learners (ELs). Her company creates and delivers professional development, designs curriculum, conducts research, and provides technical assistance to clients. Clients include the American Federation of Teachers, American Museum of Natural History, Center for Applied Linguistics, Council of Chief State School Officers, Florida Department of Education, Massachusetts Department of Education, National Education Association, SEED Schools, and World-Class Instructional Design and Assessment (WIDA). Dr. Staehr Fenner is also the National Council for the Accreditation of Teacher Education (NCATE)/Council for the Accreditation of Educator Preparation (CAEP) program coordinator for TESOL International Association, where she oversees the application of TESOL's P–12 Professional Teaching Standards to teacher licensure programs throughout the nation.

Prior to forming DSF Consulting, Dr. Staehr Fenner gained research and EL policy experience at edCount and George Washington University's Center for Excellence and Equity in Education. Her instructional background includes a decade as an ESOL teacher, dual language assessment teacher, and ESOL assessment specialist in Fairfax County Public Schools, Virginia. Dr. Staehr Fenner has served as an expert on numerous EL education committees and was a committee member to revise the National Board for Professional Teaching Standards' English as a New Language Standards. She is a frequent presenter at conferences across the nation. She writes a weekly Common Core blog for teachers of ELs for the Colorín Colorado website. Her first book, coauthored with Natalie Kuhlman and published by TESOL International Association, was *Preparing Effective Teachers of English Language Learners* (2012).

I dedicate this book to all educators who share the responsibility—and joy—of teaching English learners.

I also dedicate this book to my husband David and children Zoe, Maya, and Carson Fenner—for always supporting me and for being as proud of me as I am of them.

Introduction

One of the more unspoken and unexplored factors which is central to the success of English learners (ELs) in K–12 schools is teachers and administrators serving as effective advocates for these students. While ELs are the most rapidly growing segment of the U.S. PreK–12 population, they do not always possess a strong voice in their own education due to many factors that may work against them such as their developing English language skills, their parents' unfamiliarity with the U.S. school system, and their families' level of understanding of community resources that are available. Yet, despite all of these challenges, ELs bring multiple strengths to the educational landscape. The time has come for us to approach the education of ELs from an advocacy perspective, defining and operationalizing the multiple forms advocacy for ELs can take so that teachers and administrators can be better poised to provide them an equitable as well as excellent education in the United States.

Advocating for English Learners focuses on supporting teachers and administrators as they examine their views on advocacy for English learners and develop their EL advocacy toolkit to better support ELs' success. The goal of the book is for all educators to share the responsibility for teaching ELs and to hone their advocacy skills for ELs inside and outside the walls of the classroom. This book is intended to start a much needed conversation around EL advocacy in four overarching ways. First, the book creates the argument that advocacy for ELs is essential for ELs' academic success. Second, it provides tools for determining educators' beliefs and awareness around educating ELs. Third, it helps individual educators as well as groups of teachers, administrators, schools, and districts prioritize which facets of advocacy are in need of their attention. Fourth, it uses hands-on application activities to shine a light on how to improve advocacy of ELs in the areas that warrant further action in their specific context.

This book is applicable to multiple audiences, including pre-service teachers, current ESL teachers, and content or general education teachers.

The book's content is also relevant to school administrators, district administrators, and state administrators. It can be used for individual professional development efforts or as part of a larger professional development initiative at the school, district, or state level. Professors in teacher education programs will also find the content of the book useful, as it is the first book of its kind to focus solely on what it means to advocate for ELs at the K–12 level.

All chapters contain margin notes which will help readers reflect on the content and relate the content back to their particular context. Each of the chapters is grounded in relevant research and begins with a section titled What the Research Tells Us. The chapters then contain examples of advocacy efforts taking place in different areas of the United States. Most chapters contain quotes and examples of how different types of educators advocated for ELs in their contexts. All chapters contain a framework for choosing areas of advocacy to focus on and implement in readers' contexts.

Chapter 1: Need for Advocacy for English Learners. Chapter 1 presents the research base that supports the call to better advocate for our nation's English learners. This chapter also defines the concept of advocacy for ELs that will frame the contents of the book. Chapter 1 also describes the increased focus on advocacy in the National Board for Professional Teaching Standards as well as TESOL International Association's P–12 Professional Teaching Standards. While this chapter contains frequent references to research, the chapters that follow contain more of a focus on practical applications of research on facets of advocacy for ELs.

Chapter 2: Creating a Shared Sense of Responsibility for Teaching English Learners. The focus of this chapter is on the need to create a sense of shared responsibility to teach ELs and on some steps teachers can take to help shift their colleagues' thinking on this topic. The chapter contains several exercises to gauge educators' feelings toward working with ELs. It is also intended to build educators' empathy for ELs by providing them a sense of what it feels like to be an EL with low English language proficiency. The chapter also contains an activity that will help readers gain more perspective on the EL parent experience.

Chapter 3: How ESL Teachers Can Collaborate to Expand Advocacy Efforts for ELs. The focus of Chapter 3 is to provide an advocacy overview directed at—but not limited to—ESL teachers. The chapter examines advocacy from the unique perspective of ESL teachers and offers suggestions on how ESL teachers can help influence other educators to share the responsibility for teaching and advocating for ELs. It offers many hands-on activities for self-reflection and application of information presented.

Chapter 4: Advocacy Overview for School and District Administrators. Chapter 4 approaches EL advocacy from the perspective of school and district administrators. It contains considerations for creating a culture conducive to EL advocacy, hiring staff who share a disposition toward effectively educating ELs, and providing professional development to staff. Other topics include interacting with EL parents, considering how teachers of ELs are evaluated through teacher observations, and creating effective policies related to EL education. Chapter four presents several ideas for how to advocate at the school or district level even when resources are scarce and funding is tight.

Chapter 5: Increasing EL Families' Involvement Through Building Their Advocacy Capacity. Chapter 5 examines advocacy for EL parent and family involvement and offer ideas for harnessing educators' creativity and flexibility to increase EL family involvement in their children's education. The chapter examines the makeup of EL families, their hierarchy of needs, and provides a snapshot of the different forms EL family involvement can take. It offers opportunities for educators to examine their expectations of EL family involvement and provides insight into EL families' perspective on their children's education. The chapter suggests many examples of creating an environment that is welcoming to EL families and that values their language and culture. The chapter provides options to circumvent typical challenges EL families face in terms of school involvement. Finally, Chapter 5 focuses on providing tools so that EL families can learn to advocate for themselves.

Chapter 6: Advocacy Through Effective Instruction of ELs. Chapter 6 provides considerations and examples of how EL advocacy is intertwined with the effective instruction of English learners. This chapter focuses on what *all* teachers of ELs can do to instruct ELs more effectively, drawing upon their students' strengths and providing extra support to address their potential linguistic and cultural challenges. The chapter shares some considerations and exemplars in instructing ELs and culminates with a content unit based on the Common Core State Standards that models multiple effective EL instruction strategies.

Chapter 7: Advocacy for ELs in Assessment. Chapter 7 takes on advocacy of ELs in assessment issues. It focuses on equitable assessment of ELs for placement in ESL programs and exit from those programs. In addition, it examines how to advocate for ELs' thoughtful inclusion on formative assessments and summative content and annual English language proficiency assessments. It examines how to advocate for ELs when they are referred for special education consideration. Finally, it addresses ELs' inclusion in gifted and talented programs from an advocacy perspective.

Chapter 8: Advocacy for ELs' Success Beyond Grade 12. The final chapter examines advocacy for ELs so that they will be on a path that will lead them toward graduation and meaningful employment or postsecondary education. Chapter 8 includes considerations for advocating for ELs' placement in courses that will lead to their graduation. It also offers suggestions on ensuring ELs take and succeed on Advanced Placement courses. Finally, the chapter provides guidance on how educators can advocate for their ELs to take part in the college application process and/or to be prepared when seeking employment.

1 Need for Advocacy for English Learners

Ms. Ritter, an English as a Second Language (ESL) teacher at a midwestern elementary school, has been a teacher for seven years. She has noticed the population of her ELs rise dramatically during her tenure, and she has also become keenly aware of her shifting role within her classroom as well as within the larger context of her school. She has gone from being "only" a language teacher to taking on responsibilities beyond teaching that include helping her students' families acquire affordable housing, translating documents for parents, providing professional development to grade-level general education teachers on using EL strategies, and trying to persuade her principal to devote more resources to the school's ESL program.

Frankly, Ms. Ritter is starting to feel burned out this year, as she senses she is fighting an uphill battle. In her eyes, her principal is not fully on board that the school culture needs to become more accepting of its EL population and take the extra steps necessary to ensure their academic success as well as their emotional well-being. Ms. Ritter absolutely loves working with her ELs, who bring rich linguistic and cultural diversity to her school. However, she is not sure where she should turn for some additional support to help her school draw upon and realize her students' full potential. She has just learned that another school with a large EL population is going to be hiring an ESL teacher and is considering applying for the position, as she knows the other school's principal has embraced its EL population. She is not sure what to do.

CONTENT OF THIS CHAPTER

This chapter will outline the areas that provide the theoretical framework for the book, drawing on EL demographics, research, and recent events that support the argument that educators must consider approaching the education of ELs from an advocacy perspective in addition to focusing on EL education solely from an instructional stance. In order to effectively teach ELs, all educators who work with these students must realize that they share the responsibility to teach these students who have so much to offer. This chapter contains multiple references to theory and research, so please keep in mind that subsequent chapters are more focused on the application of information you will read in this chapter.

After providing a definition of EL advocacy that will be used in this book, I will present theory and research in such areas as the achievement gap, teacher preparation to work with ELs, the EL deficit paradigm, and applicable social justice theory that will situate this advocacy perspective and allow for you to apply it throughout the book. The chapter will conclude with an examination of the new focus on advocacy for ELs highlighted in the influential TESOL (Teachers of English to Speakers of Other Languages) P–12 Professional Standards and in the National Board for Professional Teaching Standards (NBPTS) English as a New Language (ENL) Standards.

CALL FOR AN ADVOCACY PERSPECTIVE ON TEACHING ELs

Given the challenges of teaching ELs as well as the often unpublicized multiple joys and rewards that come from supporting ELs to achieve in school and beyond, there is a need to focus on EL education from a new perspective. There is a growing number of methods and resources available for teaching ELs (e.g., sheltered instruction observation protocol or SIOP, specially designed academic instruction in English or SDAIE, and various software products), but none of these resources focuses on providing an equitable education for them from an advocacy perspective.

Specifically, the often unexplored concept of advocacy for ELs lies at the heart of teachers' expectations for ELs, their interactions with these students, and their ability to support their students' success through collaboration with colleagues, administrators, and the community as a whole. In short, a content area or general education teacher can be trained on many of the academic strategies necessary for ELs to achieve (e.g., scaffolding content instruction, creating appropriate formative assessments, teaching language and content simultaneously). However, if that teacher does not first buy in to the idea that ELs are capable of achieving with some extra support, and if that teacher doesn't share a sense of responsibility for teaching ELs so that they can achieve, that teacher will be less likely to successfully implement the instructional strategies that are known to be effective.

In order to be effective advocates for ELs, educators[1] must be aware of the areas in which ELs require advocacy efforts and the reasons these efforts are needed. Educators will also benefit from explicit instruction, ideally at both the preservice and inservice levels, in advocacy tools in order to serve as a voice for their EL students who might not yet be able to advocate for themselves.

Defining Advocacy

The majority of teacher education courses that prepare general education and content area teachers do not include instruction on teaching ELs (Ballantyne, Sanderman, & Levy, 2008), much less on how to advocate for ELs' equitable education. We can extrapolate from that research base that there is not one common definition of what it means to advocate for ELs so that they can receive an education that is equitable when compared to their non-EL peers[2]. This book will begin by providing a working definition of advocacy for ELs that will ground the rest of the book's contents and applications.

The *Oxford English Dictionary* defines an advocate as "a person who publicly supports or recommends a particular cause or policy" or "a person who puts a case on someone else's behalf." The dictionary further describes *advocate* as the Scottish and South American term used in place of the terms *barrister* or *attorney*. The term *advocate* echoes its cognates in Romance languages—*abogado* (Spanish), *advogado* (Portuguese), *avocet* (French)—meaning *attorney*, or representative of others who cannot effectively represent themselves. The notion of serving as someone's attorney involves taking actions on that person's behalf (Athanases & de Oliveria, 2008). Similarly, Dubetz and de Jong (2011) note that advocacy emphasizes acting on behalf of others.

The definition of advocacy for ELs I will use in this book draws upon both definitions and is based on acting on behalf of ELs both inside and

---

1. I will refer to teachers and administrators collectively as educators.

2. The term *non-EL peers* refers to those students who are either native English speakers or who do not qualify for ESL services due to their high level of English language proficiency. However, non-EL students may still speak or be exposed to a language in addition to English in their homes.

outside the classroom. I define advocacy for ELs as working for ELs' equitable and excellent education by taking appropriate actions on their behalf. To me, advocacy for ELs means stepping in and providing a voice for those students—and their families—who have not yet developed their own strong voice in their education. Advocacy for ELs also means knowing about each of my EL students' and families' backgrounds to be able to know which appropriate action I need to take on each person's behalf. It is not a one-size-fits-all approach, as each EL and his or her family differs from the next in terms of which kinds of advocacy are needed for them.

Scaffolded Advocacy

The concept of advocacy that will be used in this book is further influenced by the concept of *scaffolding*. Scaffolding is an instructional strategy that provides ELs an appropriate level of support as they access content material in a language in which they are developing proficiency. One of the basic principles of scaffolding instruction for ELs is that the teacher must know his or her ELs' backgrounds, including their linguistic, cultural, and socioemotional strengths as well as areas of need in order to determine which scaffolds to use and also when to remove the scaffolds. Because no two ELs are exactly the same, the types and amounts of scaffolding used for one EL (e.g., visuals, graphic organizers, first language support) will be different from the types and amounts of scaffolding used for another EL with a different background. In addition, teachers who are familiar with scaffolding for ELs also know that scaffolding is not meant to be a permanent support to ELs. By their very nature, scaffolds should be gradually removed as ELs' levels of English language proficiency (ELP) increase. In this way, the students eventually do not require scaffolded instruction, as they have developed enough ELP to access content and achieve without scaffolding alongside their non-EL peers. It is our goal as teachers of ELs to help get our students to a place where they no longer require our scaffolding.

Much like scaffolded instruction, the concept of advocacy for ELs that will be used in this book is one of *scaffolded advocacy*. Educators tend to advocate more actively for ELs who fit into one or more of the categories below, although the list is by no means exhaustive:

- Are at lower levels of ELP
- Are newly arrived to the United States
- Are from lower socioeconomic groups in the United States
- Attend schools in which there are low rates of EL achievement and/ or graduation

- Are from families who are most unfamiliar with their children's educational rights and community resources in the United States
- Come from families whose levels of ELP are at the lower end
- Belong to families who have limited or interrupted educational backgrounds
- Have undergone trauma

It is known that ELs will require fewer instructional scaffolds to access challenging content as their ELP levels increase. Similarly, educators anticipate that ELs will require fewer advocacy scaffolds in order to obtain an education that is equitable with that of their non-EL peers as they and/or their families acquire more English, become more familiar with the U.S. educational system, and develop their own voices as advocates for themselves. It is educators' task to help connect them with available resources and help them use these resources in order to achieve in the U.S. context. In short, educators' goal is for ELs and their families to be able to advocate for themselves. Educators therefore need to share the responsibility for teaching ELs as their voices grow stronger by providing temporary advocacy scaffolds to help ELs and their families become their own advocates in the U.S. educational arena.

> How do you define advocacy for ELs? Are your advocacy efforts static or are they dynamic? Why is this so?

EL DEMOGRAPHICS

Now that the concept of advocacy has been established as it will be used in this book, attention will shift to several key changes that have created the need for educators to develop their advocacy efforts around ELs. First, the number of ELs in P–12 classrooms who are learning English continues to grow. More than 10% of the P–12 population across the United States is composed of English learners (National Clearinghouse for English Language Acquisition, NCELA, 2011). ELs constitute a growing presence across the United States. Six states experienced more than 200% growth in their preK–12 EL populations between the 1999–2000 and 2009–2010 school years. See Figure 1.1 for a representation of this growth. In addition, the EL school-age population has grown more than 63% since the 1994–1995 school year, while the non-EL school-age population has only increased slightly more than 4% (NCELA, 2011).

> What are your school, district, and state EL demographics? What is your EL rate of growth? Which languages do your ELs speak? Which countries do they come from? Why do they move to your area?

Figure 1.1. PreK–12 EL Population Growth From 1994–1995 to 2009–2010

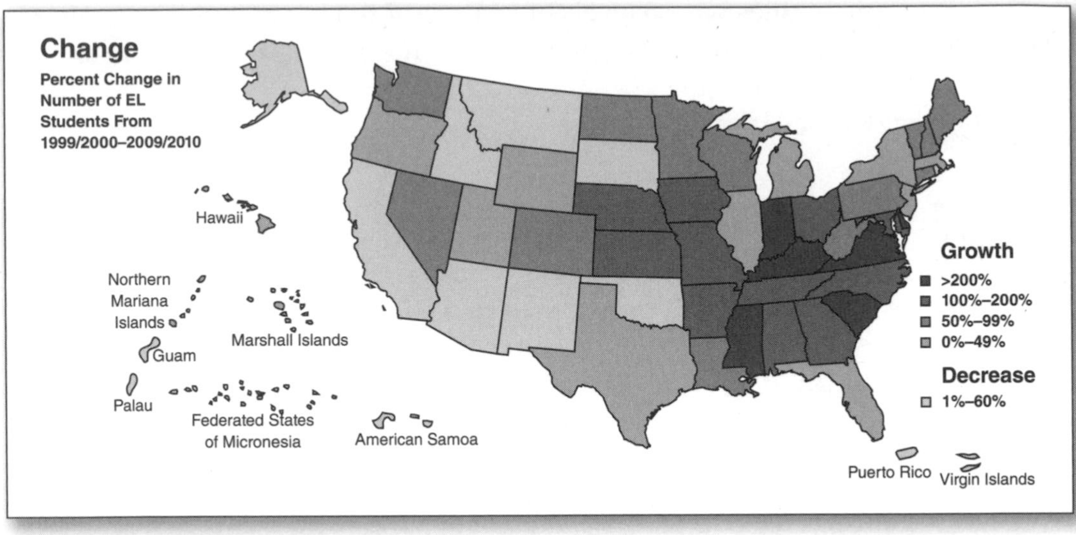

Change

Percent Change in
Number of EL
Students From
1999/2000–2009/2010

Hawaii

Northern
Mariana
Islands

Guam

Palau

Marshall Islands

Federated States
of Micronesia

American Samoa

Growth
■ >200%
■ 100%–200%
■ 50%–99%
□ 0%–49%

Decrease
□ 1%–60%

Puerto Rico   Virgin Islands

Source: NCELA, 2011.

EL ACHIEVEMENT GAP AND UNDERLYING REASONS

In addition to the sheer numbers of ELs that cannot be ignored, another area that points to the need for advocacy for ELs is the achievement gap between ELs and students who are considered to be non-ELs. Non-ELs are either native English speakers or former ELs who have exited from language support programs or placed out of them upon initial assessment of their English language proficiency.

Researchers acknowledge that EL students' achievement scores are lower than those of non-EL students (Abedi, 2002; Fry, 2008). There is also a gap between high school completion rates as well as attainment of post-secondary degrees by ELs versus non-ELs (Kao & Thompson, 2003; National Center for Public Policy and Higher Education, 2005; Reardon & Galindo, 2009). While many theories exist to explain this achievement gap, five will be highlighted in this chapter: socioeconomic status, teacher preparation to work with ELs, administrator preparation to work with ELs, ELs' access to academic English, and EL families' involvement in their children's education. There is some overlap of categories, and knowing where the categories overlap is important when considering how to improve ELs' achievement through the lens of advocacy.

How does your school's EL achievement rate compare to your school's non-EL achievement rate? How does the achievement rate vary by ELP level?

Socioeconomic Status

One reason that has bearing on the achievement gap between ELs and non-ELs is socioeconomic; that is, ELs frequently live in poverty. ELs often attend schools that serve students living in poverty, as defined by eligibility for free and reduced-price lunch (Fry, 2008). They tend to attend public schools that have low standardized test scores, high student/teacher ratios, and high student enrollments. Other researchers have determined that nearly 60% of adolescent ELs qualify for free or reduced-price lunch (Ballantyne et al., 2008). Wilde (2010) found that ELs who live in poverty score worse in math skills and reading achievement than non-ELs. When ELs are not isolated in low-performing schools, their gap in test score results is considerably narrower (Fry, 2008; Wilde, 2010). While there is a difference in achievement among ELs living in poverty and those who do not live in poverty, educators cannot view poverty as an excuse not to educate ELs.

> What percentage of your school's ELs receive free or reduced-price lunch? How does that percentage compare to the percentage of your school's non-ELs?

Access to Academic English

Another reason to explain the achievement gap between ELs and non-ELs is the role academic language plays. ELs' ability to access the content they must learn in order to be successful in school and beyond is predicated upon their ability to acquire and use complex academic language. All teachers of ELs, including content area teachers and ESL teachers, face the challenge of teaching academic language and challenging content simultaneously to ELs—quite often without sufficient resources to do so. While several definitions of academic language exist today, many have defined academic language as being distinguished from nonacademic language on several cross-cutting levels: lexical/vocabulary, grammatical/syntactical, and discourse/organizational (Bailey, 2010; Gottlieb, Katz, & Ernst-Slavit, 2009; Scarcella, 2003, 2008).

Teacher Preparation to Work With ELs

With the large number of ELs enrolled in schools across the nation coupled with the increase in the number of ELs far outpacing the growth in numbers of non-ELs, one might expect that all teachers would be fully trained in working with ELs. However, only 20 states require that all teachers have training in working with ELs. Furthermore, the breadth, depth, and quality of this training varies widely (Ballantyne et al., 2008). In addition, certification requirements for ESL teachers vary by state (Ballantyne et al., 2008; Education Week, 2009). The growing, linguistically and culturally diverse student population in K–12 U.S. schools is taught by a mostly monolingual English-speaking teaching staff (de Jong & Harper, 2008). In sum, the majority of teachers have not been fully prepared to effectively teach English learners.

To begin to address the need to prepare teachers for diverse learners, in recent years, multicultural education and diversity issues have been added to the curriculum of preservice and inservice teacher education programs in many U.S. universities (O'Neal, Ringler, & Rodriguez, 2008). Even if teacher education programs include a focus on multicultural education, de Jong and Harper (2008) posit that changes in individuals' attitudes and values will not be sufficient to prepare all teachers for the growing linguistically and culturally diverse student population.

Due to this unevenness in teacher education policies, it cannot be assumed that content area teachers[3] and ESL teachers share a uniform degree of knowledge about how to effectively teach ELs. In general, due to their differing levels of teacher preparation, many content area teachers as well as some ESL teachers are not fully equipped with the skills to be able to effectively educate ELs with multifaceted backgrounds, strengths, and challenges (Staehr Fenner & Kuhlman, 2012). This lack of uniformity in the preparation of teachers has created a national patchwork approach to teacher credentialing that does not serve the best interests of the growing population of ELs, nor the field of ESL and bilingual education.

Despite the necessity for teachers to teach content and language simultaneously so that ELs can achieve, most ELs spend the majority of their days with content area teachers who are likely not trained in working with them (Ballantyne et al., 2008). This lack of training can affect the learning of ELs. Most teachers, both ESL and content area, who work with ELs typically receive a low percentage of inservice professional development time devoted to how to instruct these students (Zehler et al., 2003). With the growing numbers of ELs in U.S. schools today coupled with the ever-persistent achievement gap between ELs and non-ELs, effective professional development of teachers who work with ELs should be a top priority for schools, districts, and states.

> What are your state's requirements for ESL teacher certification? What are your state's requirements for training content or general education teachers to work with ELs?

---

3. Content area teachers are defined as teachers who teach subjects other than ESL (e.g., science, mathematics, music, English language arts, etc.).

Administrator Preparation to Work With ELs

In addition, school administrators also often find themselves unprepared to lead their teachers to teach ELs. The principal's role is critical in strengthening a positive school culture, which includes the values, beliefs, and norms that characterize the school (Deal & Peterson, 2009). In strengthening a school culture that supports high achievement for all ELs, shared beliefs at the school level include the benefits of multilingualism, an appreciation of ELs' culture, and the need to overcome stereotypes and a deficit paradigm. The principal influences this culture in serving as a key spokesperson for the school, as an evaluator of practices, and as a model of commitment to student success (Alford & Niño, 2011).

Lack of EL Parents' Voice in Their Children's Education

Another frequently cited reason to explain ELs' tendency to achieve at levels lower than those of non-ELs is the general lack of EL parental involvement in their children's education. Research shows that parental involvement positively affects student achievement (Ferguson, 2008). However, parents of ELs tend to participate in their children's education less than parents of non-ELs.[4]

Some barriers that tend to inhibit EL parental and familial involvement include English language proficiency of families, parents' educational level, differences between school culture and parents' home culture, and logistical challenges such as securing childcare, finding transportation, and taking time off from work (Arias & Morillo-Campbell, 2008; Tinkler, 2002). In fact, although EL parents may place a high value on education, they might find it very difficult to relate to their children's U.S. school experience or understand how to help their children succeed in the U.S. school environment and continue on to post-secondary education (Suarez-Orozco, Suarez-Orozco, & Doucet, 2004).

> What role do EL families play in their children's education at your school?

UNRAVELING THE DEFICIT PARADIGM OF ELS

These factors that explain the EL/non-EL achievement gap point to a deficit paradigm in which ELs are viewed primarily for their insufficient level of English proficiency and lack of familiarity with U.S. culture. How-

---

4. The terms *families* and *parents* are used here interchangeably, as ELs may live with parents, they may live with extended families, or they may live with both parents and extended families. Chapter 6 explores family involvement in their children's education.

Miami-Dade County Public Schools (Florida) was recognized in 2012 with the Broad Prize for showing a great level of academic performance and improvement while reducing achievement gaps among poor and minority students. Miami-Dade is the fourth largest school district in the United States, and its student population is 65.9% Latino. Twenty-one percent of the district's students are ELs, and 74% of the total student population is eligible for free and reduced-priced school lunch. One effort that led to the district making such gains among achievement results is that district leaders have worked to create a districtwide culture focused on achieving results. Alberto Carvalho, the district superintendent and an English learner himself, is widely regarded as being an advocate for the district's English learners.

ever, dedicated educators of ELs know that ELs bring often-untapped strengths and have much to offer the educational system in the United States. If their educators and administrators provide them an equitable education based on a culturally and linguistically appropriate framework with high but attainable expectations and collaboration among various stakeholders, ELs can achieve. Below, two overarching examples of strengths that ELs bring to the educational arena are provided to question the idea that ELs merely present challenges to educators.

Language Diversity as a Resource

Nieto (2001) believes there is a strong need to view language diversity as a resource rather than a deficit, recognize the role that language discrimination has played in U.S. history, recognize the benefits of linguistic diversity for all students, understand the role that native language development plays in school achievement, and make the education of language minority students the responsibility of all teachers. She conceptualizes students as culturally, linguistically, and ability diverse (CLAD) when they speak a language other than English but don't necessarily qualify for ESL programs. Further, CLAD learning can be positively impacted by school policies and practices that value students' identities and are part of systemic educational reform (Nieto, 2007). While certain practices—such as first language instruction, eliminating tracking, or a culturally responsive pedagogy—can significantly improve CLAD student learning, in isolation these practices do not reflect the complexity of student learning. School policies and practices may perpetuate the structural inequalities that exist in society.

Cultural Differences as a Strength

Some see cultural differences as a root cause of the EL/non-EL achievement gap. A discontinuity exists between the culture of the schools and the home culture of culturally and linguistically diverse students, yet these students possess distinct, often unrecognized funds of knowledge (or historically accumulated bodies of knowledge and skills) that many teachers do not know exist (Moll, Amanti, Neff, & Gonzalez, 1992; Vélez-Ibanez & Greenberg, 1992). Moll et al. (1992) argue that in order to successfully educate diverse populations, including ELs, teachers' consciousness first needs to be raised so that they recognize that students come to school in possession of funds of knowledge. In addition, teachers must also incorporate students' funds of knowledge into classroom instruction in order to build on the strengths and knowledge diverse students bring with them.

Recently, researchers and educators have challenged this deficit view of culturally and linguistically diverse families and discovered diverse families possess a vast range of cognitive resources, skills, and knowledge and provide their children with a variety of learning opportunities and experiences. They argue that using students' funds of knowledge as a base for classroom discussions bridges the school and household learning and ultimately helps students make sense of abstract, theoretical concepts taught in schools (Dwordin, 2006; Hensley, 2005; Moje et al., 2004).

The polar opposite of the EL deficit model is recognizing and honoring the cultural capital and funds of knowledge that each student brings to the class-

> What funds of knowledge and rich resources do your ELs and their families bring to your school's classrooms? How do you know?

room. The term *cultural capital* was made popular by French sociologist Pierre Bourdieu (Bourdieu & Passeron, 1973) and is understood to be the cultural background, knowledge, dispositions, and skills that are passed down from one generation to another.

For example, consider Amadou, a recently arrived sixth grade Haitian student who enters a classroom with very limited English language skills. It would be quite easy to view him in terms of what he doesn't appear to possess, such as English reading skills, mathematics skills, appropriate classroom behavior, and so on. What Amadou does bring to his education is most likely an incredible sense of self-reliance, survival skills, a strong work ethic, and a strong sense of community. Acknowledging Amadou's strengths and building from them is a huge step toward supporting his achievement, whereas "to deny students their own knowledge is to disempower them," (Delpit, 1995, p. 33).

SHARING RESPONSIBILITY TO TEACH ENGLISH LEARNERS

Fortunately, the field of ESL education is now better positioned to be able to accurately articulate some research-based criteria that influence teachers' ability to effectively teach ELs. For instance, a synthesis of studies

(Gándara, Maxwell-Jolly, & Driscoll, 2005) reports that the most successful teachers of ELs have pedagogical and cultural knowledge and skills, including the ability to communicate effectively with ELs and include their families in their children's education. In short, the greater a teacher's preparation for working with ELs, the more professionally competent that teacher feels to teach them and the more responsibility that teacher takes on for ELs' achievement.

In order to provide effective professional development for those who teach ELs, teacher educators must first have an understanding of the role that content area and ESL/bilingual teachers have in teaching ELs within a systems approach. In this approach, three components (teachers, standards, and assessment) constantly interact and influence each other as parts of an inseparable system, forming a triangle of inter-action. For ELs to learn content and language simultaneously, all three components must be equally developed—as educators, we have to share the responsibility to make sure that all three components are developed when it comes to ELs. If one component is neglected, the other two will not fully develop (Staehr Fenner & Kuhlman, 2012). Figure 1.2 repre-sents the multifaceted, triangulated approach to teaching ELs that high-lights the relationship between content standards, English language proficiency (ELP)/English language development (ELD) standards,

Figure 1.2. Triangulated Approach to Teaching ELs

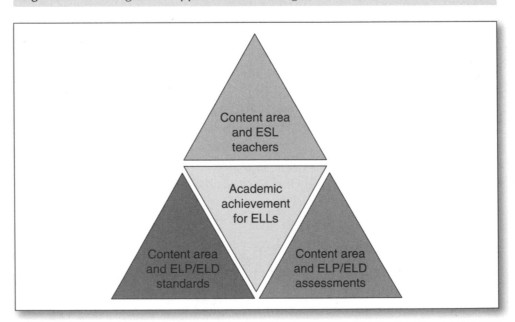

Source: Staehr Fenner & Segota, 2012.

content assessments, and ELP/ELD assessments. Educators first need to recognize that it is everyone's responsibility to equitably educate ELs, and all types of teachers need to collaborate so they can capitalize on each other's strengths in terms of supporting ELs' achievement.

For ELs to be instructed effectively, content area and ESL teachers must have the knowledge, skills, and dispositions to work with these students. They must have a solid base of knowledge of the content but they must also be able to apply that knowledge in the classroom. Furthermore, all teachers must have a disposition that embodies their desire to work with ELs to support them as they achieve, or a sense of responsibility to ensure their ELs' academic success. Teachers must also design their instruction for ELs around high-quality content as well as ELP/ELD standards that outline the content students are responsible for. In addition, teachers must determine the academic language students need to acquire at each stage of English language proficiency/development so that students can access that content. Teachers' needs and levels of preparation must form the central piece of this relationship so that ELs can achieve in school and beyond.

> How do your school's content area and ESL teachers collaborate to support your ELs' success? What kind of disposition do they have toward working with ELs?

Advocacy for ELs as Social Justice

In order to increase awareness of advocacy for ELs, it is also beneficial to take a look at how social justice can inform advocacy for ELs. Social justice education grew out of social reconstructionism, which speaks to the need to ask social questions in an effort to create a more just and democratic society. Similar to social reconstructionists, critical theorists such as Paulo Freire (1985, 1993) conceptualized education as a means for structural and social change and a way in which the oppressed could overcome oppression. There are currently a variety of names for a model of education that seeks to transform society and instill in students greater appreciate for difference and a sense of agency to work against injustice and inequity. While there are some differences in what educators using various methods advocate, the basic assumptions and desired outcomes are fundamentally similar in scope. Social justice education views two components as taking place simultaneously—individuals changing and working to change society, which in turn fosters greater individual change (Sleeter & Grant, 2009). Social justice can inform educators' dialogues about the need to advocate for ELs by raising awareness of how educators can help change the school climate for the better for ELs and support ELs and their families to be able to advocate for themselves.

Components of Social Justice as They Relate to Advocacy for ELs

This first stage in the social justice transformation is signified by individuals thinking critically about themselves in relation to their political circumstances. Freire (1985) refers to this process as *conscientizaco* or *concientization*, stating, "It is as conscious beings that men are not only *in* the world but *with* the world, together with other men" (p. 68). Freire explains that only once individuals become open in this way, able to view the events of the world more objectively, can they begin to make change. With these new eyes, individuals are more open to hearing what members of oppressed groups have to share, are more reflective about oppressive practices and structures, and are more motivated to work for change. It is at this point that such educators are ripe for discussions concerning the political nature of education and how knowledge is constructed. This book will attempt to help raise educators' awareness about current inequities in ELs' education and how these inequities can be overcome.

Nieto (2006) argues that teaching is political work. She describes social justice education as fundamentally about power, including who has the power to make decisions and who benefits from those decisions. She also describes social justice as being a democratic project, because it aims to promote inclusiveness and fairness. Nieto also identifies key characteristics of teachers who are making a positive difference in the lives of marginalized students. She describes these qualities as a sense of mission; solidarity with and empathy for their students; courage to challenge mainstream knowledge; improvisation; and a passion for social justice. Darling-Hammond (2002) believes that supporting all students, including ELs, to be readers and writers in the context of general education classrooms is a matter of social justice. These tenets of social justice certainly apply to the definition of EL advocacy proposed and operationalized throughout this book.

Equally important to consider is what Giroux (1983, 1988) refers to as the language of possibility. Just as schools have the potential to perpetuate structural inequity, they also have the potential to empower students and support personal transformation. Such a vision includes an educational process by which learning is relevant, critical, and transformative. hooks (1994) describes the classroom as "the most radical space of possibility" (p. 12). Typical reasons ELs' families immigrate to the United States include wanting a better education for their children. It is educators' responsibility to ensure that our schools serve to empower our ELs to fulfill their families' desires and make their families' sacrifices in the United States worth it in terms of their children's education.

How do you describe your stance on social justice for ELs?

CULTURE AS SOCIAL
JUSTICE AND ADVOCACY COMPONENT

Culture is a key component in social justice education as well as in advocating for ELs in terms of recognizing the role of culture in teaching and learning, using culture as a basis for student learning, viewing students through a lens of cultural capital, and connecting classrooms and schools to families and the community. The critical first step toward including culture in a social justice education and advocacy framework is the recognition of not only the importance of culture but also the understanding that everyone has a culture, and that culture shapes who we are as educators. Often, White teachers must first begin to see themselves as cultural beings and recognize the role that culture plays in their own lives before they can develop recognition of their ELs' cultures. It can be quite a journey to the point in which educators view cultural diversity as a strength and an academic resource for all students (Gay, 2000).

One final tension is the contradiction between the seriousness of social justice and beneficial nature that creativity and humor can have in advocating for ELs. When challenged by the weight of injustice and charged with the task of societal transformation, it is easy for educators to feel overwhelmed, just like Ms. Ritter. However, some of the most inspirational teachers radiate a sense of possibility and a positive outlook. Many ESL teachers share that their ELs describe the ESL classroom as the first place in which their strengths seem appreciated and they sense that they are safe to share their feelings, lowering their affective filter. Cummins (2000) writes that the classroom needs to be hopeful, joyful, kind, and visionary. "The ways we organize classroom life should seek to make children feel significant and cared about—by the teacher and by each other. Unless students feel emotionally and physically safe, they won't share real thoughts and feelings" (p. 262).

> To what degree do your school's ELs feel significant and cared about? How do you know?

Current EL Advocacy Efforts Underway

There are some movements that have begun to address educators' awareness of advocacy as well as their ability to advocate for ELs as important elements teachers must possess to effectively teach them. This section of the chapter will focus on recent efforts by TESOL International Association and the NBPTS to prominently place advocacy for ELs on the educational landscape. Since these influential professional bodies have built advocacy into their professional standards, these organizations' endorsement of advocacy supports the importance of advocacy for ELs.

PROFESSIONAL STANDARDS

The TESOL International Association's P–12 Professional Teaching Standards and the NBPTS English as New Language Standards were revised in 2009 and 2010, respectively. Given recent changes in the context of education for ELs that has been heavily influenced by assessment and accountability, advocacy is a theme that permeates both sets of the newly revised sets of professional standards for teachers.

The TESOL P–12 Professional Standards

The TESOL standards represent what preservice ESL teaching candidates earning their initial licensure in ESL should know and be able to do in order to effectively teach ELs. The TESOL standards are used for recognition by the Council for the Accreditation of Educator Preparation (CAEP)—formerly known as National Council for the Accreditation of Teacher Education (NCATE)—as well as by institutions of higher education as they create and revise ESL teacher preparation programs. They are also used to form a framework for schools' and districts' professional development for general education as well as for ESL/bilingual inservice teachers (Staehr Fenner & Kuhlman, 2012).

TESOL's eleven professional standards are organized around five overlapping domains: Language, Culture, Instruction, Assessment, and Professionalism. The domains of Language and Culture form the content knowledge that ESL teachers need to know in order to apply them to Instruction and Assessment. The fifth domain, Professionalism, is at the core of the standards; it drives who effective ESL teachers are and what they can do. It is in this fifth domain, Professionalism, where advocacy plays an important role through Standard 5b: Professional Development, Partnership, and Advocacy.

The NBPTS ENL Standards

More than 1,300 teachers are currently nationally board certified in English as a New Language using the NBPTS ENL Standards as a framework for national board certification. The NBPTS standards contain the following nine standards: Knowledge of Students; Knowledge of Culture and Diversity; Home, School, and Community Connections; Knowledge of the English Language; Knowledge of English Language Acquisition; Instructional Practice; Assessment; Teacher as Learner; and Professional Leadership and Advocacy.

Focus on Advocacy in the TESOL and NBPTS Professional Standards

Both the TESOL and the NBPTS professional standards contain a heightened focus on teachers' responsibilities to advocate for their ELs. Although these standards are intended for specialists who work with ELs such as ESL teachers, the content of the standards can extend to all educators, including content area teachers as well as administrators. Below, the focus turns to examining how advocacy plays a role in each of these sets of standards.

Advocacy in the TESOL Professional Standards

TESOL's Professional Development, Partnership, and Advocacy standard reads, "Candidates take advantage of professional growth opportunities and demonstrate the ability to build partnerships with colleagues and students' families, serve as community resources, and advocate for ELLs"[5] (TESOL, 2010, p. 71). Some performance indicators TESOL has defined to measure the degree to which preservice ESL licensure candidates meet this standard include the following (TESOL, 2010):

- Advocate for ELLs and their families, including full access to school resources and technology and appropriate instruction for students with special needs or giftedness. (p. 73)
- Serve as advocates and ESOL resources to support ELLs and their families as families make decisions in the schools and community. (p. 73)
- Provide ELLs and their families with information, support, and assistance as they advocate together for the students and their families. (p. 74)
- Take leadership roles on instructional teams advocating for appropriate instructional services for ELLs who may have special needs or giftedness. (p. 74)
- Help create empowering circumstances and environments for ELLs and their families. (p. 74)
- Take leadership roles with community members and policymakers with respect to issues affecting ELLs. (p. 74)

---

5. TESOL uses the term *English language learner (ELL)* in its P–12 Professional Teaching Standards. Several other organizations use the term *ELL* as well.

The TESOL P–12 Professional Teaching Standards include the advocacy standard to operationalize some of the most important facets of being an effective teacher of ELs. Staehr Fenner and Kuhlman (2012) recommend one or more teacher preparation courses and inservice professional development should contain a focus on how to access and share advocacy information with educators.

Advocacy in the NBPTS ENL Standards

Advocacy is a theme that plays two roles in the NBPTS ENL standards. It stands alone as NBPTS Standard IX, Professional Leadership and Advocacy, and also serves as a thread that weaves throughout several of the other NBPTS ENL standards. Standard IX states,

> Accomplished teachers of English language learners contribute to the professional learning of their colleagues and the advancement of knowledge in their field in order to advocate for their students. (NBPTS, 2010, p. 20)

During the revision process of the NBPTS standards, advocacy became its own standard to draw attention to the changing role of educating ELs during a time of increased collaboration among educators as well as a higher level of accountability surrounding the education of ELs.

The introduction to the NBPTS ENL standards helps define the context for the importance of advocating for ELs, stating,

> Accomplished teachers accept their ethical responsibility to advocate for their students' success in order to give both the students and their families a voice they may not have yet acquired themselves. Accomplished teachers' advocacy at the school, district, state, and even national levels extends beyond their students' academic needs to the unique personal needs of their students. Accomplished teachers understand that everyone in the school shares the responsibility for the success of all students, and they collaborate with other stakeholders to ensure that success for English language learners. (NBPTS, 2010, p. 14)

Standard IX's pertinent text is provided below:

> Accomplished teachers challenge misconceptions about English language learners, arbitrary requirements, inappropriate curricular and assessment assumptions, cultural misunderstandings, and other factors that may limit their students' achievement. Teachers

ensure that valid assessments, placements, and referral procedures occur so that English language learners receive appropriate and equitable services. (NBPTS, 2010, p. 92)

They advocate for their students' admission to special programs, such as those for gifted and talented students, and they argue against inappropriate placements in compensatory or remedial programs. Teachers recommend, and, when possible, help establish, new programs, courses, and curricula to build on the knowledge, skills, and interests that ELs bring to school, addressing students' individual needs and fostering a positive self-image for each one. Teachers also advocate for equal access to extracurricular activities and enrichment programs:

> **One Example of a Promising Practice in EL Advocacy:** One example of including advocacy at the preservice education level is in the English Language Development course at Purdue University. As a part of this course, preservice teacher candidates complete a four-week module on The Role of the Teacher in the English Language Development of ELs. One week focuses solely on teachers learning to advocate for ELs. Candidates read about inequities that warrant advocacy acts in schools and beyond. In this course, teacher candidates discuss their roles as teachers of ELs in the context of advocacy efforts in their classrooms, schools, and communities and what they can do to ensure ELs receive an equitable education. They discuss how they can advocate for ELs and obtain resources for these students.

Accomplished teachers advocate for students and their families to ensure that their voices are heard. . . . Teachers engage families in practices that empower them to become advocates for their children. . . . They promote educational opportunities for their students by advocating for local, state, and federal funding of programs that advance instructional programs and services for English language learners. (NBPTS, 2010, p. 93)

CONCLUSION

Since all teachers share responsibility for ensuring ELs' achievement, educators must examine EL achievement from the perspective of advocacy. In this chapter, the need to advocate for ELs was framed around such factors as EL demographics, the EL/non-EL achievement gap, and the lack of preparation for teachers to effectively work with ELs. Advocacy for ELs was defined and presented within a scaffolded approach, in which each EL's background variables must be known and addressed through advocacy in order to truly serve and support each EL student. In addition, the EL deficit paradigm was examined, and ELs' strengths were highlighted. The chapter closed with a description of the TESOL and NBPTS professional teaching standards' new focus on advocacy as necessary for all teachers of ELs. Chapter 2 will focus on creating a sense of shared responsibility for teaching ELs.

REFERENCES

Abedi, J. (2002). Standardized achievement tests and English language learners: Psychometrics issues. *Educational Assessment, 83*(3), 231–257.

Alford, B. J., & Niño, M. C. (2011). *Leading academic achievement for English language learners: A guide for principals.* Thousand Oaks, CA: Corwin.

Arias, M. B., & Morillo-Campbell, M. (2008). *Promoting ELL parental involvement: Challenges in contested times.* Tempe: Education Policy Research Unit, Arizona State University.

Athanases, S. Z., & de Oliveria, L. C. (2008). Advocacy for equity in classrooms and beyond: New teachers' challenges and responses. *Teachers College Record, 110*(1), 64–104.

Bailey, A. L. (2010). Implications for assessment and instruction. In M. Schatz & L. C. Wilkinson (Eds.), *The education of English language learners: Research to practice* (pp. 222–247). New York, NY: Guilford Press.

Ballantyne, K. G., Sanderman, A.R., & Levy, J. (2008). *Educating English language learners: Building teacher capacity.* Washington, DC: National Clearinghouse for English Language Acquisition.

Bourdieu, P., & Passeron, J. C. (1973). Cultural reproduction and social reproduction. In R. K. Brown (Ed.), *Knowledge, education and cultural change* (pp. 71–112). London, UK: Tavistock.

Cummins, J. (2000). *Language, power and pedagogy.* Buffalo, NY: Multilingual Matters.

Darling-Hammond, L. (2002). Learning to teach for social justice. In L. Darling-Hammond, J. French, & S. P. Garcia-Lopez (Eds.), *Learning to teach for social justice* (pp. 1–7). New York, NY: Teachers College Press.

de Jong, E., & Harper, C. (2008). ESL is good teaching "plus": Preparing standard curriculum teachers for all learners. In M. E. Brisk (Ed.), *Language, culture, and community in teacher education* (pp. 127–148). New York, NY: Erlbaum.

Deal, T. E., & Peterson, K. D. (2009). *Shaping school culture* (2nd ed.). San Francisco, CA: Jossey-Bass.

Delpit, L. (1995). *Other people's children: Cultural conflict in the classroom.* New York, NY: The New Press.

Dubetz, N. E., & de Jong, E. J. (2011). Teacher advocacy in bilingual programs. *Bilingual Research Journal, 34*(3), 248–262.

Dwordin, J. (2006). The Family Stories Project: Using funds of knowledge for writing. *Reading Teacher, 59*(6), 510–520. doi:10.1598/RT.59.6.1

Education Week. (2009). *Quality counts: Portrait of a population, 28*(17). Bethesda, MD: Editorial Projects in Education. Retrieved from http://www.edweek.org/go/qc09

Ferguson, C. (2008). *The school–family connection: Looking at the larger picture.* Austin, TX: National Center for Community and Family Connections with Schools.

Freire, P. (1993). *Education for critical consciousness.* New York, NY: Continuum.

Freire, P. (1985). *The politics of education: Culture power and liberation.* South Hadley, MA: Bergin & Garvey.

Fry, R. (2008). *The role of schools in the English language learner achievement gap.* Washington, DC: Pew Hispanic Center. Retrieved from http://www.pewhispanic.org/topics/?TopicID=4

Gándara, P., Maxwell-Jolly, J., & Driscoll, A. (2005). *Listening to teachers of English language learners: A survey of California teachers' challenges, experiences, and professional development needs.* Santa Cruz, CA: Center for the Future of Teaching and Learning. Retrieved from http://www.cftl.org /documents/2005/listeningforweb.pdf

Gay, G. (2000). *Culturally responsive teaching.* New York, NY: Teachers College Press.

Giroux, H. A. (1983). *Theory and resistance in education.* South Hadley, MA: Bergin & Garvey.

Giroux, H. A. (1988). *Teachers as intellectuals: Toward a critical pedagogy of learning.* South Hadley, MA: Bergin & Garvey.

Gottlieb, M., Katz, A., & Ernst-Slavit, G. (2009). *Paper to practice: Using the English language proficiency standards in PreK–12 classrooms.* Alexandria, VA: TESOL.

Hensley, M. (2005). Empowering parents of multicultural backgrounds. In N. Gonzalez, L. Moll, & C. Amanti (Eds.), *Funds of knowledge* (pp. 143–151). Mahwah, NJ: Lawrence Erlbaum.

hooks, b. (1994). *Teaching to transgress: Education as the practice of freedom.* New York, NY: Routledge.

Kao, G., & Thompson, J. S. (2003). Racial and ethnic stratification in education achievement and attainment. *Annual Review of Sociology, 29*(1), 417–442. doi:10.1146/annurev.soc.29.010202.100019

Moje, E. B, McIntosh-Ciechanowski, K., Kramer, K., Ellis, L., Carrillo, R., & Collazo, T. (2004). Working toward third space in content area literacy: An examination of everyday funds of knowledge and discourse. *Reading Research Quarterly, 39*(1), 38–70.

Moll, L. C., Amanti, C., Neff, D., & Gonzalez, N. (1992). Funds of knowledge for teaching: Using a qualitative approach to connect homes and classrooms. *Theory Into Practice, 31*(2), 132–141.

National Board for Professional Teaching Standards (NBPTS). (2010). *English as a new language standards* (2nd ed.). Arlington, VA: Author.

National Center for Public Policy and Higher Education. (2005). *Income of U.S. workforce projected to decline if education doesn't improve.* Retrieved from http://www.highereducation.org/reports/pa_decline/pa_decline.pdf#search=%22minorities%22

The National Clearinghouse for English Language Acquisition (NCELA). (2011). *The growing number of English learner students.* Retrieved from http://www.ncela.gwu.edu/files/uploads/9/growing_EL_0910.pdf

Nieto, S. (2001). We speak in many tongues. In C. Diaz (Ed.), *Multicultural education for the 21st century* (pp. 152–170). New York, NY: Longman.

Nieto, S. (2006, Spring). *Teaching as political work: Learning from courageous and caring teachers.* Longfellow Lecture, Sarah Lawrence College, Bronxville, NY.

Nieto, S. (2007). School reform and student learning. In J. Banks & C. Banks (Eds.), *A multicultural perspective in multicultural education* (6th ed.) (pp. 424–443). Hoboken, NJ: Wiley.

O'Neal, D., Ringler, D. D., & Rodriguez, D. (2008). Teachers' perceptions of their preparation for teaching linguistically and culturally diverse learners in rural eastern North Carolina. *The Rural Educator, 30*(1), p. 5–13. Retrieved from http://www.ruraleducator.net/archive/30–1/30–1_ONeal.pdf

Reardon, S. E., & Galindo, C. (2009). The Hispanic–White achievement gap in math and reading in the elementary grades. *American Educational Research Journal, 46*(3), 853–891. doi:10.3102/0002831209333184

Scarcella, R. (2003). *Academic English: A conceptual framework* (Tech. Rep. No. 2003–1). Irvine: University of California, Linguistic Minority Research Institute.

Scarcella, R. (2008, August). *Defining academic English.* Webinar presented for the National Clearinghouse for English Language Acquisition. Retrieved from http://www.ncela.gwu.edu/webinars/event/1/

Sleeter, C. E., & Grant, C. A. (2009). *Making choices for multicultural education: Five approaches to race, class, and gender* (6th ed.). Hoboken, NJ: Wiley.

Staehr Fenner, D., & Kuhlman, N. (2012). *Preparing effective teachers of English language learners: Practical applications for the TESOL P–12 Professional Teaching Standards.* Alexandria, VA: TESOL International Association.

Staehr Fenner, D., & Segota, J. (2012). *Standards that impact English language learners.* Washington, DC: Colorín Colorado. Retrieved from http://www.colorincolorado.org/article/50848/#authors

Suarez-Orozco, C., Suarez-Orozco, M., & Doucet, F. (2004) The academic engagement and achievement of Latino youth. In J. Banks & C. Banks (Eds.), *Handbook of research on multicultural education* (pp. 420–437). San Francisco, CA: Jossey-Bass.

Teachers of English to Speakers of Other Languages (TESOL). (2010). *TESOL/NCATE standards for the recognition of initial TESOL programs in P–12 ESL teacher education.* Alexandria, VA: Author. Retrieved from http://www.tesol.org/s_tesol/seccss.asp?CID=219&DID=1689

Tinkler, B. (2002). *A review of literature on Hispanic/Latino parent involvement in K–12 education.* Retrieved from http://www.huildassest.org/products/latinoparentreport/latinoparentrept.htm

Vélez-Ibáñez, C., & Greenberg, J. (1992). Formation and transformation of funds of knowledge among U.S. Mexican households. *Anthropology and Education Quarterly, 23,* 313–335.

Wilde, J. (2010, May). *Comparing results of the NAEP long-term trend assessment: ELLs, former ELLs, and English-proficient students.* Paper presented at the annual meeting of the American Education Research Association. Denver, CO. Retrieved from http://www.ncela.gwu.edu/files/uploads/16/AERA_2010_Wilde.pdf

Zehler, A. M., Fleischman, H. L., Hopstock, P. J., Stephenson, T. G., Pendzick, M. L., & Sapru, S. (2003). *Descriptive study of services to LEP students and LEP students with disabilities.* Washington, DC: U.S. Department of Education, Office of English Language Acquisition, Language Enhancement, and Academic Achievement of Limited English Proficient Students.

2

Creating a Shared Sense of Responsibility for Teaching English Learners

One of the first steps toward effectively advocating for ELs' equitable education is recognizing that everyone involved in ELs' education must share the responsibility for ensuring their success. All school stakeholders who impact ELs' lives, including content and general education teachers, music teachers, special education teachers, art teachers, cafeteria workers, guidance counselors, physical education teachers, janitors, and administrators will have an effect on the education ELs receive. However, educators may not fully realize the extent to which they have the opportunity to positively impact an EL's education. All educators must first share a sense of responsibility for providing an equitable education for ELs so that they will be willing to change the ways in which they work with ELs to recognize ELs' unique strengths as well as address ELs' specific linguistic and cultural needs through instruction. In addition, if they feel responsible for teaching ELs, they will also be more likely to go beyond teaching ELs effectively and also advocate for ELs' equitable education.

INTRODUCTION

This chapter will begin by presenting a framework from which to establish the need to build shared responsibility for equitably educating ELs to

> What does the term *shared responsibility to educate ELs* mean to you?

prepare educators to begin to advocate on their behalf. It will first focus on the importance of creating a sense of empathy for the EL experience, bearing in mind that ELs are not a monolithic group, and each EL's academic experience is different. This framework will also recognize that ELs' experiences transcend the more visible facet of their U.S. academic experience, extending to ELs' social and community lives in the United States and their country of birth or their parents' countries of birth.[1] It will also ground the need to build a shared sense of responsibility for working with ELs in research and best practice as well as show the necessity for all teachers to seek and gain their ELs' trust.

THE COMMON CORE STATE STANDARDS' CALL FOR SHARED RESPONSIBILITY

In addition to the need for educators to share responsibility rooted in their moral imperative to do so, the Common Core State Standards (CCSS) support the need to share the responsibility to include ELs. The CCSS do so by insisting that instruction in reading, writing, speaking, listening, and language be a shared responsibility within schools by the very nature of the standards' structure and content. For example, the K–5 standards define expectations for reading, writing, speaking, listening, and language that are applicable to a range of subjects, not only English Language Arts. Standards in Grades 6–12 are divided into two sections, one for English language arts and the other for literacy in history/social studies, science, and technical subjects. With this paradigm shift brought forth by the CCSS, every teacher must now simultaneously be a teacher of language, literacy, and content. In order for ELs to be successful in achieving the CCSS, all teachers must first examine what sharing responsibility to foster ELs' academic success looks like in their context. In addition, teachers must collaborate so that ELs can access the Common Core.

Definition of Shared Responsibility

This chapter uses the term *shared responsibility* to describe the mind-set that all educators must see themselves as equal stakeholders who must strive to positively influence the education of ELs in the classroom as well

---

1. The majority of ELs are born in the United States, so it cannot be assumed that all ELs have been born in a country outside the United States. In addition, a student's or parent's country of birth may be different from the country in which the child has received schooling.

as outside of school. Many ESL teachers express that they feel that content area or general education teachers see ELs only as the "ESL teachers' kids." That is, compared to content teachers, ESL teachers sometimes feel that they are expected to make the majority of choices with respect to ELs' education. ESL teachers may also feel more immediately accountable for ELs' academic success (Staehr Fenner & Kuhlman, 2012).

For example, ESL teachers may find themselves determining which accommodations ELs receive on assessments, taking the lead on seeking out resources available in the community for EL families, and serving as ad hoc language interpreters as necessary. It is completely understandable that content teachers and administrators often turn to ESL teachers to assume a lead role in these areas, as ESL teachers have tended to receive more specialized training in working with ELs and their families through preservice teacher education programs.

In addition, many teachers and administrators may depend on ESL teachers to advocate for ELs, because they have not had the experience of learning a language in addition to English and/or traveling to a foreign country, let alone having been immersed in a school in which the culture and language are completely new. For these reasons, many teachers and administrators may not fully understand the EL experience in terms of what ELs' needs are or be familiar with community resources that are available and appropriate for ELs or their families. Yet it is everyone's charge to ensure ELs succeed; the responsibility for ELs' success both in school as well as outside the school walls should extend to all educators who interact with them.

In particular, teachers' desire to share responsibility for ELs and advocate for their equitable education is inextricably intertwined with their expectations for ELs and beliefs about educating them. This desire is also linked to their ability to support their students' success through collaboration with colleagues, administrators, and the community as a whole. However, until now, most content area teachers have not realized that serving as a voice for ELs and their families is a prerequisite for their students to be able to fully engage in instruction and succeed in school and beyond. Only after teachers and administrators realize the great sense of urgency that all educators must share the responsibility for equitably educating ELs can the best available research, methods, strategies, and professional development (PD) for working with ELs be truly beneficial and worthwhile.

Theoretical Framework for Sharing Responsibility

This chapter will begin by examining several factors that impact how educators can move through a process to more actively share the responsibility for providing an equitable education for ELs. These factors influence shared responsibility. Each factor will be described and applications of it will be provided through activities. Educators should examine each of the factors in the sequence outlined. First they will examine their beliefs and expectations about working with ELs, and then they will reflect on their own culture and its impact on their teaching. Next, educators build empathy for ELs and their families, and finally they collaborate with various stakeholders involved in ELs' education. The process is iterative and requires continually moving through the sequence so that shared responsibility for ELs changes to accommodate new ELs and their families as well as new issues that arise with current ELs. Figure 2.1 is a graphic representation of this process.

Figure 2.1. Factors That Influence Shared Responsibility

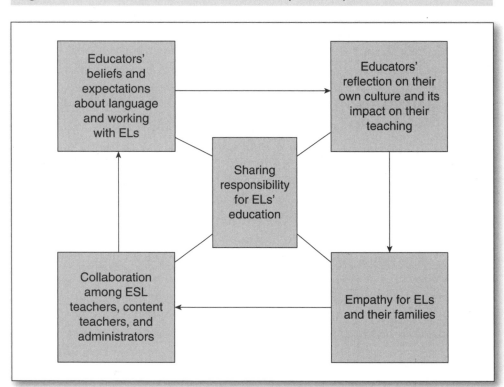

WHAT THE RESEARCH TELLS US

Some researchers (e.g., English; Lewis-Moreno) have recently begun investigating the creation of a sense of shared responsibility for educating ELs as one component of the effective education of these students. For example, through analysis of top-down and bottom-up discourses among various teaching professionals, English (2009) attempts to deconstruct the ideological assumptions about how ELs learn. English believes that professional development (PD) can help to promote pedagogical change that incorporates shared responsibility into educating EL students. This researcher found general education teachers need support to improve their practice of sharing responsibility for teaching ELs.

Lewis-Moreno (2007) argues that general education classroom teachers are just as responsible for the success of EL students as administrators and EL specialists. She posits that all teachers have a moral responsibility to ensure the success of ELs, and that every teacher, regardless of role or specific job description, must be given the charge to incorporate strategies that develop the language acquisition of ELs. She also believes that school districts may see more success from ELs if everyone is provided the right tools to teach these learners.

Issues of content teacher attitudes and the importance of developing trust between EL students and their teachers are also related to the concept of sharing responsibility to educate ELs. For example, Reeves (2006) investigated teacher attitudes toward teaching EL students and discovered that most teachers had a neutral to positive attitude toward teaching ELs in general education classes. Her quantitative study, however, revealed that many of the teachers are misinformed about how ELs learn

> How would you rate your own attitude toward working with ELs?

and acquire language. Moreover, many of these same teachers were ambivalent about learning how to teach ELs. Her findings point to a disconnect between the teachers' generally positive attitudes toward teaching ELs in their content area classrooms and their reluctance to take action to improve upon their abilities to better educate those same students.

Developing trust between ELs and their teachers is one key to ELs' success in school. Wassell, Hawrylak, and LaVan (2010) found that, for many of the EL students they studied, gaining the trust of a teacher was tantamount to being given the opportunity to learn English successfully. If they felt that the teacher respected their culture, the ELs were more apt to take certain risks and make important mistakes that facilitated their learning. Without developing such trust, learning opportunities remained hidden.

Finally, Honigsfeld and Dove (2010) posited that several factors point to the need for collaboration in schools so that ELs can succeed. They point out that sociocultural, socioeconomic, affective, linguistic, and academic factors can impact an EL's success. The authors also report that administrators face several challenges in creating a collaborative environment in their schools to ensure the equitable education of ELs. Among these challenges are ESL program compliance and accountability, creating a positive school culture for ELs, and balancing the needs of all stakeholders.

In sum, research tells us that shared responsibility for teaching ELs contains many layers of complexity. This emerging area of study includes the role of PD in shaping educators' dispositions toward working with ELs, building trust between ELs and their teachers, and fostering collaboration among all stakeholders who work with ELs so that ELs can succeed. Educators should consider how developed all of these factors are in their own practices so that they can contribute to creating an environment that is conducive to ELs' success.

PROFESSIONAL DEVELOPMENT TO SHARE RESPONSIBILITY FOR TEACHING ENGLISH LEARNERS

The remainder of the chapter details sample activities educators can use individually or with groups of educators to

- Raise awareness about their beliefs regarding language and teaching ELs
- Examine the cultures that they bring to their experiences as educators
- Explore what it feels like to be an EL at a beginning stage of English proficiency in an academic classroom setting
- Feel what it's like to be the parent or family member[2] of an EL with beginning English proficiency and little knowledge of the U.S. school system
- Increase collaboration among content teachers, administrators, and ESL teachers[3]

Even if educators don't find themselves in that more formal situation, they can still use these tools for their personal PD. Admittedly, these sample PD activities only begin to skim the surface of the EL and EL family member experience in order to increase educators' empathy for this population of students, and the activities are also not meant to be prescriptive in nature. It is also not possible to fully experience the multifaceted world of an EL in just one PD session. The intent of these activities is to

---

2. I use the term *parent* interchangeably with *family member* here, because ELs may have extended family such as older siblings, aunts, uncles, grandparents, and trusted family friends that serve the expected role of parents. In addition, some ELs may arrive in the United States after long periods of separation from their biological parents; in such situations, these parents of ELs may not be as informed of the ELs' prior schooling and life experiences as other family members may be.

3. I use the term *English as a Second Language (ESL) teacher* to encompass any specialist that provides linguistic support to ELs; this would also include bilingual education teachers.

apply some of the current research and best practices to move the needle in the direction of creating a shared sense of responsibility for educating ELs through an experiential approach.

Survey of Teachers' and Administrators' Beliefs on Educating ELs

Teachers should first ascertain their perspectives on language as well as their feelings regarding working with ELs. Use of the two-part survey[4] in Figures 2.2a and 2.2b is one way to begin this dialogue. The survey should be taken anonymously, and it can be taken prior to a PD session so that the PD facilitator can tabulate the scores before beginning of the PD to more effectively tailor the PD to the needs of the group.

The sample survey consists of two interrelated parts: Part One: Perspectives on Language and Part Two: Preparation for Teaching. Part One, Perspectives on Language, examines educators' beliefs and values regarding the political and sociocultural aspects of using English and other languages in the home, school, and society. Part Two, Preparation for Teaching, focuses on respondents' self-reported level of expertise and comfort in designing and implementing instruction for English learners. The first survey will most likely be more politically charged and may very well evoke strong feelings by PD participants. While originally developed for future teachers of ESL, the second survey builds on the first and focuses on the degree to which teachers self-report skills needed by classroom teachers to effectively teach ELs.

After participants have taken each survey, the PD facilitator can lead them through a discussion of their responses to gain a sense of where the educators are coming from individually in their thinking and where the school as a whole falls on the continuum as a vehicle to advocate for ELs. When educators are analyzing the results of survey such as this, they will need to keep in mind that respondents are self-reporting their data. For example, respondents may overestimate their skill level in working with ELs on the survey. In addition, when they are sharing with a group rather than filling out a paper form, they may be less willing to share their true convictions regarding immigration and language policy in the United States for fear of repercussions.

Any discussion of the Language Use survey's results must take place in a climate of trust, and all participants should know that they won't be judged for their responses. Otherwise, a sense of finger pointing could take over and cloud the intent of the exercise. After individuals take the survey, they can compile their scores individually and privately compare

---

4. Part 1: Perspectives on Language, is adapted from: Byrnes & Kiger (1994). Part 2, Preparation for Teaching ELs, is adapted from Lucas, Reznitskaya, & Villegas, (2008).

them to general descriptions of the scores provided below. Depending on previous knowledge of the school climate, the PD facilitator might choose to have the respondents tally up their score and respond to the score in a private journal instead of having a group discussion on the topic.

Figure 2.2a. Language Use

Part 1. Perspectives on Language Use

Please circle the number that best captures your agreement or disagreement with each statement below.

Note: The term *linguistic minority student* refers to a student who speaks or is exposed to a language other than English in the home; that student may or may not be proficient in English.

1 = strongly agree   6 = strongly disagree

1. To be considered American, a person should speak English fluently.	1	2	3	4	5	6
2. I would not support the federal, state, and local government spending additional money to provide better programs for linguistic minority students in public schools.	1	2	3	4	5	6
3. Parents of students who are not proficient in English should be counseled to speak English with their children whenever possible.	1	2	3	4	5	6
4. It is not important that people in the United States learn a language in addition to English.	1	2	3	4	5	6
5. It is unreasonable to expect a general education classroom teacher to teach a child who does not speak English.	1	2	3	4	5	6
6. The rapid learning of English should be a priority for students who are not proficient in English even if it means they lose the ability to speak their native language.	1	2	3	4	5	6
7. Local and state governments should require that all government business (including voting) be conducted only in English.	1	2	3	4	5	6
8. Having a student who is not proficient in English in the classroom is detrimental to the learning of the other students.	1	2	3	4	5	6

	1	2	3	4	5	6
9. General education classroom teachers should not be required to receive preservice or inservice training to be prepared to meet the needs of linguistic minority students.	1	2	3	4	5	6
10. Most K–12 students who are not proficient in English are not motivated to learn English.	1	2	3	4	5	6
11. At school, the learning of the English language by children who are not proficient in English should take precedence over learning content area subject matter.	1	2	3	4	5	6
12. English should be the official language of the United States.	1	2	3	4	5	6
13. Students who are not proficient in English often use unjustified claims of discrimination as an excuse for not doing well in school.	1	2	3	4	5	6
Total score	___ points					

Source: Adapted from Byrnes & Kiger, 1994.

Language Use Survey Score Categories

13–26 points: You feel that being American is equated with speaking English and see the value in English being used for official purposes in the United States. You agree that students need to learn English quickly in order to succeed in school, and you don't think it's as important for those students to maintain their first language. You think that some English learners are not motivated enough to learn English and might be taking advantage of their status as ELs to justify their lack of successful academic performance in school.

27–52 points: You may not feel as strongly that being American is equated with speaking English and may not agree that English should be used for official purposes in the United States. While you believe that ELs need to learn English in order to succeed in school, you may think these students should also maintain their first language and also learn content simultaneously with English. You may think some English learners are motivated to learn English and might believe ELs contribute to the classroom climate.

53–78 points: You believe that it is possible to be an American even if a person does not speak English fluently. You most likely do not believe that only English should be used for official purposes in the United States.

While you believe that ELs need to learn English in order to succeed in school, you also believe these students should also maintain and develop their first language and also learn challenging content simultaneously with English. You think English learners bring strengths to their schools and are motivated to learn English.

Guiding Questions

After taking the survey, either respondents can write a journal passage about their reactions to it, or the facilitator can use these guiding questions to facilitate small group or full group discussions. This examination of beliefs will help individuals and groups of educators get a better sense of where they are coming from in terms of their openness to share the responsibility to teach ELs.

- How did you feel after taking the survey?
- Did certain questions surprise you? Which ones? Why?
- Do you think your final score on the Language Use survey is in line with the description of the category you fall into? Why or why not?
- Which areas of language use did you have the strongest reaction to? Why?

As with the Language Use survey, after respondents take the Preparation for Teaching ELs survey, they can compile their scores individually and compare them to general descriptions of the scores provided below. They can then reflect upon their answers individually or discuss them as a group. The second survey should not be as controversial as the first, and the results of the second survey can be used to guide further PD topics for teachers.

Language Use Survey Score Categories

13–26 points: You are aware of the challenges you face when teaching ELs but need a great deal more information on language, culture, prior knowledge, and modification of instruction for ELs. You also don't have an in-depth understanding of the interplay between language, culture, instruction, and learning.

27–52 points: You are aware of the challenges you face when teaching ELs and have a beginning understanding of language, culture, prior knowledge, and modification of instruction for ELs. You have an understanding of the interplay between language, culture, instruction, and learning.

Figure 2.2b. Preparation for Teaching ELs

Part 2. Preparation for Teaching ELs

Note: The term *English learner* refers to a student who is exposed to or speaks a language other than English and is not yet fully proficient in English.

Please circle the number that best captures how well or poorly prepared you feel in each area below.

1 = Extremely *Poorly* Prepared   6 = Extremely *Well* Prepared

1. Understanding of how people learn a second language.	1	2	3	4	5	6
2. Understanding of the nature of academic English and the challenges it poses for ELs.	1	2	3	4	5	6
3. Skills and strategies for learning about the cultural backgrounds of ELs.	1	2	3	4	5	6
4. Skills and strategies for teaching academic content to English language.	1	2	3	4	5	6
5. Understanding of how culture influences learning.	1	2	3	4	5	6
6. Understanding of how language influences learning.	1	2	3	4	5	6
7. Understanding of language variation and dialects.	1	2	3	4	5	6
8. Ability to assess ELs' academic abilities in a classroom setting.	1	2	3	4	5	6
9. Understanding of the differences between proficiency in oral language and in written language.	1	2	3	4	5	6
10. Ability to modify classroom instruction for ELs.	1	2	3	4	5	6
11. Ability to access ELs' prior knowledge and experience as part of instruction.	1	2	3	4	5	6
12. Ability to link ELs' prior knowledge and experience with new ideas and skills.	1	2	3	4	5	6
13. Skills and strategies for reaching out to ELs' parents/guardians/family members.	1	2	3	4	5	6

Source: Adapted from Lucas, Reznitskaya, & Villegas, 2008.

However, you could still use some more information and strategies on how to effectively instruct ELs.

53–78 points: You have an in-depth understanding of language, culture, prior knowledge, and modification of instruction for ELs. You have a deep understanding of the interplay between language, culture, instruction, and learning. There may still be some topics on this survey that you would like to develop further.

Guiding Questions

As with the Language Use survey, after taking the second survey, either respondents can write a journal passage about their reactions to it, or the facilitator can use these guiding questions to facilitate small group or full group discussions.

- How did you feel after taking the survey in terms of your preparation to teach ELs?
- Did your responses to certain questions surprise you? Which ones? Why?
- Do you think your final score on the Preparation to Teach ELs survey is in line with the description of the category you fall into? Why or why not?
- Which areas are the strongest for you?
- Which areas would you like to develop further?

Creating an Awareness of Educators' Own Culture

In addition to teachers examining their own beliefs around language and instruction for ELs, it is also important for them to take a closer look at their own cultures that they bring to their role as teachers and administrators. Many educators may not realize that even if they have lived in the United States all their lives and are monolingual speakers of English, they already possess a culture and worldview that influences who they are as educators.

One suggested activity for educators to become more aware of their own cultures is adapted from PD given by Dr. Paul Gorski, assistant professor at George Mason University and founder of EdChange (www .edchange.org). In this activity, which can be used as an introductory activity during PD, participants are asked to stand up if the statement that the facilitator reads applies to them. This activity is designed to raise teachers' awareness of their own memberships in cultural groups and of how these memberships have impacted their lives and also their stance on educating all students, including ELs. For example, some topics addressed in this activity are socioeconomics, gender, and linguistic issues. A brief list of sample statements is below. Others may be added as appropriate according to the makeup of the participants. While this exercise works best in a group where others can see who is participating in which way, it can also be a reflective exercise for individuals.

Stand up:

- If you worry about whether you'll be able to pay your bills
- If people routinely mispronounce your name
- If you represent the first generation of your family to attend college
- If you have ever been the only person of your race/ethnicity in a class or place of employment
- If you are often expected to work on your religious holidays
- If you never had a teacher of your racial or ethnic group
- If you have ever been teased because of the clothes you were wearing
- If you have ever been made fun of because of the part of the country or world you come from
- If you have ever felt pressured to change the way you speak, dress, or act in order to fit in
- If there is any dimension of your identity that you have to hide from most people in order to feel accepted or safe
- If there has never been a president of the United States who shared your gender identity
- If English is not your first language

After participants have taken part in the first part of the PD activity, they can debrief with a small group of colleagues and discuss which statements applied to them and which did not. They can discuss how they felt taking part in the activity and which cultural groups were referenced in the exercise. Finally, they can share how they belong to certain cultural groups they may not have realized they had membership in and how they can make connections between their own cultural experiences and those of their EL students. Next, educators can discuss how their raised awareness of their belonging to certain cultural groups would influence their teaching of ELs.

One United States–born monolingual participant who went through this exercise shared that he hadn't realized how his membership in the first-generation college graduates in his family influenced how he viewed himself. He shared that he had to change how he spoke in order to fit in better at college and often felt unprepared academically or socially because his home culture was different from his college's culture. He was able to draw connections between his own experience not fitting in and how his ELs must have felt when they had to learn a new language in order to fit in at school both academically and socially.

An extension and application of this activity asks educators to put themselves in their ELs' and EL families' shoes to determine which cultural groups their ELs and EL families are likely to belong to. More important, educators take this information and apply it to their own teaching. Educators can work with a partner to envision how all their students, including their ELs and their ELs' families, would respond to the same questions, keeping in mind that all students and their families would have different responses. The educators can discuss how they can use this information—about how their ELs and ELs' families would respond to the same questions—in their teaching. A representative from each small group can then share that group's answers with the large group of participants. A table such as the one found in Table 2.1, which has been prepopulated with sample responses to the first three "stand up" questions, can be used to facilitate this discussion.

EL IMMERSION EXPERIENCE: STUDENT PERSPECTIVE

One potentially powerful tool to help monolingual teachers and administrators experience what it's like to be an English learner, if only on a small scale and for a limited time, is to teach a lesson to them in a language they do not know (Washburn, 2008). Using a "language shock" method, Washburn believes that teachers can be given a simulated experience of what EL students go through that will in turn carry over into their own pedagogy. She believes that only through the experience of being immersed and forced to struggle with another language and culture can teachers truly begin to empathize with EL students. In turn, this sense of empathy will ideally impact an educator's sense of responsibility to teach ELs language and culture simultaneously.

This language shock technique is in my PD toolkit and is an exercise that I find to be particularly powerful with monolingual PD participants. I happen to speak German and Spanish, but since many educators have some knowledge of Spanish, I prefer to teach a sample lesson in German and sketch out the lesson below. While reading through this activity does not have the same effect as experiencing it in person, educators can adapt the exercise to an academic topic in a language other than English.

Table 2.1 Educator Cultural Awareness Activity Sample Application to Teaching

Statement	My Response: Yes or No	My ELs' Anticipated Response	My EL Parents' Anticipated Response	Comments/Application for Teaching ELs
If you worry about whether you'll be able to pay your bills	No	Yes (depending on their age)	Yes	Increased awareness that some high school age ELs can't take part in afterschool activities because they have to work and/or that other ELs may have to care for younger siblings and family members so their parents can work; knowledge that some ELs' parents work two jobs or more and may not see their children often and consequences of this lack of child–parent interaction and supervision
If people routinely mispronounce your name	Yes	Yes	Yes	ELs appreciate it when teachers take the time to learn how to pronounce their names; they begin to build more trust in their teachers when teachers make this gesture that may seem insignificant on the surface
If you represent the first generation of your family to attend or who will attend college	No	Yes	No (haven't attended college)	Many parents of ELs have not attended college; even if they have attended college in their home countries, they are likely not aware of the college admissions process as well as the courses, afterschool activities, and level of college admissions test preparation U.S. students must have to present a strong college application; teachers must present this information to students and parents in a form they will understand in different modes (e.g., in person, by phone, in writing)

EL Empathy PD Activity Step 1

The facilitator lectures by reading the following aloud:

Wir werden heute einen Würfel, einen Quader, einen Kegel, einen Zylinder, eine Pyramide und eine Kugel beschreiben und erklären.

***Ein Würfel** ist einer der fünf platonischen Körper, genauer ein dreidimensionales Polyeder mit sechs kongruenten Quadraten als Begrenzungsflächen, zwölf gleichlangen Kanten und acht Ecken, in denen jeweils drei Begrenzungsflächen zusammentreffen.*

***Ein Kegel** ist ein geometrischer Körper, der entsteht, wenn man alle Punkte eines in einer Ebene liegenden, begrenzten runden Flächenstücks geradlinig mit einem Punkt (Spitze beziehungsweise Apex) außerhalb der Ebene verbindet. Das Flächenstück nennt man Grundfläche, deren Begrenzungslinie die Leitkurve und den Punkt die Spitze oder den Scheitel des Kegels bildet.*

***Ein Zylinder** wird laut der allgemeinen Definition von zwei parallelen, ebenen Flächenund einer Mantel- bzw. Zylinderfläche, die von parallelen Geraden gebildet wird, begrenzt. Das heißt, er entsteht durch Verschiebung einer ebenen Fläche oder Kurve entlang einer Geraden, die nicht an dieser Ebene liegt.*

***Eine Pyramide** ist ein dreidimensionaler Körper in der Geometrie. Dieses Polyeder besteht aus mehreren nahtlos aneinanderliegenden ebenen Flächen, von denen eine ein Polygon und alle anderen Dreiecke sind. Die Dreiecke bilden die Mantelfläche.*

***Eine Kugel** hat keine Kanten und keine Ecken.*

The facilitator asks these questions of participants aloud:

Wer kann diese Fragen beantworten? Zeigt bitte auf!!

- *Was ist ein Würfel?*
- *Wie nennt man das Flächenstück eines Kegels?*
- *Wer kann eienen Zylinder beschreiben?*
- *Wieviele Dimensionen hat eine Pyramide?*
- *Wieviele Kanten und Ecken hat eine Kugel?*

When none of the participants answers the questions (unless there happens to be someone with knowledge of German), the facilitator begins to start speaking louder and more slowly. The facilitator begins showing frustration with the students' lack of answers and changes the tone of voice and body language to show students that they are not meeting expectations. If someone attempts to answer in English, the facilitator does not allow that answer. When I am facilitating, I also don't allow participants to talk to each other.

Guiding Questions

I continue this way for about 5 to 10 agonizing minutes and then allow the teachers a chance to debrief (in English) in small groups about their experience, providing them guiding questions such as these:

1. How did it feel to be a German as a Second Language student?

2. What kind of extra help did you need to understand the lesson?

3. What did you do to try to understand the content?

4. How did the facilitator adapt instruction to meet your linguistic needs?

5. Do you have or have you had any students who might have been in a situation similar to the one you were just in?

Once they have debriefed about Step 1 in small groups, several groups share their experiences with the large group.

EL Empathy Professional Development Activity Step 2

The facilitator then adds the additional scaffold of visual and written information to help slightly lighten the linguistic load for the participants to allow them to demonstrate, in a language that is unfamiliar to them, the academic content they presumably already know. Participants are also allowed to work together and use English to solve the problems. Some samples of the visuals and written information provided for this German lesson are the following:

Du findest hier einen Würfel, einen Quader, einen Kegel, einen Zylinder, eine Pyramide, und eine Kugel. Schreibe den richtigen Namen unter die entsprechende Darstellung!

Versuche anschließend zu entscheiden, ob die angeführten Aussagen wahr (w) oder falsch (f) sind. Kreuze Entsprechendes an!

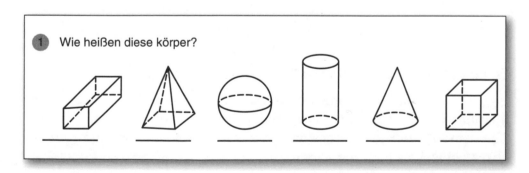

Aussage	w	f
Der Würfel hat 10 Ecken		
Die Kugel hat keine Kanten und keine Ecken.		

Guiding Questions

The participants then debrief with a partner or in a small group, using the following sample guiding questions:

1. How did it feel to be a German as a Second Language student in Step 2 as compared to Step 1?

2. What were you being asked to do in this exercise? How do you know?

3. What skills do you possess that allowed you to understand some of the content?

4. What kind of extra help did you receive to meet your linguistic needs in order to understand the lesson?

5. What kind of help would you still need to understand the lesson and take part in the informal assessment?

At this point, participants tend to feel slightly more at ease due to the facilitator's use of some preliminary language supports. They will also have previous knowledge of the content, they will recognize some German/English cognates such as *Pyramide/pyramid,* and they will know how to respond to fill-in-the-blank and true/false questions. Because of this background knowledge, most of the educators would ascertain that they were being asked to match the name of the geometric figure to the visual. They should be able to point out that the written and verbal information provided helped them to at least figure out what they were supposed to do, even if they weren't exactly sure of the language of the tasks and could not fully access the meaning of the content. Some participants will also express that they were relieved that they could work with a partner and/or discuss the problem in English.

EL Empathy Professional Development Activity Step 3

Finally, the facilitator provides the participants the additional scaffold of a written bilingual glossary to help them complete the task given in Step 2. They can still work in pairs or small groups and use English to figure out the answers together.

GLOSSARY

Würfel–cube
Quader–cuboid
Kegel–cone
Zylinder–cylinder
Pyramide–pyramid
Kugel–sphere

Darstellung–figure
wahr–true
falsch–false
Ecken–corners
Keine–no
Kanten–edges

They are then given the correct answers below.

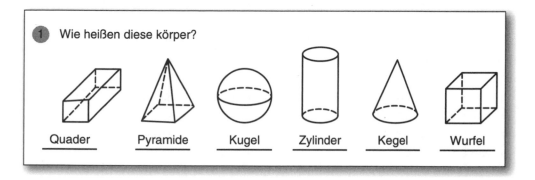

1 Wie heißen diese körper?

Quader   Pyramide   Kugel   Zylinder   Kegel   Wurfel

Aussage	w	f
Der Würfel hat 10 Ecken		✓
Die Kugel hat keine Kanten und keine Ecken.	✓	

Guiding Questions

At the end of this activity, participants debrief about the overall experience in small groups using guiding questions:

1. How did your feelings about taking part in the lesson change as we progressed from Step 1 to Step 3?

2. Which modifications to the lesson helped you? Why?

3. What happened to your level of anxiety as the lesson progressed? Why?

4. Do you think these modifications would work for all ELs? Why or why not?

5. What did the facilitator do that helped or hindered your learning?

6. What has changed about your knowledge of working with ELs?

7. What can you apply from this experience to your own teaching of ELs?

At the conclusion of this activity, participants come away with an increased sense of what it is like to be an EL. They also realize this short experience is just a small window into an EL's world. ELs at low levels of English proficiency encounter situations like these all day, every day in school as they acquire English proficiency. Through Step 1 of this activity, the facilitator modeled what not to do in teaching ELs challenging content. The teacher in Step 1 did not feel it was his or her responsibility to teach language and content simultaneously; instead, the teacher focused only on content.

The participants also become aware that they are already at a large advantage over some ELs, since they most likely already have learned the geometry content in their dominant language, English, and they can transfer this knowledge of the content to the lesson in German. They also already know how to participate in a classroom environment and understand the facilitator's questioning format, knowing that they are expected to raise their hands to answer. The bilingual glossary is beneficial to them because they are already literate in English and also know the geometry content in English.

EL FAMILY EMPATHY BUILDING EXPERIENCE

Building a sense of shared responsibility to educate ELs also extends to the need for all educators to be inclusive of ELs' families and to be willing to serve as their advocates. I am a United States–born, native English-speaking parent of school-age children, and I have classroom teaching and administrative experience in the same public school district in which my children are in school. Even so, I sometimes find myself unsure about my children's classroom and school and about district policies and expectations. I subsequently contact my children's teachers or administrators via phone or by e-mail with questions. I can advocate for my own children's education in a Spanish immersion public school program due to my knowledge of the following factors:

1. How the public school system "works" from my experience as a teacher and administrator in the district

2. My understanding of my expected place in the district's school system as a parent

3. My understanding of the teachers' and school's expectations for how I should interact and communicate with teachers and administrators

4. My ability to communicate fluently in English—and occasionally drop an education jargon term—within the expectations for K–12 school discourse

I often try to put myself in the shoes of ELs' families as best I can as they try to comprehend the expectations and policies of their children's classrooms, schools, districts, and states, not to mention federal requirements of EL education and accountability that do not apply to me or my own children. EL families will likely not have the same four strengths to draw upon as I do. They may not know of the opportunities that are available to them or their children that could potentially be hugely beneficial to them in the immediate future and for the duration of their academic careers (such as afterschool tutoring, extracurricular activities, or SAT preparation for college). Educators must share the responsibility to support ELs' families so that they can learn to navigate the policies, expectations, and opportunities for their children in their school. In order to help EL families in this way, educators must first get a taste of what it's like to be an EL parent to begin to get a sense of which areas require their support.

EL Parent Empathy Professional Development Suggestion

One way to help educators construct a more comprehensive view of what it's like to be an EL family member is through having them fill out forms in a language that they do not speak or read. A form that seems innocuous for the majority of United States–born parents may present a more nuanced, complex situation for families of ELs. The activity below helps provide experiential learning to educators about what it is like to fill out one such simple form for two different parents of ELs. Both EL parents speak the same language, but their prior experiences are worlds apart.

There are many school forms translated into languages other than English available for download online, and many districts have also often translated parental forms into the top language group(s) spoken by EL families. The form I have chosen for the PD activity that follows is a sample free and reduced-price lunch form that has been created for the U.S. Department of Agriculture for school districts to modify and download (Figure 2.3).

For purposes of this activity, teachers assume one of two identities (Ahmed or Mojtaba), which they use to complete the form individually. They know only that the form is required by the school.

The first identity:

You are Ahmed, a 45-year-old mechanical engineer from Dubai who has moved to the United States for two years on a work visa to provide specialized support to an international company. You have two children enrolled in your district's school system. You speak and read English at an intermediate level, and this is your children's second year in U.S. schools.

The second identity:

You are Mojtaba, a 30-year-old refugee from Darfur, Sudan. You have four children enrolled in U.S. schools and have two toddlers at home. You attended school through the third grade in Sudan and arrived in the United States two weeks ago. You don't speak or read English, and you are able to read Arabic at the first grade level.

Guiding Questions

After the participants have attempted to fill out the form through the eyes of Ahmed or Mojtaba, all the participants who filled out the form as Ahmed work as a small group to discuss their experience using the sample guiding questions below. All the participants who filled out the form as Mojtaba would also discuss their questions together. If participants take part in this exercise individually, they can still choose one of the identities and reflect on the guiding questions:

- What do you think this form is used for? Why do you think so?
- How much do you think Ahmed/Mojtaba will understand what is written here? Why?
- What do you think Ahmed/Mojtaba could perceive as unintended consequences for filling out this form incorrectly?
- What other life circumstances could affect how Ahmed/Mojtaba would complete this form?
- What information do you take away from this experience as an educator that you can apply to your own classroom or school context when working with families of ELs?

Once both groups have debriefed under the guise of their assumed identities, educators can compare the two groups' responses to the guiding questions as a large group; then the facilitator can inform them that the form is a free and reduced-price lunch form. As U.S. educators most likely are aware, all families of U.S. students have to fill out such a form if their child is to qualify to receive a free or reduced-price lunch. The information the family provides is based on self-reported income.

Figure 2.3. Free and Reduced-Price Lunch Form in Arabic

جزء 1: جميع أفراد الأسرة			
أسماء جميع أفراد الأسرة (الاسم الأول، أول حرف من الاسم الثاني، اللقب)	اسم المدرسة لكل طفل، أو اذكر NA ان لم يكن الطفل في المدرسة.	قم بالإشارة هنا اذا كان الطفل متبنى(تحت المسؤولية القانونية لوكالة ويقدر أو محكمة* اذا كان جميع الأطفال المذكورين ادناه متبنين، تخطى هذا الجزء ه الى ان تصل الى الجزء ه 5 لتوقيع هذه الاستمارة)	قم بالتأشير هنا ان لم يكن هناك دخل

جزء 2: المعونات

اذا كان اي عضو من أعضاء الأسرة يحصل على معونات من، أعطي اسم ورقم ملف الشخص المستلم للمعونات واذهب الى جزء ه 5. ان لم يكن هناك اي شخص يستلم هذه المساعدات، تخطى هذا الجزء ه واذهب الى جزء ه 3.

الاسم _____

رقم الملف _____

(Continued)

Figure 2.3. (Continued)

جزء 3 . إذا كان أي طفل تقدم طلبا بشأنه مشرد أو مهاجر أو هارب قم بتأشير المربع المناسب وتصل ب

□ مشرد □ مهاجر □ هارب

جزء 4. مجموع الدخل الإجمالي لكل الأسرة/البالغ وفترات الاستلام / يجب ان تخبرنا بالمبلغ وفترات الاستلام

2. الدخل الإجمالي وتكرار القبض

جزء 1.1 الأسم (اذكر فقط اسماء اعضاء الأسرة الذين لديهم دخل)

الأسم	الدخل من العمل قبل المقتطعات	المساعدات الحكومية، النفقة، إعالة الطفل الزوجية	معاشات التقاعد، الراتب التقاعدي، الضمان الاجتماعي و SSI و مخصصات VA	أي دخل آخر
مثال: جون سميث	$199.99/ اسبوعيا	$50.00/ شهريا	$99.99/ شهريا	$149.99/ كل اسبوعين
	$/____	$/____	$/____	$/____
	$/____	$/____	$/____	$/____
	$/____	$/____	$/____	$/____
	$/____	$/____	$/____	$/____
	$/____	$/____	$/____	$/____
	$/____	$/____	$/____	$/____

جزء 5. التوقيع واخر اربعة ارقام من رقم الضمان الاجتماعي (يجب ان يوقع من قبل شخص بالغ)

يجب ان يوقع هذه الاستمارة شخص بالغ من اعضاء الاسرة. اذا كنت قد املت جزء و 4. يجب على الشخص البالغ والموقع على الاستمارة ذكر اخر اربعة ارقام من رقم الضمان الاجتماعي او يقم بتأشير مربع "ليس لدي رقم ضمان اجتماعي ".(انظر الى البيان في الجانب الخلفي لهذه الصفحة)

انا اؤكد (اعد) ان جميع المعلومات الواردة في هذه الاستمارة صحيحة وانني قد قمت بالتبليغ عن كامل دخلي. انا اعرف ان المدرسة سوف تحصل على تمويل فدرالي بناءً على المعلومات التي اوردها. انا اعرف ان مسؤولين في المدرسة قد يتحققون من المعلومات. انا اعلم انني اذا اعطيت معلومات خاطئة متعمداً فقد اطالب بمعوضات الوجبات، وقد تتم مقاضاتي.

رقم هنا :

الاسم بوضوح:

التاريخ:

العنوان:

المدينة:

الاسم بوضوح2:

رقم الهاتف:

الولاية:

الرمز البريدي:

اخر اربعة ارقام من رقم الضمان الاجتماعي :

* * * – * * – _____

☐ لا املك رقم ضمان اجتماعي

جزء 6. الهوية العرقية والاثنية للاطفال (خياري)

المعلومات التي اذكرها زوجها. انا اعرف ان مسؤولين في...

قم بتأشير اثنية واحدة:

☐ اسباني او لاتيني

☐ غير اسباني او لاتيني

اختر واحد او اكثر (بعض النظر عن العرق)

☐ اسيوي

☐ ابيض

☐ هندي امريكي او من سكان الاسكا الاصليين

☐ من السكان الاصليين لهاواي او جزر اخرى في المحيط الهادئ

☐ اسود او افريقي امريكي

Source: http://www.fns.usda.gov/cnd/frp/frp.process.htm.

However, the seemingly simple act of completing this form can be more high stakes for families of ELs, even if the form has been translated into their native language. For example, parents of ELs who understand the content of the form can be embarrassed that their child qualifies to receive a free or reduced-price lunch and might not fill in this information correctly or at all, ultimately spending family funds that may already be tight. Other families who lack immigration documentation may not wish to fill out the form because they do not know what the information will be used for, even if they have reassurance from the school that it will be used only to determine if their child can qualify for a free or reduced-price lunch.

How Ahmed's and Mojtaba's Experiences Impact Them

Ahmed and Mojtaba bring vastly different sets of experiences to the task of completing a form, and each of them will require varying amounts of support from their school's personnel to assist them with this procedure. Ahmed, a college educated mechanical engineer, already possesses literacy in Arabic and will most likely not experience difficulties completing the form, assuming it is an accurate translation into the dialect of Arabic he speaks. Since he is a career professional, his income will probably preclude his children from receiving free or reduced-price lunch at their school. In addition, if he has any questions about this form, his level of English proficiency and familiarity with schooling in general as well as one year of experience with his children's school in the United States will be an asset to him if he decides to contact the school for more information. Ahmed will therefore require much less assistance from school personnel in order to complete this form.

The experience of Mojtaba, who also speaks Arabic, will be markedly different from that of Ahmed. Mojtaba legally resides in the United States but is most likely functionally illiterate in Arabic. She would first and foremost experience difficulty understanding the content of the form, since she can barely read Arabic. Thus, despite the school's good intentions of giving her a form in her native language, she most likely will not understand its content. Mojtaba would require someone to speak with her in Arabic about the purpose and content of the form and to work with her to complete it, since she can most likely not write more than her name or some very basic information in Arabic. For example, she may not be able to write her new address or phone number (if she has a phone). Since she has not received schooling beyond the first grade and is not familiar with the U.S. school system, she might be unaware that lunch is provided at her children's school. Furthermore, she may be fearful about providing too much personal information to school authorities, fearing that her refugee status may be revoked at any moment. Due to all the potential roadblocks for her in completing this form, it is unlikely that she will complete it without help. If she does not complete the form, she will forfeit her children's access to free or reduced-price lunch, increasing the economic burden on her family. She won't be able to contact the school with questions about the form if the school does not have an Arabic-speaking person on staff to assist her. Even though the school has made the laudable effort to provide the form in her native language, Mojtaba still requires concerted advocacy efforts from school personnel in order for this form to be meaningful to her and for her to complete it.

CONCLUSION

In order for educators to serve as advocates for the English learners in their classrooms and in their schools, they must first become open to the notion that everyone in the school is responsible for the success of its ELs. Since educators' own cultures, experiences, and education influence their beliefs about language practices and policies as well as their classroom and societal expectations of ELs, they must first examine their personal beliefs about students who are acquiring English. Because most educators haven't had experiences of being schooled in another language and have not had to adjust to life in a different culture, it is also important to offer educators a glimpse into the challenges ELs face in the classroom as well as uncertainties families of ELs experience as they learn more about the U.S. school system. Chapter 3 focuses on EL advocacy through the ESL teacher perspective.

> Has your definition of shared responsibility to educate ELs changed after reading this chapter? If so, in what ways?

REFERENCES

Byrnes, D. A., & Kiger, G. (1994). Language attitudes of teachers scales (LATS). *Educational and Psychological Measurement, 54*(1), 227–231.

English, B. (2009). Who is responsible for educating English language learners? Discursive construction of roles and responsibilities in an inquiry community. *College and Education 23*(6), 487–507. doi:10.1080/09500780902954216

Honigsfeld, A., & Dove, M. (2010). *Collaboration and co-teaching: Strategies for English learners.* Thousand Oaks, CA: Corwin.

Lewis-Moreno, B. (2007). Shared responsibility: Achieving success with English-language learners. *Phi Delta Kappan, 88*(10), 772–775.

Lucas, T., Reznitskaya, A., & Villegas, A.M. (2008, April). *Exploring the attitudes and preparedness of regular classroom teachers to teach English language learners.*

Presentation at the annual meeting of the American Educational Research Association, New York, NY.

Reeves, J. (2006). Secondary teacher attitudes toward including English-language learners in mainstream classrooms. *Journal of Educational Research, 99*(3), 131–142.

Staehr Fenner, D., & Kuhlman, N. (2012). *Preparing effective teachers of English language learners: Practical applications for the TESOL P–12 Professional Teaching Standards.* Alexandria, VA: TESOL International Association.

Washburn, G. (2008). Alone, confused, and frustrated: Developing empathy and strategies for working with English language learners. *The Clearing House, 81*(6), 247–250.

Wassell, B.A., Hawrylak, M. F., & LaVan, S. (2010). Examining the structures that impact English language learners' agency in urban high schools: Resources and roadblocks in the classroom. *Education and Urban Society, 42*(5), 599–619. doi:10.1177/0013124510375598

3 How Teachers Can Collaborate to Expand Advocacy Efforts for ELs

This chapter is targeted primarily at ESL teachers[1] who find themselves in a situation in which they would like to make a positive impact on their school's ELs' academic experience and who could benefit from some practical guidance. There are also content or general education teachers[2] and administrators who may find themselves in the position of serving as their ELs' voice in an advocacy role, and this chapter applies to them as well. This chapter focuses on how committed teachers can make a positive change for ELs through advocacy even when they feel the majority of teachers at their school are not as likely to support ELs.

INTRODUCTION

This chapter is centered on how ESL teachers can utilize their unique skill set to collaborate with general education teachers and administrators to

---

1. Although this chapter refers to ESL teachers, it also applies to any educator or administrator who would like to change a school's culture to become more supportive of ELs. For purposes of clarity, only the term *ESL teacher* is used in the chapter.

2. The terms "general education" and "content teachers" are used interchangeably in this chapter even though their roles may be different.

bring about positive change for ELs. It also touches on ways in which content area teachers and administrators can collaborate with ESL teachers. It begins with an examination of the varied roles ESL teachers play in different contexts and highlights the benefits of empathy and collaboration between ESL teachers and content teachers. The chapter then provides considerations and suggestions for ESL teachers to begin to extend their advocacy efforts outside the walls of their individual classrooms to work with general education teachers and administrators to more effectively instruct ELs and serve as their advocates, progressing to a schoolwide advocacy effort.

OPERATING WITHIN TEACHERS' SPHERE OF INFLUENCE

In the field of international relations, a *sphere of influence* functions as a spatial region or conceptual division over which a state or organization has significant cultural, economic, military, or political influence. The term is also used to describe nonpolitical situations. For example, a shopping mall is said to have a sphere of influence that marks the geographical area where it dominates the retail trade. My colleague Paul Gorski adapted this term to education and shares the following perspective:

> Any sort of change is hard, not only because it requires us to reshape our own thinking, but also because, when we upset people's comfort, we are sure to face resistance. This is especially the case when we're advocating for ELs or other groups of students on whose backs a lot of nasty political wrangling is happening. Also, for those of us who do not see ourselves necessarily as activists or change agents, it can be easy to imagine the challenges, like colleagues' bias toward ELs, as too big and overwhelming to overcome. How am I, a classroom teacher, supposed to find the energy and voice to push back against a whole society's worth of bias?
>
> This is why I encourage people to think not about how they can create massive change, like the elimination of societal bias against immigrants from Mexico or Central America, but about how they can commit, at the very least, to creating an equitable and just learning environment within their own spheres of influence. Certainly there are people who have dedicated their lives to battling global discrimination, but most of those people do not go to work at a school or district office every day. Most of them do not have

grading and lesson planning to do. That level of advocacy and activism is not within everybody's purview.

However, each of us does have a sphere in which we have the power to decide just how equitable an environment we want to make for students and their families. Maybe that sphere is a classroom or department within a school. Maybe it's a school or a district or state. Whatever it is for you, just ask yourself this: What do I have control over in this environment? What do I not have control over here? Make yourself a t-chart or a list. Then make a commitment: Within this sphere, based on the circumstances over which you do have control, commit to doing all you can do to provide an equitable, safe, welcoming, and validating learning environment for EL students and their families.

You need not fret that you are not equipped to eliminate societal racism or advocate on a national stage for ELs (although imagine the world we could create if we all spent just a little time on such endeavors). Instead, focus on building that equitable space within your sphere of influence. Then, when you begin to feel like you have a handle on that sphere, you might consider growing it, from classroom to school, perhaps, or from school to district. This way you do not try to take on too much, risking advocate's burnout; you don't feel the weight of the entire equity enterprise on your shoulders. But you commit, at least, to being an advocate for students who, sitting right before you, need an advocate right now. (personal communication, 2012)

> Sketch your current sphere of influence in terms of advocating for ELs. Now sketch your ideal EL advocacy sphere of influence. What do you think it will take for you to move to your ideal model?

WHAT THE RESEARCH TELLS US

Research reveals that the role of the ESL teacher extends beyond that of a language teacher, expanding into the affective realms of nurturer and also of cultural mediator. The next section of this chapter will focus on research defining the role of the ESL teacher and supporting collaboration among different types of educators.

The Role of the ESL Teacher

With the changing demands on ESL teachers, the role of ESL teachers in schools is also constantly evolving. Several recent studies highlight the varying role of the ESL teacher that extends beyond teaching language skills to ELs. For example, Abu-Rabia's (2004) research findings prompt questions about the important role of the ESL teacher as a kind, nurturing filter of affective learning, which has implications for the role of the ESL teacher as a nurturer and not merely a taskmaster who ensures students strictly follow English speaking guidelines.

In her analysis of narratives, interviews, and questionnaires of inner city junior high school ESL teachers, Ajayi (2011) explores the role of ESL teachers as cultural bridges to their students. Her study recommends immersion service-learning types of teacher education programs that can prepare teachers to learn how to act as this bridge between cultures. The findings demonstrate the unique role of the ESL teacher as cultural ambassador and not just instructor of English grammar and syntax. Ghanizadeh and Moafian (2010) found that teachers' emotional intelligence is critical in facilitating their students' process of learning and productive acquisition of English. This study implies that in order to become successful ESL instructors, ESL teachers must be well versed not only in English content but also in managing emotions.

> How would you describe your role with ELs at your school?

Collaboration Among ESL and Content Teachers

In addition to embodying multiple roles, ESL teachers also collaborate with general education teachers and administrators to support ELs' success in their schools. To that end, several authors (e.g., DelliCarpini, 2009; He, Prater, & Steed, 2011; Honigsfield & Dove, 2010) have touted the multiple benefits of collaboration for all teachers of ELs and for the ELs themselves. However, successful teacher collaboration that benefits ELs takes careful planning and forethought among ELs' teachers and general education teachers (Arkoudis, 2006; DelliCarpini, 2009; Honigsfeld & Dove, 2010).

Arkoudis (2006) argues that negotiating collaborative teaching practices between content area teachers and ESL teachers is a complex undertaking. She posits that ESL teachers are challenged with the task of asserting the importance of their subject matter within the mainstream content area curricula of secondary schools while making sure that their position as the ESL teacher is not relegated to a secondary assistant status. She stresses the importance of all the social actors—in this case, the general education or content area teachers, administrators, students, and ESL teachers—being aware of the fluid dynamics involved with their positions and negotiating their role for each evolving circumstance. Arkoudis (2006) concludes that ESL teachers must position themselves to be on equal footing with general education teachers by not only knowing and confidently asserting their expertise but by also knowing the general education teachers' agendas and the standards under which they are held.

DelliCarpini (2009) states that creating and maintaining a collaborative space where ESL and content area teachers regularly meet, learn, and plan together is tantamount to success with their EL students. Unfortunately, this space is often neglected and is not something that naturally occurs without a great deal of prompting. She argues that this necessary collaborative space does not have to be highly structured—it can occur in small conversations in which goals, students, and materials can be discussed. She suggests that without collaboration, teachers operate with only one piece of the information they need to determine whether or not their ELs students are "getting it." If teachers begin by purposefully building relationships with one another, this collaboration can begin to develop naturally, which ultimately feeds ELs' success.

Honigsfeld and Dove (2010) stress that collaboration among ESL and general education teachers is necessary due to the multiple factors that affect ELs' socioeconomic, sociocultural, linguistic, affective, and academic spheres. They encourage collaborating teachers to become familiar with and agree upon the model(s) that will work best for the particular curriculum they will be instructing. Regardless of which model is espoused, the authors recommend that teachers make an effort to establish good working rapport with one another, taking mutual advantage of the skills and talents that each educator brings to the classroom.

Some authors (Davison, 2006; Fu, Houser, & Huang, 2007) argue that ESL teachers must establish themselves as equal partners in their ELs' education in order to effectively collaborate with general education teachers. For example, Davison (2006) offers that the idea of classroom teachers and ESL teachers being equal partners is not easy and nearly always fraught with tension, primarily because general education teachers may view themselves (albeit sometimes unconsciously) as having primary authority over their students.

Fu et al. (2007) argue that part of the tension that content area teachers and ESL teachers face in collaboration is based on presumptions that (1) ESL teachers teach only the basics of language and nothing about content (e.g., reading, writing, math, science, or history), and (2) classroom teachers do not know how to develop ELs' reading, writing, or vocabulary skills so the ELs' can understand the content they are supposed to learn. To deal with difficulties that may arise with two coauthorities in the classroom, the researchers recommend continual planning and collaboration that enables ESL teachers and content teachers to communicate their observations, goals, and student assessments with one another.

TESOL International Association recently produced a report related to the role of the ESL teacher during the implementation of the Common Core State Standards. Major findings included that the ESL teachers' expertise is often misunderstood, often relegating them to a lower status.

Due to the new demands of the Common Core, ESL teachers' roles are now shifting to those of collaborators, advocates, and experts (TESOL, 2013). The report suggested that administrators provide vehicles for ESL teachers to develop their leadership voices in order to have a more visible impact on policy decisions that affect ELs in their school.

Leveraging the role of the ESL teacher to create effective collaboration between ESL teachers and general education teachers hinges on more clearly defining the ESL teacher's seminal role in the achievement of ELs. Effective ESL/general education collaboration is also believed to improve ELs' achievement, but this collaboration cannot happen without stakeholders carefully designing a space in which it can successfully take place. The next section of this chapter is about how to design a space in which collaboration to foster EL advocacy can take root and flourish.

> What are some ways in which ESL and content teachers collaborate at your school? What works well? What could be improved?

THE ROLE OF THE ESL TEACHER: VOICES FROM THE FIELD

I have been collecting quotes from ESL teachers as I provide them professional development on various topics, including collaboration and advocacy for ELs. In one recent session, I asked a group of teachers from across Pennsylvania to define their role as it currently stands. Some of their shorter responses included social worker, advocate, mentor, interpreter, and a trusted adult.

Some of their other, lengthier responses were as follows:

- I improve ELs' social and academic language, monitor their ability in content curriculum, and help (general education) teachers learn to modify instruction.
- My role is an integral part of ELs' achievement. I am the liaison between the EL and U.S. culture and all that is necessary for success here.
- I am their advocate. I provide a comfortable, nurturing environment in which they're not afraid to take risks when participating orally in their learning.
- I am compassionate and patient and provide a comfort zone for the students. I enjoy learning about them as well.
- I prepare them to be able to participate with their peers.
- I help them navigate the school environment.
- I am like the mama bear taking care of her cubs!

- I am the anchor for my ELs.
- My role is to help ELs succeed in all academic subjects and help them access resources to aid navigation in this country.
- As a middle school ESL teacher, I have a huge role in my ELs' achievement. I collaborate with the English language arts teacher on a daily basis to make sure instruction is modified for and comprehensible to them.
- I am the advocate who goes to bat for the ELs with their content teachers.
- I'm the biggest supporter of ELs' education in my school. My advocacy for them sometimes gets me in trouble; administration gets tired of hearing me.
- I prepare them for what may come in their general education classrooms and give them tools to become more successful in the general education classroom.
- I have a huge role—for some students I've been told I'm the only person that actually teaches them.

A quick analysis of the quotes above tells us that these ESL teachers see themselves as more than just content specialists in language acquisition and scaffolding instruction for ELs, which in itself requires a deep degree of content knowledge. However, as these teachers describe it, the role of the ESL teacher often extends beyond supporting students' academic success. These roles underscore the extensive expertise ESL teachers possess that can be leveraged to support ELs' success in school.

In working with ESL teachers, I often ask them what expertise they bring to the table that they can build on with the rest of the school. Quite often, they first acknowledge their expertise around empathy for ELs instead of recognizing their strengths in instructional strategies for ELs. ESL teachers often report that they have a love of language and culture that drives their interactions with ELs. Many times, they share that they have been Spanish learners, Tagalog learners, Swedish learners, et cetera, at some point in their lives, facing challenges living in another culture and speaking another language, and at times attending school in another language. The experience some share with ELs has built many teachers' sense of empathy for how difficult it can be to function in a language in which they're not proficient, and it often carries over to their work with ELs.

All the while, teachers recognize that their experiences abroad were most likely driven by different purposes than those of their ELs' families; instead of immigrating

> Which skills and experiences in terms of working with ELs do you bring to the table that you could leverage when collaborating with other teachers?

to a new country for economic or political reasons as ELs often do, ESL teachers may have studied abroad during college or taught abroad by choice for the experience of living in another country. Quite often, the empathy facet of ESL teachers' role can be just as powerful as their expertise in language acquisition and teaching techniques, depending on the context in which they find themselves. One of educators' tasks is to "bottle" ESL teachers' empathy for ELs and determine how to replicate it appropriately within and across schools.[3]

ESL Teachers' Opportunities for Collaboration and Advocacy

Once ESL teachers recognize that they possess unique skills in working with ELs, they can begin to leverage their expertise to bring about positive changes for ELs on the schoolwide level. Despite the valid challenge of there not being enough time for ESL and content teachers to collaborate and lack of a structure to facilitate this formal level of collaboration, many less traditional opportunities exist for ESL teachers to use their expertise to increase general educators' and administrators' repertoire of skills and approaches to better meet their ELs' needs.

ESL teachers typically begin their advocacy efforts on a small scale by first focusing their energy with individual students. For example, a teacher may notice that an EL who is still developing English language proficiency should be considered for a gifted and talented program or may work to ensure an EL has access to afterschool tutoring. After teachers experience success advocating for their ELs in their own classrooms, they may feel empowered to begin to make changes happen with students and teachers outside their own classrooms by collaborating with other teachers. These teachers could then have a wider impact on more ELs at their school and possibly begin advocating for ELs at the district level. The image in Figure 3.1 portrays the ripple effect that advocates for ELs can have, beginning with their own students and, after developing advocacy skills, eventually having an impact on more ELs, teachers, and policymakers in larger numbers. As the ripple grows wider, the number of ELs that are positively impacted by these advocacy efforts increases dramatically.

Collaboration to Bring About Change for ELs

Collaborating and making positive changes occur for ELs does not need to be as formal as providing planned, ongoing professional development with an entire school or hosting an event for parents of ELs. It can—and should—start with smaller, more personal teachable moments. Teachers

---

3. See the empathy-building activities described in Chapter 2.

Figure 3.1. Ripple Effect of EL Advocacy

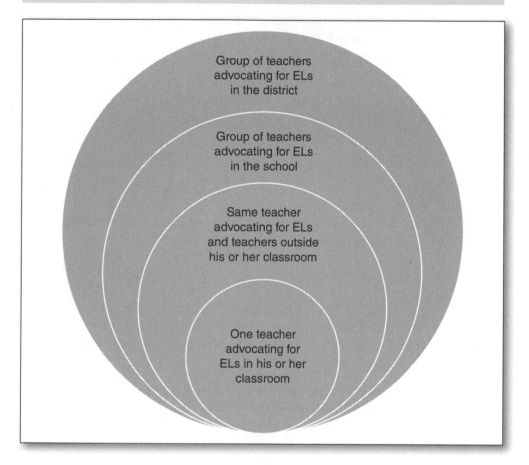

should also consider how their efforts will be perceived by other teachers and administrators. If they are perceived as supportive of content teachers' efforts and as professionals who acknowledge these educators' expertise, their advocacy efforts will have the potential to reach a wider audience. On the contrary, if they are perceived as confrontational or disrespectful of content teachers' knowledge of their subject matter and experience teaching, they will likely face more roadblocks to their advocacy for ELs.

> How do you think other teachers and administrators perceive your current EL advocacy efforts? Why?

SCALING UP EL ADVOCACY IN DIFFERENT CONTEXTS

Teachers will first need to take into consideration what kinds of collaborative opportunities present themselves most easily in their context. Opportunities for ESL teachers to begin their EL advocacy efforts by first focusing on their

EL caseloads are likely dependent upon the context in which ESL teachers find themselves, as contexts vary widely depending on the state, region, district, and school. Table 3.1 outlines some different roles ESL teachers can play to advocate for their students within their own classrooms first and suggests opportunities for collaboration and advocacy within those contexts.

Table 3.1. Examples of Different Roles ESL Teachers Can Play and Opportunities for Collaboration and Advocacy

ESL Teacher Role	Potential Opportunities for Collaboration and Advocacy
Itinerant ESL teacher	This scenario may be among the most challenging, since an itinerant teacher is not based at one school but serves two or more. Itinerant ESL teachers might be providing pull-out classes or push-in support, or they might be coteaching, depending on their context. They will have to make their presence and expertise known at the schools they serve and possibly be more assertive about collaboration with ELs' teachers of record and advocating for their ELs.
Stand-alone ESL teacher (Pull-out ESL at elementary level)	These teachers will likely be coordinating with several grade-level teachers who are their ESL students' teachers of record. This scenario presents multiple opportunities for collaboration related to ELs' instruction and assessment. If ESL teachers have ELs at the same grade level taught by different content teachers, they could have a brief meeting with the group once a week or so to provide input on EL strategies for the content teachers' lesson plans and to learn what content will be taught in the upcoming week, so the ESL teacher can support their ELs' language and content development and check in on their ELs' progress.
Stand-alone ESL teacher (Pull-out ESL at secondary level)	In many cases, middle and high school ESL teachers will have their students for a separate period or more of ESL instruction. This scenario presents benefits as well as challenges: ESL teachers may be regarded as more responsible for their ELs' acquisition of English, yet at the same time, they may have to exert more effort to collaborate with content teachers to ensure they are supporting the content teachers' efforts.
Push-in ESL teacher	In this scenario, the ESL teacher works with groups of ELs within a content or general education class for limited amounts of time. This scenario presents multiple opportunities for collaboration related to EL strategies and techniques. However, ESL teachers must exercise caution to be sure they are regarded teachers of equal stature, not teachers in a subordinate role.

ESL Teacher Role	Potential Opportunities for Collaboration and Advocacy
ESL coteacher	There will be ample opportunities for ESL teachers who coteach a general education or content class to collaborate with their partner teacher(s) and model what advocacy for their shared ELs can look like. Like the push-in ESL teachers, they must also exercise caution to ensure their teaching is seen as just as important as the content teacher's instruction. Some teachers have compared coteaching to an arranged marriage—sometimes the relationship clicks immediately and other times it takes considerable effort to build an effective relationship between coteachers.

I suggest ESL teachers begin to build their reputations for having EL expertise and being a source of support to other teachers in their building by first focusing on smaller, more personal moments in which they dialogue informally with individual content teachers. ESL teachers may wish to begin checking in with each of their EL students' content teachers to first acknowledge the content teachers' efforts to do their best with their ELs, empathizing with them and pointing out concrete examples of what the ESL teacher knows the content teacher is doing to better serve the needs of their EL students. ESL teachers should begin a dialogue with content teachers by drawing their attention to the steps content teachers are taking to equitably educate their ELs, even if they are small steps.

ESL teachers may wish to share a checklist or menu of topics in which content teachers could use extra support and focus on one or two topics at a time. ESL teachers can check in with content teachers quarterly or as needed to facilitate an ongoing dialogue. See Table 3.2 below for a sample collaborative menu list.

Table 3.2. ESL/Content Teacher Collaboration Checklist

Area of EL Support	ESL Teacher Support Needed	Comments
Knowledge of second language acquisition	Yes / No	
Teaching academic vocabulary to ELs	Yes / No	

(Continued)

Table 3.2. (Continued)

Area of EL Support	ESL Teacher Support Needed	Comments
Planning lessons for ELs at different levels of English language proficiency	Yes / No	
Teaching academic language to ELs	Yes / No	
Teaching reading to ELs	Yes / No	
Teaching writing to ELs	Yes / No	
Creating content and language objectives for ELs	Yes / No	
Understanding and using English language proficiency scores to design instruction for ELs	Yes / No	
Designing formative assessment for ELs	Yes / No	
Understanding federal and state policy for ELs	Yes / No	
Communicating with families of ELs to increase parental involvement	Yes / No	
Providing ELs access to community resources	Yes / No	
Understanding and incorporating ELs' culture in instruction	Yes / No	
Creating a safe classroom environment for ELs	Yes / No	
Other areas (describe)	Yes / No	

Collaboration Action Plan for ESL and Content Teachers

One idea to self-assess areas in which collaboration is needed to foster ELs' success in school is for teachers to participate in a reflective exercise. Ideally, a content teacher and an ESL teacher would complete this exercise together and use the results to brainstorm an action plan collaboratively. The template shown in Table 3.3 can be used for this purpose. This exercise leads ESL teachers and content teachers to focus on one area that they can take steps to strengthen together. It can be undertaken quarterly so that progress can be gauged and results noted.

Table 3.3.   ESL/Content Teacher Collaboration Action Plan

Action Plan Consideration	Explanation
An area in which collaboration is needed	
Why it's needed	
How I'll collaborate	
Who I'll need support from	
How I'll measure success	

After organizing her thoughts with the action plan, Maria invited a group of content teachers to meet with her and showed them some translation websites, and also showed them some homework assignment schedules that she had already translated as a model. She also explained that the teachers might need to work with the school's parent liaison to call the parents if the parents were unable to read in their primary language. Maria also decided to check in with her assistant principal, Karyn, with whom she shared a good relationship, to apprise Karyn

Maria, an ESL teacher, shared the following information in her collaboration action plan, as shown in Table 3.4. She decided to focus on one area where she felt her efforts could have an immediate impact for ELs and their families. After the content teachers she was collaborating with remarked how many of their ELs weren't turning in their homework, instead of blaming them for not providing the assignment information in a language the students' parents could understand, she thought more deeply about the issue, and she also asked her ELs about why they weren't turning in their content teachers' homework. She determined that her students' parents did not understand the content teachers' expectations, so she decided to provide some EL advocacy on a small scale.

of the situation and ask for her support. Together, Maria and Karyn determined that this issue was more pervasive at the school and that Maria should provide a short session to the school's teachers on translation websites and interpretation services that were available. Maria recognized that there would still be errors using websites for translation, but she thought temporarily tolerating a few linguistic errors, until a better solution could be found, would be better than parents not understanding their children's homework schedules.

Table 3.4. Maria's Completed ESL/Content Teacher Collaboration Action Plan

Action Plan Consideration	Explanation
An area in which collaboration is needed	Providing translations to parents of ELs in their home language.
Why it's needed	My ELs shared that their parents are confused about when their children must turn in their homework assignments.
How I'll collaborate	I'll share some translation websites with the content teachers so that they can translate information for parents about when the homework assignments are due; I'll also model some translated homework assignment schedules and check back in with them weekly via email to see if they need more support until they start doing this automatically.
Who I'll need support from	I don't technically need support from administration, but I'll see if this is an area multiple teachers need support with. I'll then approach my assistant principal to see if she could let me give a 10-minute presentation on this during the next staff meeting.
How I'll measure success	If all the content teachers I work with report providing a translation of the homework schedule, and if all my ELs tell me that their parents now understand when their assignments are due, I'll know my plan has succeeded. The next step would be for me to work with content teachers to have them provide a translation of the actual content of the homework assignments, but I'll work on that after teachers get used to sending a translated homework schedule home first.

Examples of Tools to Foster Collaboration

One way to continue to foster collaboration between ESL and content teachers is to create a form for each EL in the school that serves as a collaborative tool to guide teacher discussions about each student's "story," including his or her background, English language proficiency level, strategies for instruction, and assessment considerations.

As a point of comparison, all students who are eligible to receive special education services, including ELs who are dually identified for special education, are required by law to have a 504 plan or an individualized education program (IEP) that documents these students' classroom and testing accommodations as well as instructional goals. Parents, teachers, and school staff are part of the process of completing the 504 plan or IEP. Each student who qualifies for a 504 plan or IEP receives a plan that is tailored to that student's particular strengths and areas of need.

However, ELs who are not dually identified are not required by federal law to have a similar individual plan that outlines their classroom and testing accommodations, language goals, and instructional methods according to the student's background variables such as English language proficiency (ELP), level of schooling in the first language, and amount of literacy in the first language. I believe all ELs should have an individual plan that encourages collaboration among all the stakeholders in the EL's education so that all ELs receive instruction that is built upon their unique background variables and personalized to improve their English language proficiency and allow them access to challenging content material.

There are several ways ESL teachers can go about creating a collaborative tool to foster effective instruction of ELs. One example of a collaborative tool used across a school district is found in Figure 3.2. (see p. 71). Manassas City Public Schools is a school district in Northern Virginia that has experienced an explosion of EL student growth during the past decade, currently serving more than 2,200 ELs who constitute approximately 35% of all students enrolled in the district. Manassas City Public Schools realized they needed to provide a consistent approach across all schools in the district to ensure the equitable education of their ELs through collaboration among all educators who taught ELs. The district has created several tools to increase school and district personnel's understanding of who the population is and how to better serve their needs.

> Would a collaborative tool help support your EL collaboration and advocacy work? If so, how? If not, what roadblocks are currently in your way, and how can you address them?

One tool they have created is the individualized instructional plan (IIP). The IIP contains information on each student, and each ESL teacher in the district is assigned a caseload of EL students for whom they ensure that collaboration among stakeholders occurs so that each EL receives individualized instruction based on accurate English language proficiency assessment results and instructional needs. Manassas City Public Schools' IIP documents two or more learning goals for each EL each semester that are framed around World-Class Instructional Design and Assessment (WIDA) English language proficiency standards, which the state has adopted. Virginia has also adopted WIDA's *ACCESS for ELLs* annual English language proficiency assessment.

The IIP is completed collaboratively by the student's caseload manager and classroom/core content teachers. The classroom/core content teacher and the ESL teacher meet to discuss the appropriate classroom accommodations and strategies that will best meet the language needs of each EL. Then, the caseload manager and classroom/core content teacher review the spring English language proficiency assessment score on WIDA's *ACCESS for ELLs* and check off the subject area in which the goal is to be set and what language domain the goal covers (speaking, listening, reading, or writing). Classroom/core content teachers and the ESL teacher then determine two learning goals per EL per semester. The learning goals are based on the *ACCESS for ELLs* spring scores, descriptors for the student's level of English language proficiency, performance model indicators, state content standards, and the academic needs of the EL. Learning goals must be academic in nature and supported by assessment data. ESL case managers are responsible for working with and sharing the learning goals with the EL's classroom/content area teacher(s) and other available teachers/specialists (physical education, special education, etc.) who may work with the student each semester. The lead teacher is responsible for ensuring all learning goals are completed by the end of each semester. Caseload managers fill in information on each IIP electronically and then save the IIPs to the district's shared drive for all teachers in the school to access. It is a district expectation that all staff will know where the IIPs are and how to access them.

Ways in Which Teachers Can Share EL Expertise

There are many ways in which ESL teachers can spread their knowledge about instructing and advocating for ELs, and many scenarios do not require formal professional development sessions with teachers and administrators. Table 3.5 outlines different levels of collaborative opportunities for ESL and content teachers and administrators, highlighting the potential benefits and detractors of each scenario.

HONING PEOPLE SKILLS TO EXTEND ADVOCACY EFFORTS

Many ESL teachers I have worked with have described their successes and challenges in collaborating with other teachers and administrators in order to advocate for their ELs. The majority of ESL teachers agree that they need to demonstrate empathy as well as "people skills" or

Figure 3.2. Manassas City Public Schools EL Individualized Instructional Plan

---

English Language Learner Individual Instruction Plan—Manassas City Public Schools

Student Name: Last ☐ First ☐		Gr. ☐	School Year: ☐
School: ☐	Caseload Teacher: ☐		Student's ACCESS composite score /W-APT[4] Score ☐ ☐

Possible Recommendations to Address Instructional Methods, Learning Needs, and English Acquisition for
Content Areas of ☐ Language Arts, ☐ Social Studies, ☐ Science, and ☐ Math (check all that apply)

☐ scaffold responses
☐ use high interest/low vocabulary materials
☐ scribe prewriting activities while student brainstorms

☐ sheltered instruction
☐ read texts to student when appropriate
☐ scribe activities completed under time restraints

☐ paraphrase directions for tasks
☐ engage in academic conversations
☐ scribe instructional activities requiring written responses

☐ administer assessments in small groups
☐ highlight the instructions/directions
☐ use an English dictionary daily

☐ use visual cues daily
☐ read aloud for language modeling
☐ use a thesaurus as needed

☐ use graphic organizers
☐ introduce academic vocabulary
☐ use a bilingual dictionary as needed

☐ pair with a peer tutor
☐ link instruction to prior knowledge
☐ model language and task completion

☐ break tasks/directions into sub tasks
☐ provide content and language objectives
☐ speak slowly and face student when speaking

☐ increase wait time
☐ print instead of using cursive writing
☐ support essential vocabulary/concepts in content area

☐ label items in a classroom
☐ extended time for assignments and assessments
☐ shorten assignments

☐ use books on tape
☐ build background knowledge
☐ other _____

(Continued)

---

4. The W-APT is the WIDA-ACCESS Placement Test. It is WIDA's English language proficiency assessment "screener" administered to students who indicate a language other than English is spoken by the student or in the student's home on the home language survey. The screener is given to students who may be designated as ELs and helps with the identification and placement of ELs.

Figure 3.2. (Continued)

Work with the classroom/teacher to identify two or more learning goals in each content area for the current school year. Learning goals should be based on W-APT or ACCESS score reports, ELP standards, and language learning needs of the student. Goals are to be developed each semester.

Category	Domain	Objective 1—1st Semester	Objective 2—2nd Semester
Social Instruction	▪ Listening ▪ Speaking ▪ Reading ▪ Writing		
Language Arts	▪ Listening ▪ Speaking ▪ Reading ▪ Writing		
Math	▪ Listening ▪ Speaking ▪ Reading ▪ Writing		
Science	▪ Listening ▪ Speaking ▪ Reading ▪ Writing		
Social Studies	▪ Listening ▪ Speaking ▪ Reading ▪ Writing		
Classroom/Content Teacher(s)		Date 1st Semester	Date 2nd Semester
ELL Teacher		Date 1st Semester	Date 2nd Semester
		LEP[5] Plan Completed On	LEP Plan Revised On
		Notes:	

Source: Manassas City Public Schools

5. *LEP* or *limited English proficient* is the term the federal government uses for ELs. Although EL educators tend to use the term EL, many districts and states must use the term LEP on their forms.

Table 3.5. Opportunities for Collaboration With Educators: Pros and Cons

Collaborative Opportunity	Explanation	Potential Pros	Potential Cons
Candid conversations	Provide an avenue for informal conversations with teachers and administrators about ELs ESL teachers can share suggestions and resources targeted at specific students and teachers	Can take place anywhere—in the hallway, in the lunchroom, or before or after school Tend to be low stress for ESL and content teachers Help build rapport between ESL and content teachers	Might be sporadic and not ongoing Reach only one person at a time
ESL teacher observations of content teachers' classrooms	After observing a content teacher's class, an ESL teacher offers specific strategies for that teacher to reach his or her ELs	Provides a first-hand look at the classroom context ELs are in, so the ESL teacher can design targeted strategies	Content teachers may not feel comfortable with someone else observing their classroom When an observer is present, observed teachers may not teach the way they normally do
ESL teacher strategy modeling	ESL teachers model strategies for ELs in their own classrooms or in a content teacher's classroom	Content teacher can see how ESL teacher applies a particular strategy in the content teacher's own context	Requires planning and time Students may not be used to ESL teacher and may not immediately warm up to him or her
Content/ESL teacher conferences	Meetings at an agreed-upon time in which content teacher(s) meet with ESL teacher(s) to share challenges and strategies for teaching ELs	More formal in nature than candid conversations May reach a larger number of teachers	May be challenging to schedule due to time restrictions May not be ongoing
Professional development	ESL teacher leads school staff through activities aimed at effectively educating ELs based on a needs assessment	Will reach a larger number of teachers Provides the opportunity for teachers and administrators to have a dialogue about ELs	Some teachers may not want to attend Must put in effort to make professional development ongoing

(Continued)

Table 3.5. (Continued)

Collaborative Opportunity	Explanation	Potential Pros	Potential Cons
Professional learning communities	ESL teacher leads an ongoing process to establish a schoolwide culture that develops teacher leadership focused on building and sustaining school improvement efforts related to ELs	Can be a leading force behind ongoing improvement related to ELs Freedom to choose topics relevant to EL equity and achievement	May already need to have PLC infrastructure in place; if not, will need to work with administrators to establish a PLC focused on ELs
Peer coaching	ESL teachers with colleagues to reflect on current practices; expand, refine, and build new skills; share ideas; teach one another; conduct classroom research; or solve problems collaboratively	Is individualized to teachers' needs and level of comfort working with ELs and collaborating with professionals	May require a significant time commitment if it is ongoing

> Which people skills do you see as your strengths? Which areas do you need to work on to connect with your colleagues and collaborate with them?

"soft skills" in addition to content knowledge in order to bring other teachers and administrators on board to advocate for ELs at the school level and beyond. ESL teachers must possess deep knowledge of their discipline and also have highly developed interpersonal skills to support other teachers to make changes in their teaching and advocacy efforts on behalf of ELs.

Gaining Others' Respect in the School

Some ESL teachers I have worked with on collaboration shared the challenges they have experienced in working to broaden their sphere of influence outside their classroom. While most ESL teachers reported successes to varying degrees in sharing the responsibility to teach ELs, some ESL teachers still felt their EL expertise was not being fully recognized in their school. Their feelings on the topic included the following:

> I wish I could say my opinions and knowledge were more valued, but I don't feel it. It's as though it's a big bother for classroom teachers to have to adapt (to teaching ELs).

At this point this (recognition of my expertise) is a mystery—until I have been working longer in the ESL field, some people are not going to see me as knowledgeable.

Even though ESL teachers noted some challenges remained, I suggest ESL teachers focus on a few areas of professionalism to support their work with teachers and administrators on improving ELs' education.

Respecting Content Teachers' Expertise

It may go without saying, but if ESL teachers wish for other teachers to respect their EL expertise, they should begin by consciously respecting content teachers' expertise in their content areas. Many content teachers did not anticipate teaching ELs and/or were likely not trained in EL strategies or methods. To help build their empathy for content teachers, ESL teachers can imagine how they would feel if they were suddenly required to teach calculus without a strong desire to do so and without training in the subject. Content teachers who did not "sign up" to teach ELs may feel the same way—pressured to teach ELs without enough resources to do so effectively. I suggest ESL teachers begin expanding their EL advocacy efforts by seeking out teachers they feel do have a level of respect for ESL teachers' expertise and who are open to working with ELs.

> Which one or two teachers in your school would you say are open to working with ELs? What do they do that makes you feel this way?

Serving as an Example for EL Advocacy

ESL teachers can also serve as an example or model of how to better instruct ELs and advocate for them. By meeting with teachers informally in a nonthreatening setting, ESL teachers can demonstrate some techniques for working with ELs or some resources to draw upon to better serve ELs in their communities. For example, instead of telling content teachers they need to scaffold or differentiate lessons for ELs, ESL teachers can show them some ideas for how to scaffold a particular lesson content teachers have already developed.

Another way to model advocacy is to exemplify respect for ELs. ESL teachers need to constantly affirm their ELs' academic and cultural strengths and, in many cases, sing ELs' praises with general education teachers and administrators. By modeling this vocal support of ELs' strengths and achievements—in essence, putting a positive spin

> What do you currently do to highlight ELs' accomplishments in your classroom and school?

on ELs—ESL teachers can create a ripple effect to help other educators warm up to the idea that ELs can and do achieve academically despite challenges.

Showcasing EL Student Achievement

One way to generate momentum behind positive EL public relations is to share EL success stories with content teachers and administrators. For example, ESL teachers will have access to English language proficiency test scores that may be confusing for content teachers and administrators to interpret. One way to highlight ELs' linguistic growth is for ESL teachers to meet with their building's educators and provide them an overview of what the English language proficiency test scores mean, shining a light on individual student growth from the previous year or a certain point in the past, perhaps when the student enrolled in the country. This sharing of data helps demonstrate ELs' gains in terms of linguistic growth. Another way to share ELs' successes is by calling attention to them in the school's yearbook. Susan LaFond, a former ESL teacher in upstate New York, shared with me that her high school's yearbook advisor worked with her to give their school's ESL program a full page in the school yearbook where they could showcase their students, their program, and their work.

The following vignette illustrates how an ESL teacher worked collaboratively with his peers to advocate for his ELs.

Binh Nguyen is a fourth grade ESL teacher who realized through multiple conversations with other fourth grade teachers that they often felt challenged working with the ELs in their classrooms. He practiced being an empathetic listener and put himself in the teachers' shoes, knowing that they were doing their best to accommodate the needs of their ELs but also had to work with the full continuum of other students in their classes. These included students who received special education services, students in the gifted and talented programs, "average" students, and native English speakers who lacked the academic language to access the content of the general education teachers' instruction.

After a month of mentally noting the teachers' concerns, he decided to first focus his EL advocacy efforts on supporting Emily and James, two content teachers who were challenged with teaching ELs but who seemed most open to receiving advice in how to help their ELs succeed. He first asked if he could observe their classes, and after observing the classes, he met with the teachers on several occasions, modeling strategies they could try in their classes. All the while, Emily and James shared how valuable Mr. Nguyen's help was with the other fourth grade teachers in their school, who in turn became more receptive to Mr. Nguyen when he offered to observe their classes and provide them with support a month later.

Mr. Nguyen began to feel that he was better positioned to scale up his advocacy efforts beyond the fourth grade. So, prior to the school's winter inservice day, he asked his assistant principal if he could bring back Meena, an articulate, likable former EL who was now a successful high school student, to speak to the school's general education and ESL teachers about ways in which elementary teachers helped her learn English and feel valued as an EL while she was a student at the school. Mr. Nguyen envisioned that Meena's informal presentation would highlight some of the strategies he shared with the fourth grade content teachers. The inservice was a success, and he continued his efforts at the next inservice by showcasing other ELs' academic achievements and modeling strategies for other content teachers to use with their ELs. He also followed up with teachers and administrators between professional development sessions to ensure that ELs' strengths and needs were on educators' radar screens.

Using People Skills to Advocate for ELs: Begin Slowly and "Gently"

The focus now turns to how ESL teachers can use their professional or people skills as a tool to improve ELs' equitable education at schools or districts. The first suggestion is to begin EL advocacy efforts slowly and thoughtfully. ESL teachers should decide to work on one or two issues with individual teachers they feel might be receptive to receiving more support. All the while, ESL teachers should make themselves available to listen to content teachers, empathize with them, and follow up with them to keep the lines of communication open.

Withhold Comments as Appropriate

When ESL teachers work with other teachers who may not share the same values related to educating ELs, such as recognizing their culture and language as strengths and generally viewing them from an asset perspective, ESL teachers will most likely hear remarks that reflect beliefs that are not similar to their own. In fact, ESL teachers may hear other teachers' statements about ELs that are offensive, racist, or otherwise caustic. Some teachers may not be afraid to hold back their feelings when they interact with ESL teachers, transferring their frustration to ESL teachers or even treating ESL teachers as scapegoats.

If general education teachers share a deficit or even racist view of ELs with ESL teachers (or if ESL teachers overhear someone making an uninformed statement about ELs), I recommend ESL teachers take a breath and pause before they immediately defend the students. ESL teachers should defend the ELs, but it should not be a knee-jerk reaction. ESL teachers will have a chance to more effectively work to improve the students' educational experience if they approach such situations carefully. When a teacher or administrator with whom ESL teachers are interacting makes a questionable statement regarding ELs, I recommend first acknowledging that person's statement. ESL teachers should keep in mind these individuals' feelings may be stemming from their frustration in working with ELs or another entirely unrelated issue. ESL teachers may then wish to reframe some of the other teachers' comments in more positive terms and then try to work on a solution together.

Here's a sample conversation:

Bob: I wish I didn't have Margarita in my class. All she does is speak Spanish with her neighbor and distract everyone else I'm trying to teach.

Lilia: I understand how it can be distracting to the other students when Margarita speaks Spanish with her neighbor. It can also be frustrating for you when you're trying to teach everyone. How long has this been happening?

Bob: Oh, she's been doing it all year. I just wish it would stop.

Lilia: We don't know this for sure, but Margarita may be reaching out to her neighbor to get some clarification on instruction. Do you think that could be possible?

Bob: I'm not sure. I suspect she might just be gossiping about the other kids and goofing off.

Lilia: Right. We can't be sure until we talk to her. How about if I observe your class this week and see how she's doing? We can then speak with her together after class to see if she needs some extra support in class. How does that sound?

Bob: Sure. We can do that, although it may not solve anything.

Lilia didn't immediately jump to defend Margarita, as she may have wanted to do. Instead, she listened to Bob and restated his concerns to show she was listening and comprehending what he said. She also showed empathy for his situation. Margarita may indeed be acting out, but it may also be that she doesn't understand what is happening in class and is reaching out to a peer to make sense of Bob's instruction. Lilia did not take Bob's comments personally but saw them as a way to improve Margarita's instruction. Lilia did not have an immediate solution but offered to collaborate with Bob to do some more research on what was happening with Margarita to ultimately support Bob's instruction of Margarita (and potentially other ELs in Bob's class).

As Lilia demonstrated, it's important for ESL teachers not to take teachers' unexpected comments related to ELs personally, or your message of advocacy and positive change for ELs may get derailed. ESL teachers should try to allow their passion for ELs to shine through their collaboration with teachers and administrators, modeling the kind of professional interactions they would like to ripple through the school. Lilia did not blame Bob for the situation but instead offered to support his efforts in the classroom. ESL teachers could potentially unravel their professional reputation in one confrontation with a teacher—the ripple effect can also be detrimental. ESL teachers should remain patient and recognize that change may come about slowly and in small pieces, but their calculated efforts will indeed be worthwhile for their schools' ELs.

> What would you do if faced with caustic remarks about an EL in particular or ELs in general?

CONCLUSION

This chapter focused on ways in which ESL teachers can collaborate with general education teachers and administrators to advocate for ELs. The chapter suggested that ESL teachers begin advocacy efforts thoughtfully and slowly so that later they can scale up advocacy efforts, creating a larger ripple effect of EL advocacy. The chapter also examined how ESL teachers can leverage their people skills, including demonstrations of empathy, to support their message of equity and advocacy for ELs. Chapter 4 shifts the EL advocacy perspective to the school- or district-level administrator, highlighting challenges and suggesting steps these individuals can take to advocate for ELs in their roles.

REFERENCES

Abu-Rabia, S. (2004). Teachers' role, learners' gender differences, and FL anxiety among seventh-grade students studying English as a FL. *Educational Psychology, 24*(5), 711–721. doi:10.1080/0144341042000263006

Ajayi, L. (2011). Exploring how ESL teachers relate their ethnic and social backgrounds to practice. *Race, Ethnicity and Education, 14*(2), 253–275. doi:10.1080/13613324.2010.488900

Arkoudis, S. (2006). Negotiating the rough ground between ESL and mainstream teachers. *International Journal of Bilingual Education and Bilingualism, 9*(4), 415–433. doi:10.2167/beb337.0

Davison, C. (2006). Collaboration between ESL and content teachers: How do we know when we are doing it right? *International Journal of Bilingual Education and Bilingualism, 9*(4), 454–475. doi:10.2167/beb339.0

DelliCarpini, M. (2009). Success with ELLs. *English Journal, 98* (4), 133–137.

Fu, D., Houser, R., & Huang, A. (2007). A collaboration between ESL and regular classroom teachers for ELL students' literacy development. *Changing English, 14*(3), 325–342. doi:10.1080/13586840701712014

Ghanizadeh, A., & Moafian, F. (2010). The role of EFL teachers' emotional intelligence in their success. *ELT Journal, 64*(4), 424–435. doi:10.1093/elt/ccp084

He, Y., Prater, K., & Steed, T. (2011). Moving beyond "just good teaching": ESL professional development for all teachers. *Professional Development in Education, 37*(1), 7–18. doi:10.1080/19415250903467199

Honigsfeld, A., & Dove, M. (2010). *Collaboration and co-teaching: Strategies for English learners.* Thousand Oaks, CA: Corwin.

Teachers of English to Speakers of Other Languages (TESOL). (2013, April). *Implementing the Common Core State Standards for ELs: The changing role of the ESL teacher.* Alexandria, VA: Author.

4

Advocacy Overview for School and District Administrators

In this opening piece, Esta Montano reflects upon her advocacy efforts for ELs. Dr. Montano is the director of English language education special programs for Boston Public Schools. She shares,

> I never realized that I was advocating for my students because I always thought that what is now referred to as "advocacy" was actually part of my job as a teacher. For me, advocacy took many forms, but it always began with relationships. In thinking back to my days as a teacher, it is without a doubt that the most monumental advocacy that I ever undertook was the formation of a student affinity group called *Adelante*, which in Spanish means "forward." In the spring of my first year teaching a Spanish language and literature class for Latino ninth graders (composed of a combination of English learners and former English learners), we began to talk about college. It became clear to me that my students had absolutely no idea as to how to access higher education, nor did their parents. They expressed how lost they felt, and how impossible the idea of college seemed to them. I asked them if they wanted to form an afterschool group so that we could explore this together, and they eagerly embraced the idea.

Adelante became a stronghold for Latino students in this high school and at its peak boasted 70 members, more than could fit into a classroom. Not only did it become a venue for exploring higher education, but it became a forum for Latino students to construct their identity and build leadership skills. Members became resolute about showing the school community that they would be known for their positive contributions rather than the negative stereotypes that they knew all too well. Community service, fund-raising, and mentoring younger students became a part of their mission. And in the saddest moments, when members faced the death of their peers, *Adelante* offered a place to grieve together and to move into action, beginning a scholarship to memorialize a friend and taking contributions to help send a fellow student's body home. *Adelante* lasted for 10 years and served countless Latino students. It was featured in the local newspaper on numerous occasions, and *Adelante* members were recognized in award ceremonies and at other community events.

INTRODUCTION

Administrators such as Dr. Montano, whether at the school, district, or state level, can have a huge impact on EL advocacy that takes place in their setting. A supportive administrator who embraces and embodies advocacy efforts for ELs can positively affect ELs' experiences in school and beyond. This chapter is geared toward administrators at the school, district, and state levels and provides ideas and examples of some areas in which advocacy for ELs should be considered. It focuses on the overarching goal of creating a school or district culture conducive to EL advocacy. Although geared toward administrators, this chapter will also help give teachers some insight into the varied roles as well as challenges administrators face in moving EL advocacy forward.

WHAT THE RESEARCH TELLS US

The research highlighted in this chapter is centered on four topics. The first is creating a school or district culture conducive to EL advocacy. The second is considerations in hiring staff who are likely to be advocates for ELs. The third is the importance of professional development in terms of advocacy for ELs. Finally, research related to teacher evaluation systems that are inclusive of ELs is shared.

Creating a School or District Culture Conducive to EL Advocacy

In order to build and support a culture of academic success for all students, including ELs, whole campus intervention and knowledge of ways to effectively educate ELs are needed (Shefelbine, 2008). To meet these goals of equitable EL education, schools must ensure that their ELs are encouraged as well as supported so they can take part and succeed in advanced courses. These types of changes cannot occur without strong leadership, however. The school's principal holds a key role in determining as well as shaping this culture that supports equitable education of ELs (Leithwood, Seashore Louis, Anderson, & Wahlstrom, 2004). Alford and Niño (2011) state that the principal serves as the school's primary communicator of the vision of high expectations for student success, including ELs. Furthermore, the principal has multiple opportunities each day to serve as the school's spokesperson in both formal and informal settings. Administrators at the district level also hold a great deal of influence in their ability to shape a districtwide culture that is conducive to EL advocacy and achievement.

> What kind of messages are you sending about creating a culture conducive to EL achievement in your school or district?

Hiring Staff Who Will Be Advocates for ELs

As the number of ELs continues to increase in the United States, principals and district administrators will need to consider the qualities they would like teachers of ELs to possess. One responsibility that falls upon the school principal or district administrator is making hiring decisions that will impact instruction for ELs. Researchers and policymakers are beginning to define which qualities and expertise are necessary for teachers of ELs. For example, Rogoff (2003) states that it is crucial that teaching staff have the knowledge and skill necessary to recognize ELs' cultural capital from multiple perspectives—individual, family, and community—and then scaffold or transform these experiences within new learning contexts. Meyer (2000) highlights the importance of ELs' culture and expands the definition of skilled teachers of ELs, indicating, "Teachers who instruct English learners must be skilled at lowering four significant barriers to meaningful instruction: cognitive load, culture load, language load, and learning load" (p. 229).

Given the complexities involved with finding and hiring qualified teachers who can effectively instruct all students, including ELs,[1] Garcia and Potemski (2009) emphasize six overarching strate-

> What kinds of guidelines do you use when hiring teachers who will work with ELs? How can you decide which teachers possess the skills to instruct them effectively?

---

1. Chapter 6 will focus on the effective instruction of ELs.

gies for hiring effective teachers of ELs. They suggest that principals and administrators (1) recruit teachers who are familiar with the language and culture of ELs, (2) train general education teachers to work with ELs, (3) recruit paraeducators into training programs to become certified teachers of ELs, (4) develop alternative certification programs, (5) recruit educators globally, and (6) target financial incentives.

PD Conducive to EL Advocacy

Staff development opportunities related to teaching ELs for practicing teachers tend to be underrepresented (National Center for Education Statistics, NCES, 2001). Furthermore, surveys of attitudes and feelings of preparedness indicate that content teachers tend to feel uneasy with their lack of knowledge in teaching ELs (NCES, 2001). In particular, a new survey reveals that 76% of teachers do not feel prepared to teach the Common Core State Standards to ELs (Editorial Projects in Education Research Center, 2013). Therefore, one more piece of the puzzle that is necessary for administrators to create an environment conducive to EL advocacy and achievement is through PD. Summarizing the efforts that are needed to effectively meet the needs of ELs, Alford and Niño (2011) believe that principals must work with teachers to build their "care, capacity, and confidence" in terms of their EL students (p. 64).

Rather than providing one-shot PD sessions, principals and other administrators are encouraged to implement ongoing professional development that can take place through varied formats such as peer coaching, site visits, and book studies (Alford & Niño, 2011). These authors also recommend forming professional learning communities (PLCs) so teachers can collaborate with content and/or grade-level peers as well as ESL teachers around meeting the challenges of teaching ELs. DuFour (2004) recommends that when administrators create a PLC, they should focus on learning rather than teaching, work collaboratively, and hold themselves accountable for results.

> How is the topic of teaching and advocating for ELs included in your context's PD plan? Which factors shaped this decision?

Teacher Evaluation that is Inclusive of ELs

One final area that administrators should consider is how teacher evaluation systems define and support all teachers' effective teaching of ELs to foster teachers' growth in working with these students. Creating a shared sense of responsibility to educate ELs also extends to teacher evaluation systems, in that teacher evaluation systems must define what effective teaching of ELs looks like for all teachers who work with them, not only for ESL teachers.

The National Comprehensive Center for Teacher Quality (2012) has provided a leading voice on the issue of teacher evaluation that is inclusive of ELs and outlines challenges as well as provides several recommendations in evaluating teachers of ELs based on findings from an expert forum. Their recommendations include the following:

- Develop evaluation systems that set high standards for teachers and reflect the special knowledge and skills teachers require to effectively educate ELs but that can also differentiate among teachers to ensure that teachers with ELs are included.
- Use multiple measures in evaluation systems.
- Develop exemplars of teaching practice at different levels of teaching proficiency to guide evaluators in evaluating effective teaching practices for ELs.
- Attribute growth in EL learning to teams of educators, rather than to individual teachers.
- Develop evaluation systems that can be linked to professional development.
- Connect evaluation standards to teacher preparation programs.

CREATING A SCHOOL OR DISTRICT CULTURE CONDUCIVE TO EL ADVOCACY

Administrators will be seen as leading the charge and setting the tone in creating a school, district, or even state culture that is conducive to advocating for ELs' success. If they serve as EL advocates by walking the walk and talking the talk, they are modeling the kind of vision, mission, and actions that they would like to see their staff emulate. They will also have to develop buy-in from their staff members who will possess varying skills, dispositions, and levels of knowledge to effectively instruct and advocate for ELs.

Reflective Tool

The reflective tool shown in Figure 4.1 can be used at the school, district, or state level. Working through these questions individually and then discussing them as a group can help an administrative team gauge where they find themselves in terms of their vision for the equitable education of ELs. The tool has been adapted from content created by August, Salend,

Figure 4.1. EL Administrator Reflective Tool

EL Advocacy Element	Rarely	Sometimes	Always	Comments
Does our school clearly articulate and communicate a vision for and commitment to educating all ELs effectively in classrooms? If so, how? If not, what barriers to equal access for ELs exist and how can they be addressed?				
Does our school ensure that legal and educationally sound procedures are followed when identifying and placing ELs in appropriate educational settings?				
Does our school provide ample opportunities for ELs to interact with fluent speakers of English in order for them to acquire academic and social language, and to support the acculturation of these students into the school and society while maintaining their first language and culture?				
Does our school provide all educators with access to data (e.g., grades, observations, curriculum-based assessments, formative assessments, records, and test scores) related to ELs' academic achievement and English language development?				
Do teacher evaluations use relevant performance indicators in a performance-based evaluation system that is inclusive of ELs?				
Does the school utilize strategies that help ELs develop supportive relationships with other students and teachers?				
Do ELs in our schools have opportunities to engage in extracurricular programs? If not, how can administrators redesign extracurricular offerings to ensure that ELs have access to them?				
Does the school's language support program effectively address ELs' linguistic and cultural strengths as well as needs?				
Does the district achieve and sustain a 100% graduation rate with ELs?				
Do the school's services, policies, and practices take into account the cultural, linguistic, and experiential backgrounds of all students and their families?				

EL Advocacy Element	Rarely	Sometimes	Always	Comments
Does the school provide all ELs with access to a challenging, high-quality, developmentally appropriate curriculum aligned to the state's standards within and across content areas?				
Does the school utilize a variety of valid and reliable measures to assess EL student learning progress and inform instruction? Does the school offer ELs the appropriate informal and formal assessment accommodations they need to demonstrate their learning?				
Do educators, students, families, caregivers, and community members collaborate to communicate, share resources and expertise, make decisions, and solve problems related to EL education in our school? Does the school provide educators with adequate time to collaborate with each other and to communicate with ELs' families, caregivers, and community members?				
Does the school communicate a sense of community around ELs where individual cultural and linguistic differences are valued? In what ways?				
Does the school staff embody a desire to actively include and support the school's ELs in all facets of their education and socialization?				

Source: August, Salend, Staehr Fenner, & Kozik, 2012.

Staehr Fenner, and Kozik (2012). The word *district* or *state* can be substituted for *school* as appropriate to administrators' context.

Guiding Questions

After you complete the reflective tool, you can work through these guiding questions in a group or individually:

- In which areas is your school the strongest?
- In which areas do you most greatly need to improve?
- Which areas will you prioritize that you would need to change to make the greatest impact on the effective teaching of ELs and evaluation of teachers who work with them?
- Which steps can you take to make these improvements?

Hiring Staff Who Embody EL Advocacy:
After facilitating focus groups with high school teachers who taught sheltered content[2] to ELs in a large school district on the East Coast of the United States, I learned that many teachers in the focus group were chosen to teach sheltered content to ELs primarily because they spoke Spanish, not because they were necessarily trained to teach ELs. Many of those teachers rose up to meet the challenges of teaching content and language simultaneously to ELs and reported positive experiences with ELs and fondness for teaching these students. However, not all of the content teachers in that group shared the same willingness to teach ELs due to the extra challenges involved. My takeaway is that administrators should hire new content teachers carefully. Also, when deciding how to best utilize their current staff, administrators should consider what kinds of knowledge and skills their content teachers must possess in order to successfully teach ELs. In any case, administrators should create a structure for content teachers to collaborate with ESL teachers.

Teachers of ELs in general frequently fulfill a multitude of roles in schools. All teachers who work with ELs need to be able to teach them in instructionally sound ways and advocate for ELs and their families. No matter what their position, having teachers and staff who represent some of the ELs' home cultures to the extent possible is particularly valuable in being able to connect with students and families and also provide role models for students. However, it may not always be feasible to have each student's culture represented by staff when the school educates students from multiple countries or when there is not a qualified pool of teachers. In those cases, administrators can encourage ELs' parents to volunteer as their schedules allow so that students can see the EL parents are a valued part of the school community.[3]

While it may be a bit easier to learn about current or potential teachers' experience working with ELs by looking at their résumés or asking them about their years of experience, it may prove more difficult to ascertain their underlying *disposition* to actively advocate for their ELs' equitable education. One resource administrators can use to learn more about their potential and current staff's expertise as well as dispositions toward advocacy for ELs can be found through TESOL's P–12 Professional Teaching Standards (TESOL, 2010). Due to the changing demographics in the United States and the need to devote more attention to the instruction of ELs, all teachers of ELs should be knowledgeable about TESOL's five domains of language, culture, instruction, assessment, and professionalism (Staehr Fenner & Kuhlman, 2012). TESOL's professional standards can guide formal new hire interviews, or they can be used as a framework to check in

---

2. These teachers taught separate content courses such as mathematics, science, and social studies that contained only ELs and were taken for credit toward graduation.

3. For more suggestions on increasing EL parent engagement, see Chapter 5.

with inservice teachers regarding their skills and dispositions to teach ELs.

Table 4.1 outlines each of TESOL's 11 standards for teachers of ELs and provides a guiding question as well as "look-

> How do you currently determine your new hires' dispositions to work with and advocate for ELs?

fors" related to each question. The look-fors describe some potential answers that indicate the interviewee is knowledgeable about working with ELs as described by each standard. Each look-for contains potential responses that indicate expertise and positive disposition toward working with ELs, but it cannot encompass all areas of interviewees' responses. Each look-for has been differentiated between what all teachers of ELs should know, which is described on a more general level, as well as the higher level of expertise and positive dispositions that ESL teachers should embody. Each ESL teacher look-for is additive, which means it would also contain the information in the content teacher look-for.

ESL teachers can contribute to the hiring process by reviewing the job description and suggesting questions that would help administrators determine job applicants' dispositions toward working with ELs as well as the skills they possess in working with these students. I highly encourage administrators to include ESL teachers during candidate interviews.

PROVIDING PD ON ELS TO STAFF

In addition to hiring the staff that will provide top-notch instruction for ELs and advocate for them, administrators can also consider developing EL advocacy skills in their current staff. From the administrator's perspective, it is important to consider the topics for PD related to ELs collaboratively with ESL as well as content teachers and other administrators. One suggestion is to develop a PD plan jointly with the school's stakeholders and also include EL parents to add to the conversation.[4]

Some Ideas for PD to Support ELs

Some additional ideas are provided below that incorporate the personal experience of ELs that extends beyond their effective instruction.

- Cultural workshops on lesser known aspects of the multifaceted cultures of students represented in the school (e.g., the range of school experiences in ELs' home countries, parent perspectives on education, school and parent expectations for children, career opportunities).

---

4. Information on learning more about EL families' challenges is provided in Chapter 5.

Table 4.1. Teacher Interview Look-Fors

TESOL Standard	Interview Question	Content Teacher Look-For	ESL Teacher Look-For
1a: Language as a System Candidates demonstrate understanding of language as a system, including phonology, morphology, syntax, pragmatics, and semantics, and support ELLs as they acquire English language and literacy in order to achieve in the content areas.	Tell me what you know about academic language. How would you teach ELs academic language and content simultaneously? Give an example.	A recognition that there is a difference between social and academic language, noting that ELs may sound fluent in English when talking about familiar topics but may lack the complex language needed to succeed academically.	A description of the difference between academic and social language and of the components of academic language (e.g., grammar, syntax, academic vocabulary, discourse). An understanding that it is necessary to teach academic language and content by creating student learning objectives that describe language and content.
1b: Language Acquisition and Development Candidates understand and apply theories and research in language acquisition and development to support their ELLs' English language and literacy learning and content-area achievement.	What are some factors that can impact an EL's acquisition of English? What would you like to know about your ELs so you can adjust your instruction appropriately?	The language the parents speak at home and quality of instruction can impact an EL's acquisition of English. Would like to know which languages the ELs speak and which countries they or their families were born in.	The amount of literacy in the student's first language, quality of education in the home country (if applicable), exposure to trauma, and motivation to learn would impact an EL's acquisition of English. Would like to know the amount and quality of schooling in the home language, mobility in the home country and abroad, and parents' level of literacy in the home language.
2: Culture as It Affects Student Learning Candidates know, understand, and use major theories and research related to the nature and role of culture in their instruction.	How does an EL's culture affect his or her success in the classroom?	An acknowledgment that ELs come from different cultures and may not share the same cultural background as native English speakers.	An acknowledgment that ELs' cultures are not monolithic even though students may come from the same country, and that culture extends beyond holidays and festivals. Demonstration of understanding that instruction is often based on assumptions of background knowledge that are tied in to culture, and that teachers may have to first find out how their ELs' culture impacts their background knowledge.

TESOL Standard	Interview Question	Content Teacher Look-For	ESL Teacher Look-For
They demonstrate understanding of how cultural groups and individual cultural identities affect language learning and school achievement.	Give an example of how you would ensure that your instruction builds on your ELs' cultures.	A description of a situation in which they would learn about their students' cultures and address their students' cultures during instruction (e.g., through multicultural literature, holidays, etc.).	Description of how they would learn about their ELs' cultures during instruction and integrate students' rich background experiences and culture into instruction.
3a: Planning for Standards-Based ESL and Content Instruction Candidates know, understand, and apply concepts, research, and best practices to plan classroom instruction in a supportive learning environment for ELLs. They plan for multilevel classrooms with learners from diverse backgrounds using standards-based ESL and content curriculum.	Think of a lesson you would teach. Describe the lesson. Now, tell me how you would scaffold that lesson for ELs at the beginner, intermediate, and advanced level of English language proficiency.	Awareness that different levels of scaffolding are needed for ELs at different levels of English language proficiency. An attempt to provide more linguistic support at lower levels of English language proficiency.	A description of a detailed lesson that targets specific strategies for teaching ELs at different levels of English language proficiency. Integration of English language proficiency and relevant content standards in instruction and assessment.
3b: Implementing and Managing Standards-Based ESL and Content Instruction Candidates know, manage, and implement a variety of standards-based teaching	Think of the lesson you just described. How would you use it to teach ELs listening, speaking, reading, and writing? What	The lesson contains elements that teach ELs listening, speaking, reading, and writing through academic content.	Articulation of the need to integrate the four domains into rigorous content area instruction as well as the need to base instruction around the content area as well as around English language development/ proficiency standards.

(Continued)

Table 4.1. (Continued)

TESOL Standard	Interview Question	Content Teacher Look-For	ESL Teacher Look-For
strategies and techniques for developing and integrating English listening, speaking, reading, and writing. Candidates support ELLs' access to the core curriculum by teaching language through academic content.	are your lesson's learning objectives for students that foster their development of academic language and understanding of content?	The lesson is designed around the core curriculum, and the content is not watered down for ELs.	Clear description of how the learning objectives support ELs' integrated development of academic language and content knowledge.
3c: Using Resources and Technology Effectively in ESL and Content Instruction: Candidates are familiar with a wide range of standards-based materials, resources, and technologies, and choose, adapt, and use them in effective ESL and content teaching.	Describe a text you use for your students. Which elements of that text make it challenging for ELs to comprehend? Tell me how you choose and adapt that text as well as other materials for English learners.	Acknowledgment that it may be challenging for ELs to access complex grade-level text due to their level of skill in reading English. Mention of graphic organizers and/or visuals to help provide support to ELs as well as use of technology.	Acknowledgment that it may be challenging for ELs to access complex grade-level text due to their amount of background knowledge. Description of frontloading ELs' exposure to grade-level text by providing background context for reading materials in the students' first language if possible, and integrating resources on the same topic at a less complex reading level to support ELs' comprehension of text.
4a: Issues of Assessment for English Language Learners: Candidates demonstrate understanding of various assessment issues as they affect ELLs, such as accountability, bias, special education testing,	Tell me what kinds of testing your ELs must undergo and what some issues are related to each kind of assessment.	Demonstration of awareness that ELs must be assessed annually in English language proficiency/development as well as take part in most annual content area assessments.	Teachers must be knowledgeable about each EL's background variables in order to choose effective linguistic accommodations for that student on content area assessments. Knowledge that accommodations offered on assessments should also be integrated into classroom instruction.

TESOL Standard	Interview Question	Content Teacher Look-For	ESL Teacher Look-For
language proficiency, and accommodations in formal testing situations.	How should you choose accommodations for ELs on content area assessments?	Demonstration of awareness that cultural bias may exist in testing and that it may be challenging to assess ELs for a disability. Awareness that certain accommodations are allowed to ELs on content area assessments.	Ability to articulate some reasons it is challenging to discern between linguistic difference and presence of a disability in ELs. Awareness that accommodations are allowed for dually identified ELs/students with disabilities on English language proficiency/development assessments.
4b: Language Proficiency Assessment: Candidates know and can use a variety of standards-based language proficiency instruments to show language growth and to inform their instruction. They demonstrate understanding of their uses for identification, placement, and reclassification of ELLs.	What is the state English language proficiency/ development assessment that is used with ELs? What kind of information does it give you, and how can you use this information to guide your instruction of ELs?	Awareness of the name of the English language proficiency/ development assessment used in the state and the information it provides on an EL's proficiency in listening, speaking, reading, and writing. Awareness that the teacher should be familiar with these scores in the four domains to target instruction.	Ability to describe the kind of tasks ELs must perform on the state's English language proficiency/development assessment and to describe how scores are calculated in the four domains of listening, speaking, reading, and writing. Demonstration of ability to interpret proficiency test scores to target instruction of English.
4c: Classroom-Based Assessment for ESL: Candidates know and can use a variety of performance-based	How do you design assessments so that your ELs can demonstrate their understanding of content? Give an example of a performance-based	Description of using performance-based assessments so that ELs can demonstrate what they know and can do.	Description of the utility of frequent informal assessments to gauge ELs' progress. Description of a specific

(Continued)

Table 4.1. (Continued)

TESOL Standard	Interview Question	Content Teacher Look-For	ESL Teacher Look-For
assessment tools and techniques to inform instruction in the classroom.	assessment you could use with ELs and how that assessment's results can inform your instruction.	Description of one way to assess ELs' performance and how teacher uses the assessment's results to modify future instruction of content.	performance-based assessment and how the results were used to modify instruction of academic language and content for ELs.
5a: ESL Research and History: Candidates demonstrate knowledge of history, research, educational public policy, and current practice in the field of ESL teaching and apply this knowledge to inform teaching and learning.	Tell me about what kind of rights ELs and their parents have in the educational setting.	Description of how ELs must have equal access to a quality education that enables them to progress academically while learning English.	Citation of legislation and court cases such as *Lau v. Nichols* (1974) and *Castañeda v. Pickard* (1981) and their impact on the education of ELs.
5b: Professional Development, Partnerships, and Advocacy: Candidates take advantage of professional growth opportunities and demonstrate the ability to build partnerships with colleagues and students' families, serve as community resources, and advocate for ELs.	What are some of the biggest issues and challenges facing ELs in this context (e.g., school or district)? What could you do to build partnerships and advocate for ELs so that your ELs receive an equitable education and their families feel valued and included?	Description of how the teacher could work with ESL professionals to include and advocate for ELs. Demonstration of awareness that there are community resources available for teacher to use to advocate for ELs.	Description of how the teacher could collaborate with content teachers and administration to advocate for ELs so that they have access to school and community resources. Description of ways in which the teacher could reach out to families of ELs to include them in the education of their children.

Note: The TESOL Professional Teaching Standards utilize the term *English language learner* or ELL.

94

- Courses for teachers on some of the languages represented in the school so that educators can make the effort to communicate with ELs in their own language (e.g., a Spanish for educators or Mandarin for educators course).
- Training on how to deal with student and family trauma that may pose a challenge to learning (e.g., refugee experiences; effects of civil war, natural disasters, socioeconomic stress).
- PD on community resources that are available for ELs and their families (e.g., churches that provide social services for immigrant families, housing services, workforce development).
- Sessions on health concerns for ELs presented by the school nurse and community health centers that cater to the immigrant community (e.g., vision screenings, different cultural perspectives on health and medical care).

EL Advocacy Snapshot From One School District: By Laura Kuti, Chesterfield County (Virginia) ESOL Coordinator

As a district with almost 3,000 English learners, we make many efforts to advocate for our students. We have an online learning module that all teachers and administrators must review to provide information regarding Title III requirements, second language acquisition theory, English language development standards, identification/placement/service/exit protocol, and strategies for instruction. This creates a districtwide foundation on which we base additional PD.

We provide extensive PD throughout the year to principals, counselors, ESOL teachers, and content/classroom teachers that is tailored to address their needs as educators working with English learners. For the parents of our English learners, we have one literacy program that was developed by one of our ESOL teachers that helps parents understand how to incorporate reading in the home. We also offer a technology and literacy combination series of classes that provides parents with basic computer skills and family literacy skills using online children's books.

Finally, we offer "Parents as Educational Partners" programs in which we provide parents with information about the U.S. school system and build their English skills. Babysitting for young children and tutoring for older children are provided while parents attend classes.

As part of meeting federal requirements, ESOL staff attend state conferences to ensure that they are informed of updates to policy, and they coordinate with local administrators on implementing policy. Overall, we advocate for our students at the classroom level, at the district level, and by working with families.

Focus Groups

Another suggestion to help inform PD offerings is to convene a focus group of select staff, EL parents, EL students (if they are old enough), and community members to chart a course for PD at your school. There may be issues related to advocacy for ELs that administrators are unaware of, and convening various perspectives on EL education may be an avenue to provide them access to those various voices.

A focus group is an informal tool to conduct qualitative research on people's perceptions, opinions, beliefs, and attitudes toward a product, service, concept, advertisement, or idea (Henderson, 2009). When conducting a focus group, it may be beneficial for administrators not to conduct the group or to even be present during the focus group meeting, as their presence may inhibit participants' willingness to share their experiences and open opinions about the education of ELs. Focus groups work best when participants feel at ease, respected, and free to offer their opinions without being judged (Krueger & Casey, 2009).

Sample Focus Group Guidelines

Before stakeholders are convened, a protocol of no longer than one page should be created. The protocol outlines the purpose for the focus group and selected topics that will be discussed. Once the participants have been gathered, the purpose for holding the focus group should be made clear. It will also be crucial to ensure that interpreters are present to ensure communication among the ELs, their parents, and the school staff. A sample protocol to determine EL issues at a school is shown in Figure 4.2. It should be noted that the topics listed are not survey questions. Rather, the facilitator uses the topics as a guide to pose guiding questions to the participants.

Administrators should consider having at least one note taker and recording the conversation after receiving participants' verbal consent. In addition, administrators should consult their school's or district's policy in terms of convening a focus group. After the focus group has adjourned, facilitators should synthesize the notes from the focus group and then share them with the stakeholders to determine next steps in advocating for ELs.

Professional Learning Communities

Another form of PD that administrators can integrate into their school is professional learning communities (PLCs). PLCs can be formed around salient topics related to EL education and advocacy, such as integrating ELs' families into their children's academic experience, understanding ELs' cultures, and improving the instruction of ELs. One strategy for a PLC could be to read an article together related to the instruction of or advocacy for ELs that is chosen by the ESL teacher. The PLC members could then discuss the article and apply its information to their own teaching context. Each teacher in the group could take turns choosing a

Figure 4.2. Sample Focus Group Protocol

Focus Group Topic: Successes and Challenges of English Learners in Our School

Thank you for participating in today's focus group. Today we have teachers, administrators, high school English learners, and parents of English learners who will share their perspective on the topics below. Your participation is vital in determining which issues are most important to teaching English learners in school and meeting their challenges outside of school. Thank you for speaking openly about your experiences. With your permission, we will record this session, but your statements will remain anonymous.

My successes in school (as a teacher of English learners, as an English learner, as the parent of an English learner)—20 minutes

My challenges in school (as a teacher of English learners, as an English learner, as the parent of an English learner)—20 minutes

My successes outside of school (as a teacher of English learners, as an English learner, as the parent of an English learner)—20 minutes

My challenges (as a teacher of English learners, as an English learner, as the parent of an English learner)—20 minutes

What the school is doing well for me—20 minutes

What the school can do better for me—20 minutes

reading or taking part in a webinar on a topic of interest related to ELs to suggest for discussion and application.

EL-RESPONSIVE TEACHER OBSERVATION AS PART OF TEACHER EVALUATION SYSTEMS

Another way to exemplify advocacy for ELs is to examine and adapt the teacher observation component of a school's or district's teacher evaluations so that ELs' unique linguistic and cultural needs are taken into consideration. To begin with, administrators can analyze their current teacher observation system to consider the degree to which ELs are instructed effectively in the classroom. Administrators can consider what makes teaching ELs different from teaching other students[5] and how this information is documented in the current teacher observation system. Administrators should collaborate with ESL teachers during this process to leverage the ESL teachers' expertise on the topic.

---

5. See Chapter 6 for a deeper exploration of effective teaching practices for ELs.

What makes teaching ELs different from teaching non-ELs? What does effective teaching of ELs look like in general education or content area classrooms? What would you look for during a teacher observation to document that all teachers are instructing ELs effectively?

Teacher Observation Rubrics From New York and Rhode Island

For example, five school districts in New York and five school districts in Rhode Island have worked with the American Federation of Teachers (AFT) as part of an AFT Innovation Fund and United States Department of Education Investing in Innovation grant to design and pilot a teacher evaluation system that provides evidence of teachers' skills at working with ELs as well as students with disabilities (SWD). Working collaboratively with ESL teachers and district and state administrators, participants have adapted teacher observation rubrics to help them capture multiple facets of effective teaching for ELs and SWD.

Since most teacher evaluators at the school level do not have extensive EL or SWD teaching experience or training, turnaround training was also provided to teacher evaluation leaders in the 10 districts. This training helped evaluators understand what sound instruction of ELs and SWD can look like "on the ground" for content area teachers in today's multilevel, multicultural classrooms. The PD was linked with indicators from the adapted teacher observation rubrics that tied the training in with the evaluation component. The teacher observation rubrics[6] from New York and Rhode Island, shown in Figures 4.3 and 4.4, provide a small sample of how these pilot districts define some of the considerations as well as observable behaviors all teachers of ELs should demonstrate when working with these students. Although considerations for effectively teaching students with disabilities have also been added to the rubrics, only the EL considerations have been included in the figures for purposes of this audience.

Sheltered Instruction Observation Protocol Checklist for Teachers and Administrators

Another example of observable actions that exemplify quality teaching of ELs is contained in the sheltered instruction observation protocol (SIOP) model (Echevarria, Vogt, & Short, 2008). All teachers who work with ELs can use the checklist (Figure 4.5) adapted from SIOP, for self-reflection while planning for instruction. School and district administrators can use the checklist as an observation tool to assess teachers' ability to effectively instruct ELs in the content areas. The educator's comments section provides a space for teachers and administrators to jot down notes regarding each element from the protocol.

---

6. Rubrics are awaiting final approval.

Figure 4.3. New York Sample Teacher Observation Rubric

NY Standard II: Knowledge of Content and Instructional Planning

Teachers know the content they are responsible for teaching and plan instruction that ensures growth and achievement for all students.

Element II.1 Teachers demonstrate knowledge of the content they teach, including relationships among central concepts, tools of inquiry, [and] structures and current developments within their discipline(s).

NYSED Indicators: Incorporate key concepts during instruction through the use of multiple representations and explanations. Engage students to use key disciplinary language with comprehension through instruction. Demonstrate the effective use of current developments in pedagogy and content. Design learning experiences that foster student understanding of key disciplinary themes. Demonstrate knowledge of the learning standards and their application throughout their instruction and practice.

Indicators	Ineffective	Developing	Effective	Highly Effective
Uses current developments in pedagogy and content	Teacher is not current on content-related pedagogy and is unable to cite current research to explain planned instructional decisions.	Teacher has a limited understanding of current content-related pedagogy and cites limited or dated research to explain planned instructional decisions.	Teacher understands current content-related pedagogy and cites current research to explain planned instructional decisions.	Teacher understands current content-related pedagogy and cites current research to explain planned instructional decisions. Teacher seeks out new developments to enhance practice.
Considerations for ELLs:	For teachers of ELLs, teacher understands pedagogy related to how to ensure ELLs access grade-appropriate content as well as further the development of their English proficiency. Teachers will need to have access to specialists or support personnel knowledgeable about ESL.			

Source: New York State United Teachers, 2013.

Figure 4.4. Rhode Island Sample Teacher Observation Rubric

Rhode Island Standard 1: Planning and Preparation

Component 1.2: Establishing Instructional Outcomes

Teaching is goal directed and designed to achieve certain well-defined purposes. It is through the articulation of instructional outcomes that the teacher describes these purposes. They should be clear and related to what it is that the students are intended to learn as a consequence of instruction. 21st Century outcomes must be included, as students must also learn the essential skills such as critical thinking, problem solving, communication and collaboration. (Danielson, Framework for Teaching, 2007)

Elements / Performance Indicators	Ineffective	Developing	Effective	Highly Effective
1.2 *Establishing Instructional Outcomes* *RIPTS 1, 2, 3, 4, 5*	Outcomes represent low expectations for students and lack rigor. They do not reflect important learning in the discipline, and/or are stated as activities, rather than as student learning. Outcomes reflect only one type of learning and are suitable for only some students. Outcomes are not connected to standards.	Outcomes represent moderately high expectations and rigor. Some reflect important learning in the discipline, and consist of a combination of outcomes and activities. Outcomes reflect several types of learning and are suitable for most of the students in the class. Outcomes are connected to standards.	Most outcomes represent rigorous and important learning in the discipline. All the instructional outcomes are clear, written in the form of student learning, and suggest viable methods of assessment. Outcomes reflect different types of learning and take into account the varying needs of groups of students. Outcomes are connected to standards.	All outcomes represent rigorous and important learning in the discipline. The outcomes are clear, written in the form of student learning, and permit viable methods of assessment. Outcomes reflect several different types of learning, and, where appropriate, represent opportunities for both coordination and integration with other disciplines. Outcomes take into account the varying needs of individual students. Outcomes are connected to standards.

Elements / Performance Indicators	Ineffective	Developing	Effective	Highly Effective
Considerations for ELLs:	• Lack of English language proficiency will affect student outcomes. • Pre/post conference is the opportunity to explain why outcomes may look different based on students' language needs. • Teachers must receive guidance on how to assess students with low English proficiency when the lesson and assessment are based on grade level standards. • Teachers will need knowledge of two sets of standards for ELLs—the general education standards and English language proficiency standards (e.g., WIDA standards). It will be important to have an understanding of both and how they go together. • Teachers will need to have access to specialists or support personnel knowledgeable about ESL.			

Source: Rhode Island Federation of Teachers and Health Professionals, 2012.

Figure 4.5. Checklist for Planning and Observation of Sheltered Instruction

Observer(s):_____

Teacher: _____ School:_____

Date:_____ Grade: _____ ESL Level(s): _____ Class/Topic: _____

Lesson: Multiday/Single Day *(circle one)*

Element	Considerations	*Highly Evident*	*Somewhat Evident*	*Not Evident*	**Educator's Comments**
Preparation	• Content and language objectives clearly defined, displayed, and discussed with students • Appropriate content concepts • Use of supplementary materials to support the lesson's clarity • Content and materials adapted to all levels of English proficiency • Activities that integrate content and language practice opportunities				
Building Background	• Content's concepts linked to students' background knowledge and experiences • Explicit links between prior learning and new concepts • Key vocabulary emphasized through multiple means				
Comprehensible Input	• Teachers' rate of speech and spoken language appropriate for students' English proficiency levels • Academic tasks clearly explained • Variety of techniques used to make content clear for ELs (e.g., modeling, visuals, hands-on, gestures)				
Strategies	• Students apply learning strategies throughout lesson • Consistent use of appropriate scaffolding techniques • Variety of questions and tasks that support higher-order thinking skills				

Adapted from Echevarria, Vogt, & Short, 2008.

CREATING POSITIVE CHANGES FOR ENGLISH LEARNERS AT THE SCHOOL AND DISTRICT LEVEL

As part of an EL advocacy stance, administrators can put policies in place that benefit ELs and their teachers. The examples in this section illustrate how EL advocacy ideas blossomed into impactful programs at the school and district level. These examples all began with one person noticing that the status quo was insufficient to support ELs. Advocacy for ELs can—and often does—take shape with one advocate deciding that something is not quite right for ELs and putting forth effort to make a change. In turn, these administrators collaborated with others and leveraged their expertise with ELs to make a positive impact on their teachers, ELs, ELs' families, and even on the business community.

> Which policies related to ELs work well for your setting? Which need to be improved or adapted to better serve your ELs? Why?

The Importance of Mentorship and Advocacy

by Margarita Pinkos, ESOL Director, Palm Beach County, Florida

Given ELs' circumstances, schools need to develop the advocacy support that students need in order to ensure their success. As a school administrator, I have sought to ensure that all students have at least one adult on campus that clearly understands their needs and personalizes the instructional experience for them. We all aim to provide this kind of support for all students, but in the case of English learners, the support provided must include opportunities for the students to communicate in their own language with people who understand their culture. I have struggled first hand with the specific support needed for English language learners as the director of English for Speakers of Other Languages (ESOL) in the District of Palm Beach County, the 11th-largest school district in the nation and home to over 18,000 ELs.

In 2002, I developed a partnership with the local state university to provide a cadre of teachers with specialized training to meet the specific needs of ELs. Bilingual and bicultural teachers that represent the population of the district were selected to participate in this program based on their demonstrated work in advocating for ELs. Funding from Title III was used to pay the teachers' tuition for a master's degree in school guidance and counseling. They were assigned to the schools with the largest numbers of ELs in the district to work under the mentorship of certified guidance counselors until they completed their degrees. The university adapted the courses to maintain the rigor of their program and supplemented it with a culturally relevant curriculum as well as encouraged strong collaboration among the participants in the cohort.

Within a period of five years, 58 bilingual guidance counselors completed their degrees, and they are currently serving the needs of our students. Their work is inspiring; they have become focal points for interaction among EL students, their families, the schools, and the community. Parent involvement has increased exponentially, and the district has made significant gains in the graduation rate for ELs.

One of the most important contributions of this program has been the recognition of a group of students who had been invisible in many schools. Today, the services of bilingual and bicultural guidance counselors have been institutionalized, and even in difficult budgetary times, principals, board members, and the community in general have advocated for the program to remain at current funding levels. Their influence is commonly reported by EL students and their families as the reason they were able to succeed in school.

> Would a similar initiative be beneficial to your setting? Why or why not? If so, which aspects of Ms. Pinko's efforts could you try to replicate on a smaller scale in your school or district?

EL State-Level Advocacy Examples

The following vignettes are based on EL advocacy efforts that Sara Waring, PhD, former South Dakota state Title III director, undertook in her position.

INFLUX OF ILLITERATE ENGLISH LEARNERS MIXING WITH LITERATE ENGLISH LEARNERS

Challenge: The district had a large population of Bosnian and Albanian students. These students had been well educated in their native language and had been refugees in Germany, affording them an understanding of the second language acquisition process as they acquired German. The district learned that they would be receiving students from the African nation of Somalia. The Somali students were illiterate in their native language, and most had never attended school prior to arriving in the United States. This new population required a different approach to learning English than the Bosnian and Albanian students had required.

Solution: The state provided technical assistance to the district administrators and teachers to help them increase their background knowledge on the Somali culture and prepare for the enrollment of students from Somalia. The district began an intensive language immersion program to support the intense language needs of the students and their families. The district's program changes helped the students and their families acclimate to the state, community, and school.

Guiding Questions for Discussion or Reflection

- What do you see as the benefits in the state's response?
- What else could various stakeholders have done to advocate for these Somali students? Which similar challenges does your district face?
- How would you respond to these challenges?

INCORPORATION OF ENGLISH LEARNERS' CULTURE

Challenge: A school district's administrators and teachers were not familiar with their ELs' cultures and needed more strategies to teach them effectively.

Solution: The district administration implemented a new policy that incorporated updates and new information on the cultures that were represented in the school's EL program. These updates were provided monthly at staff meetings. The EL teachers provided information on incoming student populations and updated information about cultural groups that were already being served in the program. The information included the educational background on the populations as well as teaching strategies and techniques that research and experience had shown to be beneficial. Prior to the monthly meetings, staff could submit questions to the ESL teachers about specific concerns or request recommendations to support the learning in the mainstream classroom.

Guiding Questions for Discussion or Reflection

- What were the benefits of including regular updates and new information on ELs' cultures during staff meetings?
- What are you doing in your school or district to ensure teachers and administrators are familiar with your ELs' cultures?
- How do you integrate ELs' needs during staff meetings?
- How are you utilizing your ESL teachers as resources?

SCHOOL-BUSINESS PARTNERSHIPS

Challenge: A new cheese plant was being built in the city, and the manufacturer was going to be recruiting from a community in Mexico. The influx of Mexican families would dramatically increase the number of ELs in the school district.

Solution: The school district reached out to the manufacturer to set up a committee to better understand the workforce that the plant would be recruiting from and to prepare for new EL students. The district did not have an EL program in place but began planning and preparing for the new students that would be entering the school in the following school year. Due to this advocacy on behalf

> *of the district administration, the teachers were better prepared when the new students arrived, benefiting the students and their families' transition into the new school system in the United States. The district also was better prepared to enroll the new students in school, with procedures in place and certified teachers. District administrators continued to meet monthly with the plant management to understand when new groups of families would arrive and to prepare for new enrollments.*

Guiding Questions for Discussion or Reflection

- How do you think the school–business partnership benefitted ELs and their families in this context?
- What impact do businesses in your community have on your EL student population?
- What can you do to foster relationships with local businesses to better serve your ELs and their families?
- In what ways could schools and businesses partner in your community to advocate for ELs and their families?

Getting the Good Word Out About ELs

Far too often, information we receive through the media highlights ELs' challenges instead of strengths. In striving to advocate for ELs, administrators can disseminate positive information about ELs' strengths. There are multiple avenues to share ELs' successes with the school and community at large, such as school newsletters, e-mails, social media, and the local newspaper. Yanguas (2012) suggests the following:

> All too often there are negative perceptions regarding programs for [ELs] that can be countered with a school visit or a school report. Therefore, whenever there is an opportunity to showcase [EL] students in a school, not only should notices be sent to the parents, school officials, and school board members, they should also go to other groups in the community, including the media, local elected officials, and local business and community groups.
>
> Any follow-up reports about such events or additional documents that describe the academic progress and other accomplishments of [EL] students (including those accomplishments not easily measured by standardized tests but that may be socio-affective in nature, e.g., outstanding parental involvement at different events, former [ELs]

How do you publicize ELs' accomplishments? What has been effective for you? How is this information received?

becoming teachers in the school district,) should also be sent to these different stakeholder groups. (pp. 228–229)

CONCLUSION

While this chapter offered food for thought and examples of ways to advocate for ELs as an administrator, it could not possibly capture all the areas in which advocacy for ELs is needed from the perspective of school and district administrators. This chapter can be used to begin a conversation with school staff and EL parents. While the content of this chapter was geared more toward administrators, the audience for Chapter 5 expands to teachers and administrators, as the topic is advocacy for EL families so that they increase their engagement with their children's schools.

REFERENCES

Alford, B. J., & Niño, M. C. (2011). *Leading academic achievement for English language learners: A guide for principals.* Thousand Oaks, CA: Corwin.

August, D., Salend, S., Staehr Fenner, D., & Kozik, P. (2012). *The evaluation of educators in effective schools and classrooms for all learners.* Washington, DC: American Federation of Teachers.

DuFour, R. (2004). Schools as learning communities. *Educational Leadership, 61*(8), 6–11.

Echevarria, J., Vogt, M., & Short, D. (2008). *Making content comprehensible for English learners: The SIOP model.* Boston, MA: Pearson/Allyn & Bacon.

Editorial Projects in Education Research Center. (2013). *Findings from a national survey of teacher perspectives on the Common Core.* Bethesda, MD: Editorial Projects in Education Research Center. Retrieved from http://www.edweek.org/media/epe_survey_teacher_perspctives_common_core_2013.pdf

Garcia, P., & Potemski, A. (2009). *Recruiting teachers for schools serving English language learners* (Tips & Tools Key Issue). Washington, DC: National Comprehensive Center for Teacher Quality. Retrieved from http://www2.tqsource.org/strategies/recruit/recruitingTeachersforSchoolsServingELLs.pdf

Henderson, N. R. (2009). Managing moderator stress: Take a deep breath. You can do this! *Marketing Research, (21)*1, 28–29.

Krueger, R. A., & Casey, M. A. (2009). *Focus groups: A practical guide for applied research* (4th ed.) Thousand Oaks, CA: Sage.

Leithwood, K. A., Seashore Louis, K., Anderson, S., & Wahlstrom, D. (2004). *How leadership influences student learning: Review of research.* New York, NY: The Wallace Foundation.

Meyer, L. M. (2000). Barriers to meaningful instruction for English learners. *Theory into Practice, 39(4),* 228–236.

National Center for Education Statistics (NCES). (2001). *Teacher preparation and professional development: 2000* (NCES 2001–088). Washington, DC: US Department of Education, Office of Educational Research and Improvement.

National Comprehensive Center for Teacher Quality. (2012). *Summary of expert forum on the evaluation of teachers of English language learners.* Washington, DC: Author.

New York State United Teachers. (2013). *NYSUT's teacher practice rubric.* Latham: NY: Author.

Rhode Island Federation of Teachers and Health Professionals. (2012). *Rhode Island Innovation Consortium Educator Evaluation & Support System innovation evaluation model descriptors of practice / rubrics.* Providence, RI: Author.

Rogoff, B. (2003). *The cultural nature of human development.* New York, NY: Oxford University Press.

Shefelbine, J. R. (2008). An examination of the roles and perspectives of central office supervisors of programs for English language learners. In P. Dam & M. T. Cowart (Eds.), *Current issues and best practice in bilingual and ESL education* (pp. 262–299). Denton: Federation of North Texas Area Universities.

Staehr Fenner, D., & Kuhlman, N. (2012). *Preparing effective teachers of English language learners: Practical applications for the TESOL P–12 Professional Teaching Standards.* Alexandria, VA: TESOL International Association.

Teachers of English to Speakers of Other Languages (TESOL). (2010). *TESOL/ NCATE standards for the recognition of initial TESOL programs in P–12 ESL teacher education.* Alexandria, VA: Author. Retrieved from http://www.tesol .org/s_tesol/seccss.asp?CID=219&DID=1689

Yanguas, M. J. (2012). Advocacy: Regarding English language learners, whom do we advocate with, and about what? In E. Hamayan & R. F. Field, (Eds.), *English language learners at school: A guide for administrators* (2nd ed.) (pp. 228–229). Philadelphia, PA: Caslon.

5 Increasing EL Families' Involvement Through Building Their Advocacy Capacity

INTRODUCTION

Ms. DeWitt is a third grade teacher in a midwestern suburban school district who teaches a class made up of 10 ELs and 15 non-ELs. She prepared diligently for her school's back-to-school night, which was held from 7:00 to 8:00 p.m. on September 15. She sent home invitations to all of her students' parents, and she made sure the invitations were translated into Spanish and Arabic, the languages her ELs parents spoke at home. Yet, even though nearly all of her non-EL parents attended back-to-school night, only two of her EL parents attended. The two who did come listened to her presentation and smiled politely but did not ask any questions. After two years of teaching, Ms. DeWitt wondered what she was doing wrong with her EL parents and why more of them weren't interested in learning about her expectations for their children as well as the school's policies for its students.

This chapter explores the reasons many EL parents may not participate in their children's academic settings in ways educators expect them to. It examines who EL families are, the strengths that EL families can offer to classrooms, and educators' expectations of them. Next, ideas are presented on ways in which all educators can improve EL family involvement and engagement. Finally, ways for EL families to advocate for themselves as well as their children are explored.

WHAT THE RESEARCH TELLS US

Knowledge of recent research on the topic of family involvement can greatly inform educators' practice as they strive to increase EL family involvement. Educators often hear that all parents serve as their children's first teachers. As their children's first teachers, parents set the context for their children's cognitive and social development. In this most important role, they establish the foundation for their children's orientation to the classroom in terms of their patterns for relating to peers and adults and also how they approach learning tasks (Walker & Hoover-Dempsey, 2006).

Parent Involvement

Research demonstrates that all parents' engagement in schools fosters improved student attitudes toward school, correlates with student success, and reduces the dropout rate (Mexican American Legal Defense and Educational Fund and National Education Association, 2010). Despite these findings, many schools struggle with developing effective and authentic partnerships with EL families. Henderson and Mapp's 2002 review of research uncovered the following findings:

1. Programs and interventions that assist families in supporting their children's learning at home correlate to higher student achievement.

2. The more families support their children's learning and educational progress at home, the more their children tend to do well in school.

3. Despite perceived challenges, families of all cultural backgrounds, education levels, and socioeconomic statuses have been found to encourage their children, talk with them about school, help them

plan for higher education, and keep them focused on learning and homework.

4. Parent and community involvement that is linked to student learning has a stronger association with achievement than more general forms of involvement.

In addition to the connection between parent involvement and all student achievement, schools are specifically required to address EL parent involvement under Title I (Section 1118) and Title III (Section 3302(e)) of the Elementary and Secondary Education Act of 2001 (otherwise known as No Child Left Behind). That is, EL parent involvement is more than just a good idea for districts that receive Title I and/or Title III funding.

Examining the lack of EL parent involvement from the parental side of the equation, there are several reasons EL parents tend to not become involved with their children's schools in ways educators may expect. For example, Latino parents in particular most often define the term *education* as their parental involvement in their children's lives, and as a consequence, this involvement will help their children in their academic performance in school.[1] Also, according to research, language barriers remain the main factor that discourages them from actively participating in school activities and events. The second reason cited for low Latino parent involvement is work demands that prevent them from attending school events (Zarate, 2007).

Communication with EL Parents

Despite the urgency for EL parents to become involved with their children's education, EL family involvement continues to lag behind non-EL family involvement across the United States. Poverty has an impact on family involvement, and ELs tend to live in areas with high poverty. As of 2007, 66% of ELs had a family income below 200% of the federal poverty level, compared to 37% of non-EL families (EPE Research Center, 2009). Parents from poor households were less likely to report that the school had opportunities for parent involvement than students from non-poor households.

Hierarchy of Needs

An understanding of Maslow's (1943) hierarchy of basic needs provides more insight into the issue of EL parental involvement, especially for

---

1. See more information on this view of education later in the chapter.

newly arrived or otherwise struggling EL families. Maslow's hierarchy of needs (Figure 5.1) is a framework that seeks to explain humans' stages of growth. Maslow's theory suggests that the most basic level of needs (e.g., food, love, clothing, shelter, financial security, health, safety) must be met before individuals are able to desire or become motivated to work toward meeting the higher level needs.

Many newly arrived EL families are challenged on a daily basis to provide for their own and their children's basic needs, and this challenge is often complicated by a low level of English proficiency or, in some cases, lack of legal documentation. At this basic level of needs, newly arrived EL families may not yet be able to turn their attention to becoming involved with their children's education through volunteering in their children's school; that would correlate to higher levels of Maslow's hierarchy (e.g., respect by others and achievement). While they should not pigeonhole EL parents in a particular model, educators should consider at which general stage EL parents find themselves and provide them targeted support so that they can work toward the higher levels of the hierarchy.

Educators must also maintain high expectations for their EL parents and offer them support to achieve these expectations. For example, a homeless EL family may not be interested in attending EL family literacy classes because parents are devoting a large amount of energy and resources to securing adequate housing for themselves and their children. In a case such as this, educators should consider linking them to support in obtaining housing assistance. Once the family has found adequate housing and addressed other basic needs, educators can then encourage them to attend family literacy classes.

> At which stage of Maslow's hierarchy do you imagine your EL families to be? What kind of support could you provide them so they can move to the next level of the hierarchy?

EL Health Concerns as a Barrier to Learning

Several researchers and professionals have made a direct connection between health status and student achievement for all students. The connection is also true for ELs and becomes even more complex due to linguistic and cultural influences. David Satcher, former U.S. Surgeon General, and Margie Tudor Bradford stated that numerous research studies have found that healthy students perform better in academic settings (Satcher & Bradford, 2003). Evidence continues to grow that meeting

Figure 5.1. Maslow's Hierarchy of Needs

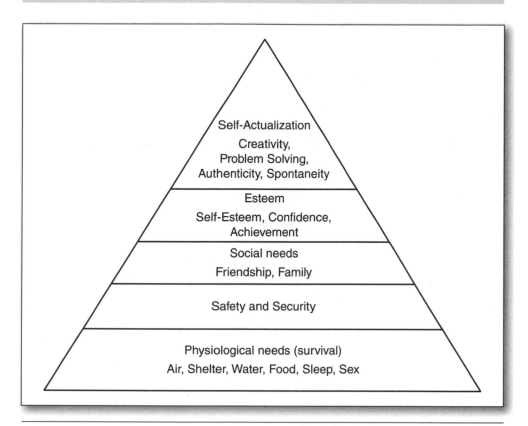

Source: http://communicationtheory.org/wp-content/uploads/2011/01/maslow-hierarchy-of-needs-diagram.jpg

students' basic developmental needs such as ensuring that they are safe, drug-free, healthy, and resilient, is critical for improving their academic performance (Mitchell, 2000). Several studies show that investing in children's physical health needs promotes learning across children's years in school and has direct effects on school readiness and early learning (Mistry, Crosby, Huston, Casey, & Ripke, 2002).

DEFINING WHO EL FAMILIES ARE

This chapter uses the more inclusive term *families* instead of *parents*, because ELs may reside with family members in addition to, instead of, or beyond parents and siblings. For example, an EL student may live with her mother, stepfather, biological siblings, stepsiblings, and half-siblings. In addition, she may also live with extended family such as her grandparents, cousins, aunts, and uncles in the same house, especially if the family is establishing themselves financially in the United States. In some cases, an EL may live with his aunt, uncle, grandmother, or grandfather instead of his parents. Some ELs—sometimes older ELs who come to the United States on their own—are the head of their own households without any other family members who can support them emotionally or financially.

One difference in working with EL as compared to non-EL families is that the definition of *family* may not fall within educators' cultural expectations if they do not share their ELs' culture. Educators should consider the many possibilities of what a family may look like to better understand their students' backgrounds in order to better serve them and their families. In some cases, the EL parents may not be the most knowledgeable about the child's educational background and preferences. For example, there are cases in which ELs have been raised in their country of origin for long periods of time—even multiple years—by individuals other than their parents (such as when a parent first immigrates to the United States to become financially established and the children follow later). In such circumstances, the EL's siblings, aunts, uncles, or grandparents may know more about that student's educational history and study habits than the parents.

Snapshot of EL Family Involvement

The tool in Figure 5.2 will help educators reflect on their school's current climate in terms of EL family involvement and advocacy.

Scaffolding EL Family Advocacy Efforts

As discussed in Chapter 1, the framework of advocacy used in this book is one of scaffolded advocacy, in which educators provide more advocacy support when needed and know when to gradually remove advocacy efforts. There is an inverse relationship between the amount of comfort and familiarity EL families feel with the school and U.S. system in general and the amount of advocacy and support educators must provide them. For example, EL families who are newly arrived, have lower levels of English language proficiency, and are not familiar with the U.S. school system will require significant advocacy efforts and support from the school. On the contrary, more established EL families who speak English fluently and are more familiar with the U.S. school system will most likely require fewer school advocacy efforts in order to take on leadership roles

Figure 5.2. Family Involvement Tool

Area of EL Family Involvement	Scale: 1 (Lowest) to 5 (Highest)
Our school advocates for its EL families who have not yet developed their own voice in the school context.	1 2 3 4 5
Our EL families participate in their children's education as much as our non-EL families.	1 2 3 4 5
Our school has high expectations of EL families.	1 2 3 4 5
Our school understands our EL families' perspectives.	1 2 3 4 5
Our school conducts home visits with its EL families.	1 2 3 4 5
Our school is flexible and creative in providing alternative schedules, locations, and kinds of events to involve its EL families.	1 2 3 4 5
Our school values its EL families' home languages and cultures.	1 2 3 4 5
Our school communicates information well to EL families.	1 2 3 4 5
Our school has an acceptable rate of EL family volunteers in classrooms and for events.	1 2 3 4 5
Our school helps EL families locate health care so that our EL children come to school healthy.	1 2 3 4 5
Our school develops EL family leadership so that families can serve as their own advocates.	1 2 3 4 5
Our school has a plan to increase EL family involvement and advocacy.	1 2 3 4 5

within their children's schools. As EL families feel more comfortable with the school and start to become more involved, educators can begin removing scaffolded advocacy supports. By knowing where EL families fall along the continuum and specifically targeting their efforts, educators can support EL families in advocating for themselves and their children to fully integrate their voices into the school context. Figure 5.3 provides a visual representation of this continuum of scaffolded advocacy for EL families.

Examining Educators' Expectations of EL Families

Educators' expectations of how they envision their students' families engaging with schools may stem from the typically White, middle class

Figure 5.3. Continuum of Scaffolded Advocacy for EL Families

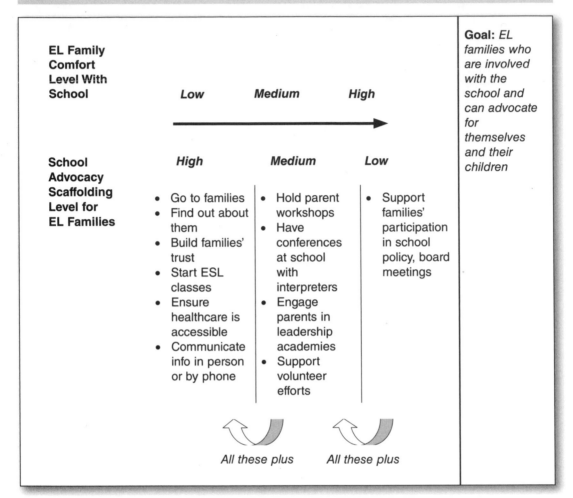

framework that defines the role parents should play in their children's education. Albert Einstein famously defined insanity as "doing the same thing over and over again and expecting different results." However, if educators keep attempting more of the same when it comes to their efforts to increase EL family involvement, they most likely will not witness a significant improvement. In order to increase EL parents' involvement in schools, educators have to first examine the cultural perspectives of EL families to understand the reasons they might not be participating according to expectations.

Once educators are more in tune with EL families' cultural perspectives on family involvement, they must then be creative and flexible to approach EL parent involvement from new angles. More of the same is not going to have a positive effect. Educators' goals in this aspect can include increasing EL families' awareness of the U.S. education

> Think of three successes and three challenges you have had with parents of ELs. Are there any commonalities?

system, contributions to their children's schools, and development of their own voices as advocates for themselves and their children.

Understanding the EL Families' Perspective

There are several ways in which families of ELs tend to differ from families of non-EL when it comes to their perspectives on their children's education. Colorín Colorado (Breiseth, 2011) defines three main areas in which culture influences EL families' perspectives on family involvement: respect for teachers, education vs. *educación*, and social group behavior.

Respect for Teachers

Many EL families were raised in cultures which hold teaching in high esteem and where the teachers are considered the pedagogical experts. As a result of their upbringing and previous experience with schooling in their countries of origin, EL families may not feel comfortable asking the teacher or school questions, because they don't want to appear as though they are questioning the teacher's authority. Alford and Niño (2011) make an analogy that one would not expect a doctor to ask a sick child's parents which complicated medical procedure parents would recommend for their child. In the same way, EL families may feel similarly uneasy about their school asking them to become involved with their children's education. If teachers are supposed to be the experts in the child's education, EL families may feel they should not interfere with that process.

Education vs. Educación

The second major cultural influence is education vs. *educación*. For some Latino families in particular,[2] the idea of *educación* focuses more on a child's personal and moral development than on academics. These parents may see the direct impact of *educación* on the child's academic development. They may believe that raising their children with good manners and

---

2. Latino families were chosen as an example since they represent the largest EL linguistic and cultural group. Other linguistic and cultural groups may have similar examples.

providing them with solid moral guidance result in good classroom behavior, which promotes higher academic achievement. However, some U.S. teachers might perceive Latino parents' focus more on the moral aspect as a lack of interest in their children's academic development.

Social Group Behavior

Finally, some EL families may stress the importance of belonging to a group more than individual achievement. Many cultures outside of the United States tend to be oriented more toward the group (e.g., the family, the society) than the individual. Therefore, the child's social behavior in a group (such as in the classroom) may be of high concern to some EL families. Being a respectful contributor to group well-being, rather than focusing on one's own achievement, may be more highly valued in some cultures.

Exploring Why EL Families May Not Fit Educators' Parent Involvement Mold

I recently attended my second grade daughter's back-to-school night at her public elementary school, which has a Spanish immersion program. Her Spanish immersion teacher was explaining the homework policy and stressed that, unlike in first grade, second grade Spanish homework would be in Spanish only with no translations provided in English. Luckily, I speak Spanish and was not too worried about this change from the previous year. However, a group of somewhat panicked non-Spanish speakers raised several questions with the teacher about (1) her reasoning for not providing a translation, (2) the weighting of homework in their children's overall grades, and (3) how their children could possibly understand their assignments in Spanish. These parents seemed to feel anxious that they would not be able to play as much of a role in their child's successful completion of homework and were concerned about how they could support their children. This meeting led me to think about how parents of ELs who are not proficient in English might feel each day, every day, with their children—wanting to support them but not knowing how to do so in a language they cannot yet fully use.

On the surface, it may seem as if EL families are not participating in their children's education if educators don't see them at many school events or receive e-mails and phone calls from them in the same proportion as they do from non-EL families. However, EL families may indeed be participating in their children's education in less visible ways, such as by providing support to make sure their children complete their homework and encouraging them to study and do well in school. Once educators learn more about EL families and the less obvious ways in which they contribute to their children's education, educators can then draw upon these strengths to increase these families' involvement in multiple ways.

Learning More About EL Families

In order to increase EL family involvement, educators must first learn about the families' lives outside of school, explore the ways in which educators expect participation to occur, and then consider reasons why EL families might not be participating in ways educators expect. Then educators will be armed with enough background knowledge specific to their EL family contexts to collaboratively construct ways to address unique challenges in their schools or districts.

One way teachers can learn more about their ELs' families in an unobtrusive way is by weaving writing instruction throughout their family background information gathering. For example, teachers can have their students at any age write about their typical daily routine. Students can include the following:

- **How they spend their time outside of school**—for example, they can fill out a weekly schedule so that teachers get a sense of what they do each day of the week including on weekends; students can then write about their weekly schedule outside of school
- **Whom they live with**—depending on their ages and comfort level sharing this information, students can bring in a photo or draw a picture of the family they live with and describe who is in the picture orally and/or in writing; they can also write about whom they lived with in a country other than the United States if applicable
- **Their home**—students can draw a picture of their home or apartment, labeling the rooms; this will provide teachers a sense of their living conditions
- **Their responsibilities**—students can write about what responsibilities they have in terms of working outside of school hours, translating for their family, and/or taking care of siblings and relatives; this will help teachers know if they have family obligations in addition to homework responsibilities
- **Literacy practices**—students can write about the types of things they read, watch, or listen to in their home language and with whom. For example, teachers can give them a list of different sources of texts (e.g., church materials, menus, signs, magazines, websites, books) and have them check whether they read these materials in

their home language and/or in English. Teachers can also check with whom they read these materials (e.g., father, mother, aunt, uncle, siblings, grandparents, cousins). This exercise will give teachers a better sense of the literacy practices occurring in their students' first languages.

Once teachers develop a sense of the ways in which their EL families are contributing to their children's education, they can confidentially share this information with school administrators and other colleagues who may teach the same students. Teachers can highlight concrete ways in which ELs' families are contributing to their students' academic achievement. They can create a family snapshot of their school's ELs to confidentially share with other educators. This family snapshot could present strengths and challenges each family brings to their children's education.

CREATING A WELCOMING ENVIRONMENT FOR EL FAMILIES

Many schools may not be aware of the messages they are sending to EL families. Such messages may be that EL families are not truly welcome, because they are different or create additional challenges for schools. Educators need to first become aware of the messages that schools are sending their EL families. In order to increase EL families' participation in school, educators must create a welcoming environment for them.

> Think of how you would feel if you lived in Korea and were entering your child's school. Imagine that there is no information available in English inside the school and that no one in the office or the hallways speaks English. How would you feel? Now imagine that you enter the same school but see signs posted in English and meet a bilingual office assistant who offers to help you. How would your experiences differ?

Yet, educators often expect EL families to participate as non-ELs would in situations that might not be the most welcoming of them. Educators must try to see their school through the lens of an EL family who is not yet proficient in English and consider the kind of message their school is sending to its EL families. Creating a welcoming environment for EL families can help increase their level of comfort with a school. Such an environment will convey that ELs' families are valued members of the school community and that the school is prepared to take extra steps to include them.

Lydia Breiseth, manager of the Colorín Colorado website, suggests that educators "keep [their ELs] visible. [ELs] are often treated as an invisible minority, but [ELs] and their families should 'see themselves' throughout the school" (Breiseth, 2011, p. 9) in the following ways:

- On the walls, through student work and photos
- In the classroom, with books and lessons that incorporate their experiences and traditions
- In schoolwide cultural activities
- In the faces of staff and volunteers who come from similar backgrounds.

She suggests some ways to make ELs' families feel welcome:

- Display student and family photos on the walls.
- Display the maps and flags of students' native countries.
- Display a large map in the front lobby where parents can mark their native countries with a pin.
- Ensure that bilingual staff and volunteers are visible throughout the building.
- Create a parent room (such as a lounge or classroom) with bilingual information and magazine subscriptions, a bulletin board, a lending library, and a computer (Houk, 2005).
- Include bilingual books in the school library and classrooms.
- Hold a special back-to-school event or picnic for EL families at which they have time to meet school leaders, their children's teachers, and school staff.
- Create a welcome DVD in languages spoken at the school or district.
- Provide staff the opportunity to learn some common phrases in ELs' families' languages as well as appropriate cultural gestures.
- Connect new families with a contact person who speaks their language as soon as they enroll in the school for guidance and information.
- Create an "ambassador" program in which students and parents are trained to give tours to newly arrived families.

EL Family Home Visits

When I was teaching in Mexico, I was often invited to my students' birthday parties, which were held at the families' homes on weekends. When teaching ESOL in the United States, I was invited to some of my Latino students' events such as their *quinceañera* ("sweet 15") birthday celebrations. I was also invited to some of my Middle Eastern families' homes in the United States for dinner. Attending my students' parties and meeting their families outside the school environment was a wonderful way to get to know them in the context of their communities. While teachers probably would not overtly invite themselves to their EL families' homes for dinner, they can reach out to these families to get to know them better within their own comfort zones, increase their trust, and build bridges between the home and school.

Figure 5.4 contends that up to 45% of all students (not only ELs) are not ready to learn under a definition that includes certain cognitive skills, physical and mental health, emotional well-being, and the ability to relate to others. In one study, a home visiting program had a profound positive impact on at-risk families, drastically increasing their children's chances of graduation.

While educators may not be able to introduce a comprehensive home visit program in their school or district in a short amount of time, they may be able to replicate some elements of successful home visits and later scale them up. One program described in *Education Week* (Sawchuk, 2011) consists of two teachers who make at least two visits to each EL student's

Figure 5.4. Results From a Study of a Home Visiting Program

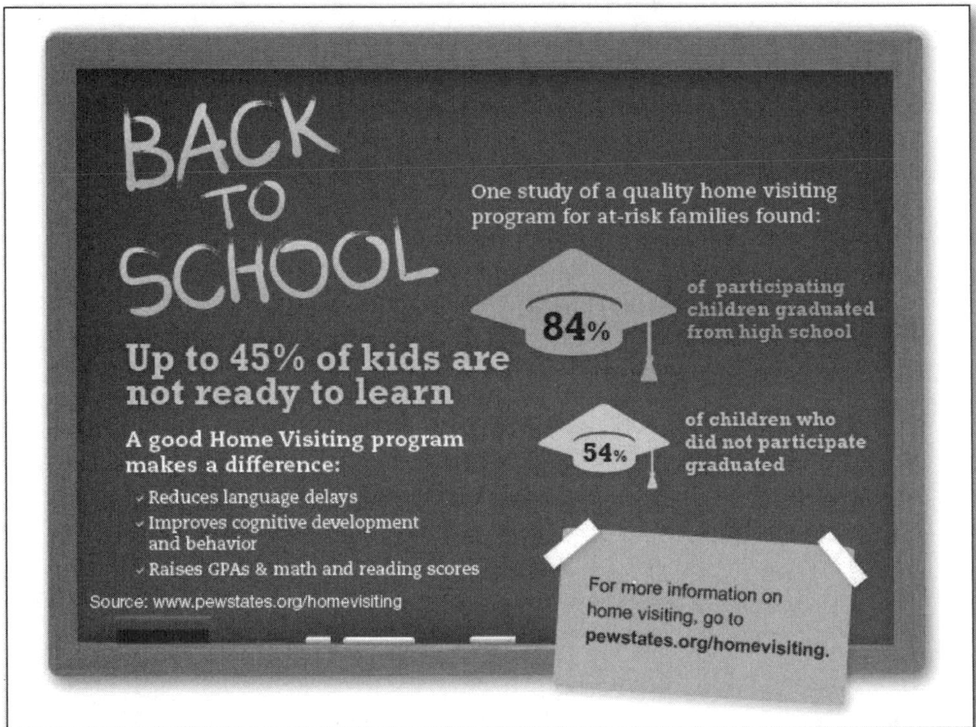

Source: http://www.pewstates.org/research/data-visualizations/back-to-school-info graphic-85899412207

home to meet with his or her parents. The visits are scheduled with the parents, and the purpose of each visit differs slightly. The goal of the first visit is to establish a relationship with the parents, learn about the child's aspirations, and find out more about factors that may affect the child's performance in school. The second visit takes place later in the academic year. In this visit, the teachers provide academic feedback to the parents, drawing upon parents to help reinforce lessons learned at school. The template in Figure 5.5 can help teachers think through considerations as they plan EL family home visits.

> What would you expect to see and learn in your ELs' homes? What do you know about their culture?

Providing Health Services to EL Families

As previously described in this chapter, children and their families who are struggling with health issues may be less likely to focus on academics. EL families will be much less likely to be involved with their

Figure 5.5. EL Home Visit Template

Information	Considerations for Teachers
Name of student	Find out the family members' names prior to the visit. Learn how the parents would like to be addressed (e.g., first names or Mr. & Mrs.). Also, learn the correct pronunciation of the family's names before the visit.
Home visit number	If it is the first home visit, goals for the meeting will likely differ from goals of subsequent visits.
Home language	It is important for teachers to know which language the family speaks at home, including whether they speak a dialect of that language or an indigenous language.
Need for interpreter	Once teachers know whether they need an interpreter for their visit, they should coordinate with that interpreter and discuss the home visit protocol and goals.
Goal(s) of visit	Teachers should clearly outline their goals for the meeting with the EL family. They should determine which goals are reasonable to accomplish during the home visit. If teachers just want to get to know the family, they should make this clear.
Positive stories to share about student	The EL family will most likely enjoy hearing anecdotes teachers can share with them about how their child is learning English and taking part in the school day. Teachers should think of any especially poignant stories they can share about the student's personality, such as a time when she may have helped another student or shown responsibility for learning.

In Fairfax County Public Schools, Virginia, there are several "entry assessment" sites that enroll ELs who are new to the school district. At these entry assessment sites, students' level of English language development and academic skills are assessed, and they are registered for school. The district's ESOL directors and entry assessment staff knew that it was often very stressful, confusing, and exhausting for EL parents to register their children for school. Often, children who had recently arrived from other countries lacked the immunizations required for school, and families would have to travel to another location to get their children immunized so they could begin school. This extra step would often cause a delay in starting school for EL children, and they would miss precious instructional time. The entry assessment staff were also aware that many EL families had to use public transportation to travel to the registration site, travel to another site to get their children immunized, and then travel back to the registration site to complete the registration. To make this process easier, Fairfax County stakeholders collaborated with a local clinic and offered school registration and immunization services at the same location near a public bus stop. In this way, they were able to greatly simplify the process for EL families and get the students placed in classrooms in a much shorter time. They were creative and flexible, and they collaborated to advocate for EL families with great results.

child's school if they and/or their children require health care. Creating a welcoming environment for ELs may mean extending support to include basic health needs so that children have a better chance at academic achievement.

In Table 5.1 educators will find some suggestions to consider as they advocate for their EL families' health.

Valuing EL Families' Home Languages

Although children's strong literacy skills in the home language correlate to strong literacy skills in English, EL parents do not always see the direct benefit of speaking and promoting literacy practices in the first language at home. EL parents may mistakenly believe first language use will hinder their child's ability to learn English. Because of this misconception, educators should actively encourage EL families to use their first language at home to develop their children's rich language experiences that will transfer to their development of English.

California and New York adopted a Seal of Biliteracy in 2012 to recognize, with the state seal, high school graduates who demonstrate academic excellence in attaining proficiency in all domains (e.g., speaking, listening, reading, and writing) in one or more languages other than English. The seal is attached to these graduates' diplomas and transcripts. These states have taken the lead in passing legislation that promotes

What messages are you sending ELs' families about the value you place on their home languages in your school?

Table 5.1. EL Health Care Advocacy Suggestions and Considerations

Facet of EL Health Care	Suggestion and Considerations
Hunger	Work with school and community resources to provide breakfast in the morning and a backpack of food for qualifying students to take home on weekends. Ensure EL parents fill out free and reduced-price lunch forms correctly.
Dental care	Collaborate with area dentists, clinics, and dental schools to provide low-cost dental care to ELs and their families (especially migrants and transient students who might slip through the cracks).
Vision screening	Make sure ELs have appropriate vision screening and follow-up care with an interpreter present as needed.
Overall health care	Seek out low-cost clinics with bilingual staff, and provide information on these clinics to families in their home languages (in written form or orally with the help of an interpreter).

multilingualism in EL students as well as non-ELs. Educators working in states other than California or New York can also advocate for their students to maintain and develop their home language(s).

Breiseth (2011) describes some ways educators can convey to EL families and the community that their school places value on ELs' languages:

Lancaster, Pennsylvania, school superintendent Pedro Rivera was worried about his ELs' health and attendance in school, so he opened clinics in three school buildings. After the clinics were opened, students' attendance improved significantly. He shares, "Every dollar we spend on kids is an *investment* in our country" (2012). If ELs are healthy, they are more likely to attend school and are therefore better positioned to achieve academically, graduate, and contribute to society.

- Posting information in school in the EL families' languages
- Discussing with families the value of their children's strong home language skills and being bilingual and biliterate. Educators may wish to bring in bilingual guest speakers (even former ESL students) who can talk about increased career opportunities for bilingual, biliterate individuals
- Encouraging families to read or tell stories to their children in their native language

- Offering parents sessions, workshops, and classes in their home languages
- Including books in EL students' home languages in the school and classroom libraries, and letting EL families know that these books are available
- Making resources (e.g., texts, video clips) available to students in their home languages to support content learning in English
- Considering the possibility of adding academic coursework (such as Spanish for Spanish speakers) in students' home languages
- Hiring bilingual staff and recruiting bilingual volunteers to the extent possible
- Providing training to all staff on the importance of maintaining and developing students' home language and on how to support students' bilingual development
- Offering high school foreign language credits if students can demonstrate proficiency in their home language
- Advocating for a seal of biliteracy at the district or state level

COMMUNICATING INFORMATION TO EL FAMILIES

It is not only a good idea to communicate well to EL families, it is also a federal requirement for school districts receiving Title I or Title III funds. Portions of Title III, Part A, and Title I, Part A, contain "to the extent practicable" language with reference to communicating with EL families. This requirement appears in most instances as follows: " . . . in an understandable and uniform format and, to the extent practicable, in a language that the parent can understand." In other words, school districts have a responsibility to adequately notify EL parents of school activities that are called to the attention of other parents. In order to be considered adequate, such communication may have to be provided in a language other than English. Educators of ELs are aware that EL parents are not always literate in their home language, so they must ensure that EL parents fully understand written communication by following up in person or on the phone if they know EL parents need extra support.

How well do you communicate with your EL families? How do you know? What are your strengths and challenges in this area?

Considerations for Translation and Interpretation

Communication with EL families extends beyond formal written communication to include all interactions with EL families, including any kind of formal or informal meetings, such as parent/teacher conferences, individualized education program (IEP) meetings, and the like. Many times, educators will need to consider using translation services to provide written materials in the families' home language, or interpreters to communicate spoken information in EL parents' home language. Some considerations and suggestions for communicating effectively with EL parents using interpreters and translators are shown in Table 5.2.

Table 5.2. Considerations in Communicating With EL Parents

Communication With EL Families	Considerations and Suggestions
Use trained interpreters for phone conversations and face to face meetings.	Meet with interpreters prior to using them as a support to make sure they understand their role and maintain objectivity when interpreting.
Investigate district translation services.	The school district may already have translation services; explore what is already in place first.
Compile a list of the languages spoken within your school or district and numbers of students/ families who speak each language.	Educators may wish to draw from some of these families for interpretation services as needed.
Translate documents into students' home languages.	Show the documents to a native speaker to see if the translated content makes sense; remember that students may speak dialects of languages and that terms may vary by country.
Collaborate with other schools and districts within the state and the state department of education to share resources.	A neighboring school or district may have already translated its documents into a language that is spoken in the educators' context.
Ask parents for preference of language for written and oral communication, and ask how they prefer to be contacted (phone, text message, e-mail, etc.).	Some home language surveys contain questions that elicit this information; parents can indicate their preference when they register their children in school or at the beginning of each school year.
Search community for interpreters (e.g., churches, hospitals, colleges).	There may be many community resources that already employ interpreters and translators.

(Continued)

Table 5.2. (Continued)

Communication With EL Families	Considerations and Suggestions
Use call-in interpretation services.	Educators may be able to use call-in services if they cannot locate an interpreter to meet with them in person; some hospitals use this resource.
Use relatives or family friends if needed (with caution).	In cases of low-incidence languages, educators may need to reach out to relatives or friends of the student's family. Make sure to stress with them that their role is to provide an objective interpretation of the language and not become involved in the content of the discussion.
Hire staff that speak the population's language(s)	This may not be possible in schools where multiple languages are spoken; in those cases, try to hire staff that speak high-incidence languages at the very least.
Avoid pulling teachers from class to translate.	If absolutely necessary, use school staff to help interpret on a rotating or scheduled basis so that the same individuals aren't frequently pulled away from instruction.
Use a parent phone or e-mail tree.	If EL parents are familiar with a phone tree, educators can consider this option. However, the concept may not exist in their cultures. If EL parents use e-mail, educators can also organize an e-mail forwarding system.
Exercise caution with translation websites.	While using translation websites is a better option than not translating documents at all, these websites' translations are often inaccurate and may confuse EL parents. If they are used, consider having someone familiar with the language check the translation if possible.
Do not have children interpret for their parents.	EL families already experience a power shift away from the parents and to the children if the children acquire English faster than the parents. Having children interpret at school meetings shifts the power even further to the child, may disrupt the family balance, and may get family members involved in sensitive topics.

Source: Adapted from Houk, 2005.

Helping With Schoolwork

Even though ELs' families may not be able to help with all homework assignments if they do not yet speak fluent English, there are ways they can support their children's learning at home. EL families can ask their children to tell them about what they learned each day in school, check to see if homework is completed when it is assigned, and ensure that the children have a place where they can do their homework with few interruptions.

> What kinds of support do you expect EL families to give their children so that they can successfully complete their homework?

Increasing EL Families' Presence as Classroom Volunteers

I once taught a multicultural education course to K–12 instructional assistants who were in a program to obtain their licensure to teach ESL. In that course, one of the teacher candidates was a kindergarten instructional assistant from an elementary school that had high Arabic- and Spanish-speaking EL populations. The assistant was happy that there were EL mothers coming in to volunteer in the school, but the classroom teacher assigned these moms only to cut, laminate, and staple papers. The assistant knew that these parents could serve as rich cultural and linguistic resources. However, the assistant was dismayed that the teacher allowed the EL volunteers to perform only menial tasks. The assistant did not feel she could advocate for utilizing the EL volunteers' skills in a more meaningful way.

Educators need to encourage EL families to volunteer in their schools, but fostering this level of parent engagement will take some creativity. Educators will need to first have a clear picture of the challenges that could prevent EL families from volunteering and seek ways to effectively address them.

Some ways educators can showcase their EL families' cultural and linguistic resources as volunteers is to have them

- Read a story from their country in their first language and/or English; the teacher could read the story in English if the volunteer does not
- Bring in food (after checking the ingredients to make sure there are no allergens) and music from their countries
- Show the students traditional clothing, art, and crafts from their country; the volunteers can then lead the class in creating their own artwork or crafts

- Teach the class some phrases from their language
- Have them do what non-EL volunteers do, such as assisting on a school trip or helping during an afterschool program

Creative Approaches to EL Family Meetings

When I was teaching ESOL at the high school level, our EL families did not attend back-to-school night in numbers proportionate to those of non-EL parents, which was often frustrating for ESL teachers. Yet, these same parents packed the school auditorium each year when it was time for International Night, an event that showcased their children performing songs from their countries and sharing authentic foods. International Night highlighted these students' languages and cultures in a positive way and celebrated their contributions to the school. In this case, EL families felt comfortable attending the event in which their children's languages and culture were the focus of the celebration. Educators need to consider ways to leverage successes with events such as International Night to encourage EL families to participate in formal and informal school events throughout the academic year.

If one goal is to increase EL parent involvement in school events such as teacher/parent meetings, educators may need to think creatively about how to approach these meetings. Sometimes, when it isn't possible for EL families to come to the school, the school has to find a way to go to the families. Meeting families in settings outside the school can provide an informal way to start building a relationship with them, especially if EL parents don't feel comfortable going to the school. Meeting with EL families outside the school might start with a gesture as simple as walking EL students to the place parents typically pick them up after school, so educators can say hello or strike up an informal conversation with them. Once educators start meeting with EL families outside the school, EL families will most likely increase their trust in teachers and, by default, their comfort level with the school. Educators can then eventually transition to encouraging EL families

> What is the state of your EL families' attendance at meetings held at your school? Which parents consistently attend? Which do not? Why?

> Raul Sanchez, who was a principal at a school with a mostly Navajo student population in New Mexico, knew that his EL families were crazy about basketball. He scheduled parent/teacher conferences on the Navajo reservation on the same nights as basketball games to increase the chances of parents attending the meetings.

to attend meetings and events at the school site if they are able to do so.

Even though EL families may feel comfortable enough to attend meetings held at the school, EL families might not be able to attend traditional meetings held during the school day due to work, transportation problems, language barriers, and/or family obligations. Table 5.3 lists each of these challenges to EL parent attendance at meetings held at school along with some possible ways to address each challenge.

Table 5.3. Potential Challenges to EL Family Participation in Meetings at School and Ways to Address Challenges

Challenge to EL Parent Participation in Meetings at School	Ways to Address Challenge
Work obligations	• Find out about EL parents' work hours by speaking with them or asking EL students and/or their students' siblings. • After contacting families' employers, meet with families before or after their work day at their workplace or during a break. • Meet with parents on a weekend.
Lack of transportation	• Provide transportation for parents (e.g., taxi vouchers, bus fare vouchers) to meet at the school. • Meet with them at their home or at a location familiar to them in their community (e.g., place of worship, community center, library). • If teachers cannot meet in person despite some creative efforts, schedule a phone conference with an interpreter.
Language barriers	Obtain an interpreter to be present at the conference and let the parents know (in their language) that an interpreter will provide assistance.
Family obligations	Provide on-site childcare at the school during parent meetings, or provide activities for children while teachers meet with their parents.

Jennifer Connors, principal at Rolling Terrace Elementary School in Montgomery County, Maryland, describes ways in which she reaches out to diverse parents:

As the principal of a school with over 65% Latino students, I have made parent and community outreach a priority. The foundation for this is building trust through defining together what our separate responsibilities are for the education of the children and where our shared responsibilities lie. I have found parents incredibly open to active participation when they feel a sense of trust in and belonging to the school community. I recommend that a position be created for a formal or informal community liaison to assist teachers and school staff in leveraging cultural backgrounds. This person has the responsibility to get to know the needs of the community and families well and to assist school staff in making decisions based on these needs. This person, as well, can assist in meeting the needs of the families within the school community by addressing food insecurity, providing referrals to mental health services, and familiarizing ELs' families with other social services.

SUPPORTING EL FAMILIES IN ADVOCATING FOR THEMSELVES AND BECOMING LEADERS

The Mexican American Legal Defense Fund and National Education Association (2010) believes that EL families tend to see the school system as the unquestionable authority and as a result often do not question decisions made by school staff. To provide EL families with key information on how schools operate in their communities, educators can give EL families information on the topics listed below, written in their languages and/or provided verbally as appropriate. It will be helpful if educators learn how these topics are approached in the EL families' home countries to anticipate any challenges families may have in working within the U.S. educational context. Information on these topics will help inform EL families in advocating for themselves:

- Their rights and responsibilities
- Components of effective parent/teacher meetings
- Structure and function of the school, the district, and the school board
- Rights and resources for students with special needs
- Rights and resources for gifted and talented students
- Information about content and English language proficiency/ development standards
- School accountability measures
- Tutoring and other afterschool resources
- Extracurricular activities

- School grading and report card policy
- College requirements and the admission process
- School disciplinary policies
- Participation in school board meetings, school council, and advisory committees
- Analysis of student and school data
- School improvement plans and how to participate in the process and monitor its implementation

Susan LaFond, former ESOL teacher in New York, writes.

I initiated many parent/teacher/counselor/interpreter conferences due to my keeping track of students' grades (interim and report cards). We were flexible in accommodating times and location for when parents were available. When off-site, I worked with an interpreter. I have gone to the houses and workplaces of these families, such as the mall, to meet with them. On one occasion, I saw that the family had very little and realized why their son was always so hungry. I acquired the application for a free or reduced-price lunch form in their language and helped them to fill it out and submit it.

EL Families Advocating for Themselves

Once EL families are comfortable coming in to the school, they can be offered workshops tailored to their strengths and areas in need of development. EL families can suggest topics, and educators can brainstorm other workshop topics. Once educators know who may be interested in attending a workshop and which topics are of interest to EL families, they will need to organize the sessions, secure interpreters, and make decisions as to the location, transportation, refreshments, and childcare. Educators should also remember to acknowledge the wealth of information that EL families bring to their children's education and exercise caution when teaching them about the school, district, or the U.S. education system.

Just as educators should hold high expectations for EL students, they need to do the same for their families. Once EL parents take part in parent workshops to learn about how to navigate the school system and begin to develop their voices to serve as their own advocates, educators can consider honing parents' advocacy skills through parent leadership academies.

In conjunction with parent workshops and leadership academies, educators can also consider avenues for strengthening families' English skills to help give them confidence as well as an avenue with which to advocate for themselves. Educators could begin by connecting parents with adult ESL classes offered

How do you develop leadership skills for your EL families?

Ayanna Cooper, independent consultant, writes,

In an effort to reach out to and involve parents of ELs, I cofacilitated a parent workshop focused on WIDA's ACCESS for ELLs test in a high school outside Atlanta, Georgia, that serves students newly arrived to the United States, including refugees. Districtwide, we were facilitating workshops for teachers about score report interpretation. I posed the idea to the principal to host a workshop for parents. She was in full support and immediately began to arrange it and schedule interpreters. We hosted a parent workshop with the goal of informing parents of the mandated English language proficiency assessment, the ACCESS for ELLs test, in Georgia. We explained the assessment, explained how it was administered, and showed participants sample test items and sample student score reports. With the help of interpreters, parents asked critical questions about the assessment, and most important, they asked how they could help their children. They were very surprised about how rigorous the test was. We encouraged them to continue talking to their children and having conversations about what the children were learning in school. If students were literate in their native language, we stressed the importance of maintaining that skill. It was truly an example of how inviting parents in to the school community is essential for community building.

The Lancaster, Pennsylvania, school district offers parent academies conducted in Spanish and English that are eight weeks long. Some topics include IEPs, technology skills, understanding the district, and book studies. These academies provide taxi vouchers for families to use, have family-style meals that appeal to EL families, and offer childcare to parents to address typical hurdles to EL familial involvement.

in the community, such as at a local library or church. This information can be sent home with students and woven in when educators speak with families. If there are not any ESL classes available, educators can work with community organizations, local universities with teacher preparation programs, and community colleges to begin one. Educators can also work with EL parents' employers to start ESL classes on site at places of employment.

Ensuring EL Families Have a Voice in School Policy

As EL families become more familiar with the school system and gain a higher level of comfort interacting within that system, educators will need to make sure families have a voice in their school's or district's policies. Several ways that educators can encourage them to take on more of a visible role are highlighted here:

- Form a committee or group of parents of ELs to represent their children's interests in school planning.
- Consider developing a workshop about the purpose and role of the school's Parent Teacher Association (PTA) or Parent Teacher Organization

(PTO). Such a meeting will help EL parents to become comfortable with their role within the school, learn more about the school, and build their capacity as leaders.

> Parents as Educational Partners (PEP) is a program that has shown success across the nation. PEP is a voluntary 10-week outreach program for parents of ELs that provides English language instruction for parents as well as educates them about the U.S. school system and culture. There are seven PEP units that address topics such as homework, report cards, parent/teacher conferences, and health clinic procedures. In one district, the program also provides a tour of the school building for EL parents in an environment that is comfortable for them. Some districts that have a PEP program provide childcare and tutoring for children while their parents attend the program.

- Call EL parents to make sure they are aware of PTA or PTO meetings, and personally invite them to attend. Tell them about the purpose of these meetings, and let them know that qualified interpreters will be available at these meetings so that parents can feel comfortable communicating their ideas in their native language.
- Personally invite EL parents to principal coffees or other informal meetings held at the school. Make sure to tell them the purpose and format of principal coffees and that there will be an interpreter present who speaks their language.
- Encourage EL parents to attend and contribute to school board meetings with an interpreter as needed.

Many ideas for engaging EL families have been presented in this chapter, and educators may feel overwhelmed at the prospect of taking on even more responsibilities to support EL families. Educators should keep in mind that they can't—and shouldn't—engage EL families on their own. Table 5.4 is a template for educators to use in order to form, implement, and evaluate an EL family involvement action plan.

Table 5.4. EL Family Involvement Action Plan

Step to Be Taken	Persons Responsible	Resources Needed	Timeline	Monitoring for Implementation	Evaluation

CONCLUSION

This chapter explored the reasons it may be challenging for EL families to become engaged with their children's schools and offered suggestions for increasing their involvement. Despite the effort needed, it is extremely worthwhile to increase EL families' involvement in their children's schools; they can provide valuable input and perspective to the school context. Ultimately, their children will benefit from educators' as well as families' advocacy efforts. Chapter 6 shifts the focus from EL families to EL classroom instruction, providing considerations for and examples of how EL advocacy is intertwined with the effective instruction of English learners.

REFERENCES

Alford, B., & Niño, M. C. (2011). *Leading academic achievement for English language learners: A guide for principals.* Thousand Oaks, CA: Corwin.

Breiseth, L. (2011). *A guide for engaging ELL families: Twenty strategies for school leaders.* Washington, DC: Colorín Colorado. Retrieved from http://www.colorin colorado.org/principals/family/

EPE Research Center. (2009). *Analysis of the U.S. Census Bureau's American Community Survey (2005–2007).* Bethesda, MD: Author.

Henderson, A. T., & Mapp, K. L. (2002). *A new wave of evidence: The impact of school, family, and community connections on student achievement. Annual synthesis.* Austin, TX: National Center for Family and Community Connections With Schools, Southwest Educational Development Laboratory.

Houk, F. A. (2005). *Supporting English language learners: A guide for teachers and administrators.* Portsmouth, NH: Heinemann.

Maslow, A. H. (1943). A theory of human motivation. *Psychological Review, 50,* 370–396.

Mexican American Legal Defense Fund and National Education Association. (2010). *Minority parent and community engagement: Best practices and policy recommendations for closing the gaps in student achievement.* Washington, DC: National Education Association.

Mistry, R. S., Crosby, D. A., Huston, A. C., Casey, D. M., & Ripke, M. (2002). Lessons from New Hope: The impact on children's well-being of a work-based antipoverty program for children. In G. J. Duncan & P. L. Chase-Lansdale (Eds.), *For better or for worse: Welfare reform, families, and child well-being* (pp. 179–200). New York, NY: Russell Sage.

Mitchell, M. (2000). Schools as catalysts for healthy communities. *Public Health Reports, 115*(2–3), 222–227.

Rivera, P. (2012, August 8). Panel discussion. A Convening of National Hispanic and Educational Organizations, Washington, DC.

Satcher, D., & Bradford, M. T. (2003). Healthy schools, healthy kids. *American School Board Journal, 190*(3), 22–25.

Sawchuk, S. (2011, December 14). Through home visits, teachers recruiting parents as partners. *Education Week, 31*(14), 10.

Walker, J. M. T., & Hoover-Dempsey, K. V. (2006). Why research on parental involvement is important to classroom management. In C. M. Evertson & C. S. Weinstein (Eds.), *Handbook of classroom management: Research, practice, and contemporary issues* (pp. 665–684). Mahwah, NJ: Lawrence Erlbaum.

Zarate, Maria Estela. (2007). *Understanding Latino parent involvement in education: Perceptions, expectations, and recommendations.* Los Angeles: The Tomás Rivera Policy Institute of Southern California.

6 Advocacy Through Effective Instruction of ELs

INTRODUCTION

One important facet of advocacy for ELs is that the students receive effective instruction in all their classes; therefore, this chapter's focus is on providing all teachers some considerations and tools in order to provide that instruction. This chapter extends beyond the basic need to put in place a quality ESL/bilingual program and provides content area teachers with exemplars and opportunities to reflect on their instruction of ELs and improve their practice. The chapter also gives administrators some examples of what effective teaching of ELs may look like in the content areas. While the chapter provides some considerations and exemplars in instructing ELs, it cannot possibly include all strategies and examples of how to teach ELs with varying background experiences and levels of English language proficiency in all the content areas.

WHAT THE RESEARCH TELLS US

This chapter's content, including exemplars of effective instruction for ELs, will be framed around current research and best practice in the field of instruction for ELs. Research findings are provided in this section of the chapter that address the areas of teacher preparation, specialized instruction for ELs, the role of academic language in EL success, and including ELs' culture in instruction.

Teacher Preparation

Since ELs tend to spend the majority of their school days with content teachers, all teachers working with ELs should possess the knowledge, skills, and dispositions to support ELs' learning. All teachers, no matter what their area(s) of certification, must be able to adapt their content instruction to meet the needs of ELs who are at varying levels of English language proficiency. They must also be able to weave instruction of academic language throughout their teaching of content, and draw on the unique strengths and backgrounds that ELs bring with them to the classroom (Staehr Fenner & Snyder, 2012). However, research gives us a better understanding of the unfortunate reality that, frequently, general education teachers do not possess the requisite knowledge and skills to work with ELs. In fact, a recent study shows that only 29.5% of teachers who have ELs in their classroom have the training to effectively educate them (Ballantyne, Sanderman, & Levy, 2008). To mitigate this lack of preparedness to teach ELs, multiple experts argue that preservice teacher education programs should begin preparing all teachers to teach ELs, and this training should continue throughout teachers' careers as ongoing professional development (Gonzalez & Darling-Hammond, 1997; Minaya-Rowe, 2004; Zetlin, MacLeod, & Michener, 1998). As educators try to advocate for preservice teacher education programs to focus on providing EL training, they can also focus their efforts on providing inservice teachers with the skills they need to effectively instruct their ELs.

> In which areas are you most and least prepared to teach ELs?

Specialized Instruction for ELs Acquiring English

Multiple authors have studied the efficacy of using EL-specific practices with English learners. They have found that EL-specific practices and preparation may be more promising for improving ELs' achievement than general best practices for all students (Graves, Gersten, & Haager, 2004; Ray, 2009; Short & Echevarria, 1999). These findings belie the saying that "good teaching is good teaching." De Jong and Harper (2007) term the effective teaching of ELs as "good teaching plus." In addition to using high-quality general instructional practices, teachers may more effectively increase ELs' achievement if they understand and adopt instructional practices that are reflective of ELs' specific needs (Goldenberg, 2008). Preliminary research on such practices suggests benefits for ELs as well as increased confidence and competency for their teachers (Echevarria, Powers, & Short, 2006; Linan-Thompson, Vaughn, Hickman-Davis, & Kouzekanani, 2003; Vaughn et al., 2006). Although some studies have found that general high-quality instructional practices show promise for improving outcomes for all students, both ELs and non-ELs (D'Angiulli, Siegel, & Maggi, 2004; Lee, Maerten-Rivera, Penfield, LeRoy, & Secada, 2008; Williams, Hakuta, & Haertel, 2007), these practices do not necessarily close the existing gaps between ELs and their English-speaking peers.

Academic Language

One facet of providing effective instruction to ELs involves teaching ELs the academic language they will need to access challenging content in school. Many experts have found evidence for the existence of *academic language*, a conceptually distinct linguistic register of language that is specific to the academic setting (Bailey, 2007; Belcher, 2006; Cummins, 1979, 1980; Scarcella, 2003). This register differs significantly from social language in terms of discourse complexity, grammatical structure, vocabulary usage, and sociocultural context (World-Class Instructional Design and Assessment, 2012). Since so many differences exist between academic and social language, ELs will need tailored instruction to ensure that they acquire the academic language that is necessary for them to access the instruction of complex content. Preliminary descriptive research suggests that ELs must be proficient in academic language in order to meet grade-level standards in content areas and on assessments (Bailey, Butler, & Sato, 2007; Bailey, Butler, Stevens, & Lord, 2007).

> What is your definition of academic language? To what extent do you teach academic language to all students? To ELs?

Culture

Another area in which teachers of ELs often require expertise is in including ELs' culture and building upon it in instruction. Although empirical research has not proven a direct relationship between student outcomes and including culture in instruction (August & Shanahan, 2006), a literature review related to effective programs for ELs has found repeatedly that these programs exemplify a strong and intentional community of respect and acceptance, both within and beyond the school (Ochoa & Cadiero-Kaplan, 2004; Williams et al., 2007). Thomas and Collier's (1997) findings also suggest that a cultural atmosphere that is accepting of ELs can make a difference in EL student outcomes. Schools and districts that view language and culture as valuable assets, rather than problematic deficits, tend to create positive environments that are more conducive to ELs' success.

FRAMEWORK FOR ADVOCATING FOR EFFECTIVE INSTRUCTION OF ELS

Two esteemed organizations also offer frameworks for defining the effective education of ELs. While the audiences and purposes for their professional standards differ, a crosswalk (Harper & Staehr Fenner, 2010) of the standards of the National Board for Professional Teaching Standards (NBPTS) and those of Teachers of English to Speakers of Other Languages (TESOL) reveals that the topics contained in both sets of standards overlap. Both sets of standards help define good teaching for ELs. These six aspects of instruction that are crucial for ELs' success are as follows:

1. Knowing ELs

2. Planning for instruction

3. Designing effective instruction for ELs

4. Teaching academic language

5. Creating content and language objectives

6. Creating assessment tools

Knowing ELs

Each EL has a multifaceted story that will affect how that student acquires English and how that student fares in school and beyond. Therefore, all teachers of ELs should be familiar with what background their students bring with them to the U.S. schooling experience in order to advocate for them.

> What is your story about how you came to educate ELs?

Table 6.1 describes some examples of ELs' widely varying background variables and shows what educators and advocates for ELs should do to ensure these background variables are considered and integrated into instruction.

Table 6.2 provides topics for discussion related to teachers' misconceptions and other factors that may impact ELs' language acquisition. Table 6.2 also offers a space for collaborators to record these misconceptions and other factors' implications on classrooms. Teachers can use the misconceptions tool individually or to collaborate with colleagues who teach at different grade levels and/or in different content areas, as well as with an ESL specialist.

> What are some of the background variables that impact your ELs' acquisition of English? How do you take these variables into account when planning for and delivering instruction?

Table 6.1 EL Background Variables, Their Impact on Language Acquisition, and Educators' Responsibility as Advocates and Effective Teachers of ELs

EL Background Variable	Possible Impact on Language Acquisition	Responsibility as Advocates and Effective Teachers of ELs
Language(s) spoken	The student's first language (L1) and additional languages spoken will affect that student's ability to use strategies such as cognates to unlock new vocabulary words in English. Some languages share cognates with English, while others don't. The type of alphabet the L1 uses will also impact the rate of the EL's acquisition of English.	Find out which languages ELs speak, including languages in which they may have received schooling in their countries of origin, as the home language may differ from their language of schooling. Ascertain whether ELs speak indigenous languages (e.g., a student from Mexico may speak Maya instead of Spanish).
Proficiency in each language in all domains	Students are poised to transfer skills in their home language to new languages they learn. For example, if a student is literate in Russian, that student already understands the sound/symbol relationship at the macro level and will learn to decode English more easily than a student at the same age who is not literate in a first language.	Learn how well each EL reads, writes, speaks, and listens in languages other than English. If districts don't have a way to formally assess ELs in their languages, teachers should do so informally.
Place of birth	Where ELs are born will probably influence where they have received schooling, which will impact how much English they have been exposed to.	Look at ELs' registration records to learn where they were born. Teachers should also look at ELs' school records to see if the students have moved back and forth from their place of birth (if outside the United States) to the United States, or if they have frequently moved from one U.S. district to another or from state to state (e.g., in the case of children of migrant workers).
Immigration status of student and/or family	If ELs and their families are worried about their immigration status, they may not seek out school and community services	Educators may not ask students or their families of their immigration status. They can listen to students' stories of how they came to the

Table 6.1 (Continued)

EL Background Variable	Possible Impact on Language Acquisition	Responsibility as Advocates and Effective Teachers of ELs
	that would be of benefit to them. They may also be preoccupied with their immigration status, which will impact their family's employment opportunities, and therefore may be more focused on immediate needs for survival[1] than on academics. Older students may not be as motivated to complete high school if they cannot gain access to postsecondary education.	United States to gain an idea of whether or not the students might have proper documentation (e.g., if a student describes walking across the desert to cross the U.S./Mexican border, that student may lack immigration documentation). Teachers should be sensitive to any potential outside stressors, such as immigration status, on students and their families that may impact ELs' acquisition of English and achievement in U.S. schools.
Educational background in home country and United States	Quality schooling in ELs' home countries (for those born outside the United States) will influence students' level of literacy and content knowledge in their first language, which will impact their acquisition of academic English and achievement in U.S. schools. As well, quality of schooling received by ELs in the United States will also have an effect on their academic achievement in the United States.	In cases where students were schooled outside the United States, educators can review students' translated transcripts (if they have them) to see what kind of courses the students took, grades received, and whether there were any gaps in their education. In the case of ELs schooled solely in the United States, teachers should look at their transcripts to see the courses they took, grades received, and number of times they may have moved and/or returned to their parent's home countries for extended periods of time.
Cultural background	A student's culture will impact his or her ability to connect with and comprehend U.S. cultural references that are often intertwined with instruction. As well, ELs born in the United States must often learn to navigate a culture at home that may be at odds with the school culture.	Educators should learn about their students' cultures, keeping in mind that cultures are not monolithic. They should attempt to relate instruction to their students' cultures to help make instruction relevant for them.

1. See Chapter 5 for an explanation of Maslow's hierarchy of needs.

EL Background Variable	Possible Impact on Language Acquisition	Responsibility as Advocates and Effective Teachers of ELs
Familial situation	Just as with non-ELs, EL students' family situations may impact their academic achievement. However, with ELs, the arrangement may become more nuanced. For example, older ELs may move to the United States to reunite with and adjust to parents and meet new stepparents and/or stepbrothers and stepsisters, coupled with a new language, culture, and school. Or, EL families may share homes and apartments with other relatives, family friends, and/or boarders.	Teachers must recognize that any new family arrangements for ELs who have recently moved to the United States may be a source of uncertainty and stress for these students. Teachers should be open to listening to students and also be aware of when to suggest further support for them, such as counseling services with the aid of interpreters.
Personal interests	ELs' personal interests will impact their interest in a particular academic topic. ELs may have learned about specific topics in their first language; this content knowledge will transfer to schooling in English.	Teachers can find out about students' interests through journals and informal conversations. The more teachers know about ELs' interests, the more they can link their instruction to what motivates and excites their students to learn.
Health	Just as with non-ELs, an ELs' health will impact their ability to learn. With some ELs, the situation may be more complex because of different health practices in other countries, different immunization requirements, and different cultural beliefs regarding doctors and medicine.	Teachers should be aware of their students' health records and advocate for students' access to care from the school clinic, or refer students and their families to community health services if appropriate. Educators should ensure that ELs' vision and hearing screening records are up to date and that an interpreter is present at these screenings if appropriate.[2]

Background Variable Vignettes

The following vignettes illustrate a small sampling of the wide variety of experiences ELs bring with them to their schools in the United States. Table 6.3 can be used as a template to reflect upon considerations for each of these students individually or to discuss them in a group. Teachers can also use the table as a guide to analyze the background variables that may impact their own ELs' acquisition of English.

---

2. See Chapter 5 for more information on advocating for addressing ELs' health issues to foster their academic achievement.

Table 6.2 Misconceptions About Second Language Acquisition, Research, and Classroom/Policy Implications

Misconception	Research	Classroom Implications
1. Young children learn second languages quickly and easily.	Adolescents and young adults are the most efficient. It is only in developing native-like pronunciation that young children have the advantage. Adolescents and young adults can also sound native-like in English, but it may take more time and effort.	
2. Students have acquired a second language once they can speak it.	While students may sound fluent, they usually acquire social English more quickly than academic English.	
3. All students learn a second language in the same way.	Cultural and social differences influence the ways in which students learn a second language.	
4. Parents of ELs should speak only English at home.	Parents should provide a strong model of rich language usage; it is best for them to speak L1 at home, as L1 skills transfer to the second or additional language (L2).	
5. Students must acquire oral language before literacy.	Oral language and literacy should be developed simultaneously. New research shows how oral language supports literacy and vice versa.	
6. Beginners must begin producing (speaking and writing) English right away.	Some students experience a silent period in which they are learning language but are not immediately ready to produce it by speaking and writing.	
7. Socioeconomic status is the strongest predictor of success in second language acquisition.	The strongest predictor of success of second language learners is a strong foundation in the L1 and quality teaching of the L2.	
8. The natural process of language acquisition can be accelerated.	Language acquisition takes time and must occur through exposure in a variety of contexts. The natural process can be hindered by inappropriate teaching methods.	
9. L1 interferes with L2; therefore, students should not speak L1 in school or at home.	Errors that reflect the structure of L1 are a part of the process and will usually disappear over time.	

Source: Staehr Fenner & Kuhlman, 2012; some material adapted from McLaughlin, 1992.

Table 6.3 EL Background Variables

Student Name: _____

Background Variable	Strengths Student Brings	What Teacher Could Do to Build on Strengths	Possible Challenges	What Teacher Could Do to Address Challenges
Language(s) spoken				
Proficiency in each language				
Nature of immigration				
Educational background				
Cultural background				
Family situation				
Personal interests				
Resiliency				

Duy Tran: Duy Tran was 8 years old when his family moved to the United States from Vietnam. He grew up in a small town, and he and his brother attended a boarding school, returning home for weekends once every two weeks, he says. Now, two years later, he is a 5th grader in an elementary school in Boston. When Duy entered the school, he spoke no English. It was a difficult beginning for Duy. "I felt very nervous. I didn't understand anything," he says. His school offers students a sheltered-immersion program, in which those who speak little or no English receive special instruction from a teacher trained in teaching English learners.

At Duy's school, 30 percent of the students are Vietnamese, and all teachers participating in the sheltered-immersion program are Vietnamese themselves, according to the Principal. Duy no longer has a hard time keeping up with his favorite subjects of math, reading, and writing. He especially likes preparing book reports, he says, because he gets to read a book and answer questions.

Source: Featured profiles, 2009.

Cesar Cervantes: Nine-year-old Cesar Cervantes is an English learner who quickly makes the transition between speaking in Spanish or English, depending on his situation. But on the playground—and at home with his Spanish-speaking parents, who moved to California from Mexico before Cesar was born—he is more likely to use Spanish. Although he was born in the United States, the 4th grader is among the 80 percent or so of children at his 980-student elementary school in his greater Los Angeles neighborhood who are classified in need of English-language support.

Cesar was originally in a bilingual class for only one year in a different school district in Los Angeles. But ever since 1st grade, his parents have chosen to have him in a general education class. He says that while math is his favorite subject, he also likes to read books such as Charlotte's Web and is helping his parents learn English as well.

His teacher says that Cesar frequently "falls back" on his first language to help him grasp new vocabulary or concepts, and is considered an intermediate or early-advanced English learner. His teacher is working with him on using complete, more complex sentences—an indication of fluency.

Source: Featured profiles, 2009.

Grendy Perez: Grendy Perez, 17, has been in the United States and attending high school in Georgia for a year and a half. She is taking the lowest-level English as a Second Language class at her school—a semester-long class—for the third time. Grendy attended school in her native Guatemala only through the 3rd grade, and couldn't read or write in Spanish when she enrolled in high school.

One of her ESL teachers says Grendy has told her she repeated 3rd grade in Guatemala before she dropped out of school. When Grendy is asked if she can read now, she says in Spanish: "No mucho en inglés" ("Not much in English.")

Her ESL teacher has been taking notes on Grendy's progress, thinking that the documentation might be useful if Grendy needs to be evaluated for special education services. Grendy has two brothers and a sister who live in the United States, and a brother who still lives in Guatemala. She doesn't identify a specific career goal but says she wants to continue to learn.

Source: Featured profiles, 2009.

PLANNING FOR INSTRUCTION

Planning for instruction of ELs tends to be more complex than planning for non-ELs. The self-assessment checklist shown in Figure 6.1 will help

Figure 6.1. Planning for the Instruction of ELs: How Often Do You . . .

EL Lesson Planning Element	Rarely	Sometimes	Often
Write language and content objectives for your lessons?			
Deliberately group your ELs so they can work with non-ELs, ELs from different language backgrounds, and ELs from similar language backgrounds, as appropriate?			
Use supplementary materials that support the content objectives and contextualize learning for ELs (e.g., pictures, visuals, video clips, translated texts, adapted texts, etc.)?			
Learn about ELs' culture, prior knowledge, and experiences and link content to these factors?			
Emphasize academic English vocabulary by combining the teaching of academic vocabulary and the teaching of content?			
Increase ELs' comprehension of spoken English by using a rate of speech appropriate for their English proficiency level, and support comprehensibility of speech through also using visuals and writing?			
Adapt content—including texts, assignments, and assessments—appropriate for students' English proficiency levels?			
Incorporate classroom activities that provide opportunities for students to practice and apply new language and content knowledge in English?			
Provide opportunities for students to demonstrate their mastery of English language and content in English?			
Include all four domains (reading, writing, speaking, and listening) in simultaneous instruction of language and content?			

teachers ascertain the degree to which they currently plan for and implement effective instruction for ELs.

Designing Effective Instruction for ELs

In order for ELs to comprehend complex content instruction, especially in the era of the Common Core State Standards (CCSS), teachers must realize that they need to do more than teach ELs isolated vocabulary words that the students will encounter in instruction.[3] They must also be taught the academic language they will need in addition to vocabulary so that they can access the content of instruction and acquire academic language simultaneously. Teachers need to appropriately scaffold their instruction for ELs. Scaffolding means providing the "just right" type and amount of support each EL needs. As ELs become more proficient in English, teachers should gradually remove scaffolding but still offer extra support when students require it. In this way, educators advocate for ELs by positioning them for academic success.

To design effective instruction for ELs, some considerations are the following:

- Be cognizant of their cultures and background experiences, and build on these factors during instruction.
- Create content and academic language objectives based on content standards as well as English language proficiency/development standards.
- To guide instruction, analyze the academic language demands of any text given to students.
- Plan for how they will be instructed before, during, and after reading complex text.
- Design appropriate assessments, so they can demonstrate what they know and can do in the English language and with the content.

Organizing Instruction of ELs

To effectively plan for and implement instruction of ELs, teachers need to build in some extra steps and considerations. One way to think about instruction for ELs is to plan for what students will do before, during, and after reading a complex text. Some considerations teachers can address in planning instruction are provided in Table 6.4.

---

3. This need also applies to instruction in states that have not adopted the CCSS.

Table 6.4   Considerations for ELs Before, During, and After Reading a Complex Text

When	What	How
Before reading	Assessing and building ELs' background knowledge	Determine students' background knowledge through informal assessment. Be sure to consider both content knowledge and knowledge related to language arts. What subject matter knowledge do the students already have in their L1 and English? What do they know about literary devices (e.g., analogy, irony, metaphor)? What connections can be made? Bring in supplementary materials (including video clips and visuals) and create minilessons to build knowledge as appropriate.[4]
	Analyzing a text's academic language	Determine areas of challenge that academic language may present for ELs at the word, sentence, and discourse level.
	Preteaching content-specific and academic vocabulary	Using an analysis of the text's academic language, determine which words and expressions to highlight before introducing the text. Also use grade-level word frequency and importance for understanding the text. Focus on abstract words and phrases for more intensive instruction prior to reading.
During reading	Teacher read aloud of text, student read aloud, and independent reading of text	Read the text aloud to students first so they will get a feel for the rhythm of it. They can then read it independently and/or with a partner. They can also summarize it in L1 and/or English or orally translate it into L1 if appropriate.
	Supplementary adapted text or text in students' L1 if appropriate	If students can read in L1 and need this support, teachers can provide a translated version of the text for them.
	Focus on academic language	Provide definitions and explanations for less frequent or more concrete words and phrases during reading. When appropriate, have

(Continued)

4. Teachers should exercise caution in how much time they devote to prereading activities, so that students spend time with the text itself.

Table 6.4 Considerations for ELs Before, During, and After Reading a Complex Text

When	What	How
		students draw on cognate knowledge, glossaries, or other skills and resources to discover the meanings of unfamiliar words. Help students understand complex syntax.
	Instructing ELs in vocabulary learning strategies	Teach students specific strategies such as how to use cognates (if they exist in L1) and English prefixes/suffixes to determine the meaning of new words.
	Teacher guided discussion	Provide students questions and graphic organizers while reading the text, and discuss the questions with them while reading.
After reading	Focus on both oral language and writing development linked to content and language objectives	Include listening, speaking, reading, and writing in instruction.
	Provide support for ELs' expressive language (speaking and writing) as well as receptive language (listening and reading)	Provide graphic organizers to help students organize their thoughts and gather text-based evidence before they begin speaking or writing. Supports such as sentence frames can be used to scaffold ELs' speaking and writing as appropriate.
	Create formative assessment	Design a rubric to assess how well students demonstrate understanding of content and language objectives.

Source: Adapted from August, Garcia-Belina, Bridgforth, King, & Haynes, 2013.

Teaching Academic Language

One way to plan for instruction of ELs is to analyze the academic English that grade-level texts require of all students, including ELs. Due to the implementation of the CCSS in most states, all students working with these standards, including ELs, will be required to work with complex text.[5] Similarly, due to the construction of the CCSS, all teachers working

---

5. In addition, many states that have not adopted the CCSS have aligned their content standards with College and Career-Ready Standards (CCRS), which also focus on complex text.

with the CCSS will share the responsibility to simultaneously teach content and academic language. Educators will be expected to expose ELs to the same grade-level, complex texts that they expose non-ELs to, to give ELs the same educational opportunities as their non-EL peers.

If ELs at a beginning or intermediate level are given a grade-level text without support, they will not comprehend it. Extra steps must be taken as necessary to adapt instruction, such as providing additional resources and giving students adapted materials that complement the grade-level texts at a reduced linguistic load. In this way, educators can construct a framework for ELs so they can eventually access the same texts as their grade-level non-EL peers. Teachers' ability to adapt instruction for ELs hinges upon their knowledge of their students' background experiences and education.

> How do you feel about ELs at different levels of English proficiency working with complex, grade-level text?

Academic language differs significantly from social language in terms of discourse complexity, grammatical structure, vocabulary usage, and sociocultural context (World-Class Instructional Design and Assessment, 2012). Figure 6.2 provides a visual representation of the various elements of academic language at the word, sentence, and discourse level, and Table 6.5 provides definitions for and examples of these elements. These academic language elements are all situated within a sociocultural context. It should be noted that analyzing and focusing on teaching academic language simultaneously with content may benefit non-ELs who also need to build their repertoire of academic language.

One way to apply the construct of academic language to instruction is to analyze the academic language found in grade-level texts used with all students. Analyzing texts' academic language will help teachers anticipate

Figure 6.2. Representation of Academic Language

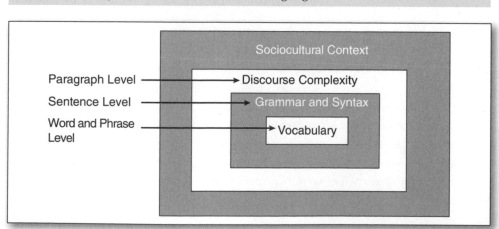

Table 6.5 Elements of Academic Language, Definitions, and Examples

Element of Academic Language	Definition and Examples
Sociocultural context	• Defining features of academic language all operate within a sociocultural context for language use. • Use of academic language occurs within a sociocultural context. • Some examples are a school's as well as a teacher's expectations for ELs and the degree to which teachers allow ELs to use their home languages in classroom settings.
Discourse complexity (paragraph level)	• The quantity and variety of oral and written text • Evidenced at the paragraph level and higher • An example is how the organization of a speech differs from that of a science laboratory experiment report.
Grammar and syntax (sentence level)	• Types, array, and use of language structures; conventions, mechanics, and fluency • Evidenced at the sentence level and higher • Some examples are clauses, verb tense, and interrogatives.
Vocabulary usage (word and phrase level)	• Specificity of word or phrase choice • Evidenced at the word and phrase level • Some examples are the use of content-specific words (e.g., *photosynthesis, integer*) and academic vocabulary words that cut across multiple contexts (e.g., *describe, quantity*)

Source: Adapted from World-Class Instructional Design and Assessment, 2012.

potential difficulties ELs will face in reading, comprehending, and working with complex text. Then, teachers can plan instruction of all domains—listening, speaker, reading, and writing—accordingly to address these challenges.

The text analysis tool in Figure 6.3 is based on World-Class Instructional Design and Assessment's definition of academic language. The tool can be used to collaborate with a colleague or group from a particular content area or grade level. An ESL specialist should also be included in collaborative efforts to determine which aspects of the text's academic language may pose challenges specific to ELs.

Figure 6.3. Text Analysis Tool

Sociocultural Context	Discourse Complexity
Grammar and Syntax	Academic Vocabulary

CREATING CONTENT AND LANGUAGE OBJECTIVES

Another element in planning for successful instruction of ELs is to design academic language and content objectives. Content teachers or general education teachers already base their lessons upon content objectives, which correlate with content area standards. Content objectives are concepts from grade-level as well as subject-area curriculum and standards. They define the goal of the teacher's lesson based on content standards and what students need to know in the subject at a given grade level.

In addition to defining content objectives, defining the academic language ELs need to access the content objectives is also necessary. While separate content and language objectives can be used, the Understanding Language initiative (http://ell.stanford.edu) argues for integrated content and language learning objectives to be used as "ways of engaging in academic practices, communicating, doing, and being by using language for different audiences and purposes" (Understanding Language, 2012, p. 2). The academic language portion of an integrated content and language objective consists of the language necessary at a student's English proficiency level to demonstrate that student's understanding of the concept you are teaching. Further, academic language objectives address what students will be able to do as they apply language to the content concept.

Teachers should think of the language functions of the lesson being planned that will support content. For example, they can brainstorm the language functions, or what students have to accomplish with language in order to access the content. Do students have to name, describe, classify, compare, explain, predict, infer, suggest, or evaluate? These are all language functions. Teachers can use Bloom's taxonomy as a reference for this task. Teachers should also consider the language structure in terms of what expressions and phrases are needed for the lesson. For example, are there any key content-specific or academic vocabulary words or phrases? Also, teachers should reflect on what type of grammar or syntax support

Table 6.6. Integrated Content and Academic Language Objective Examples

Content Area	Integrated Content and Language Objective	Academic Language and Content Constructs to Teach
Science	Students will make use of scientific terms and sequencing language to create and explain the steps in the water cycle both orally and in writing.	Scientific terms Sequencing language Water cycle steps Oral and writing support for creating and explaining the water cycle
English language arts	Students will make use of comparative language to compare three different versions of the Cinderella story in terms of plot, setting, mood, and characterization.	Comparative language Content of Cinderella stories Plot Setting Mood Characterization Oral and writing support for comparing three Cinderella stories

might be needed for ELs to be successful with this lesson (e.g., the past tense, subjunctive, the structure of interrogatives, etc.). Table 6.6 provides some examples of integrated academic language and content objectives for science and English language arts.

Creating Assessment Tools

A final element of lesson planning and implementation for ELs is creating formative assessment tools[6] that provide a means for ELs to demonstrate the degree to which they meet a lesson's academic language and content objectives. Linquanti (2011) believes that formative assessments may hold the most promise as a means for ELs to demonstrate what they know and can do in terms of knowledge of content. Formative, performance-based assessments allow teachers to gain a sense of what content and language ELs learned during instruction. Results of formative assessments can also be used to guide future instruction.

> How do you systematically gather and analyze data from your formative assessments of ELs?

---

6. Chapter 7 will focus on assessment for ELs.

As a subset of formative assessments, teachers can use informal assessments quickly and frequently to gauge students' learning. Some ideas for informal assessments of ELs are the following:

- Thumbs up—thumbs down
- Exit cards
- Think-pair-share
- Listening in on students' small group work
- One-on-one interview
- Warm-up activity
- Logs or journals
- Writing samples
- Checklists
- Cloze tests or quizzes
- Brainstorming exercises
- Story or information retelling

Performance-based rubrics also provide an opportunity for teachers to gauge the degree to which ELs access content and use academic language, and give teachers a way to use assessment results to target future instruction. Table 6.7 (see p. 158) provides an example of a performance-based assessment that is designed to determine the extent to which a student has met an integrated content and language objective of a lesson.

Content and language objective: Students will make use of pertinent scientific terms and sequencing language to create and explain the steps in the water cycle both orally and in writing.

ICE AGE UNIT

"What Thawed the Ice Age?" is a sample unit that incorporates several EL lesson scaffolding elements. The unit is based on the Common Core State Standard for Literacy in History/Social Studies, Science & Technical Subjects, CCSS.ELA-Literacy.RST.6–8.1: "Cite specific textual evidence to support analysis of science and technical text." (Common Core State Standards Initiative, 2012).

Ice Age Lesson Academic Language and Content Objective

The unit's integrated academic language and content objective is based on the related Common Core State Standard this unit addresses.

Table 6.7. Rubric to Assess Water Cycle Lesson (See objective on p. 157)

Element	Approaches	Meets	Exceeds
Demonstration of understanding of content: Creating visual representation of the water cycle	Student is unable to create a coherent visual representation of the water cycle	Student adequately creates a coherent visual representation of the water cycle	Student creates a coherent visual representation of the water cycle, adding descriptive details
Demonstration of understanding of content: Oral and written descriptions of the water cycle	Oral and written descriptions do not explain the sequence of the water cycle to the listener or reader	Oral and written descriptions adequately explain the basics of the sequence of the water cycle to the listener or reader	Oral and written descriptions explain the full sequence of the water cycle and provide additional supporting details to the listener or reader
Use of scientific terms	Student uses basic scientific vocabulary orally and in writing	Student uses basic and some technical scientific vocabulary specific to the water cycle orally and in writing	Student uses technical, precise scientific vocabulary specific to the water cycle orally and in writing
Use of sequencing language	Student does not attempt to use sequencing terms or uses sequencing terms sporadically orally and in writing	Student uses an adequate amount of sequencing terms orally and in writing	Student uses sequencing terms correctly; terms used enhance the meaning of the oral and written work

Content and language objective: Students will demonstrate understanding of the causes and effects of global warming by using academic language of cause and effect and content-specific academic vocabulary to discuss and write the factors that may cause global warming.

Ice Age Lesson Grade-Level Text

The first two paragraphs of the lengthier text that all students will read are provided below.

Roughly 20,000 years ago the great ice sheets that buried much of Asia, Europe and North America stopped their creeping advance. Within a few hundred years sea levels in some places had risen by as much as 10 meters—more than if the ice sheet that still covers Greenland were to melt today. This freshwater flood filled the North Atlantic and also shut down the ocean currents that conveyed warmer water from equatorial regions northward. The equatorial heat warmed the precincts of Antarctica in the Southern Hemisphere instead, shrinking the fringing sea ice and changing the circumpolar winds. As a result—and for reasons that remain unexplained—the waters of the Southern Ocean may have begun to release carbon dioxide, enough to raise concentrations in the atmosphere by more than 100 parts per million over millennia— roughly equivalent to the rise in the last 200 years. That CO_2 then warmed the globe, melting back the continental ice sheets and ushering in the current climate that enabled humanity to thrive.

That, at least, is the story told by a new paper published in *Nature* on April 5 that reconstructs the end of the last ice age. Researchers examined sediment cores collected from deep beneath the sea and from lakes as well as the tiny bubbles of ancient air trapped inside ice cores taken from Antarctica, Greenland and elsewhere. (*Scientific American* is part of Nature Publishing Group.) The research suggests that—contrary to some prior findings—CO_2 led the prior round of global warming rather than vice versa, just as it continues to do today thanks to rising emissions of CO_2 and other greenhouse gases. (Biello, 2012)

Analyzing The Ice Age Text's Academic Language

When teachers analyze the first two paragraphs of the text students will read using the academic language framework, they gain an overview of the multiple areas in which they will need to give ELs extra support so that ELs can comprehend the text upon which the unit is based. Table 6.8 provides a summary of these areas.

Teachers can structure their instruction to focus on any one or more of the sociocultural, discourse/organization, grammar/syntax, and academic vocabulary areas highlighted above. They may wish to read the text aloud to their students, highlighting some of the text's features that may make it challenging for ELs. Teachers could first provide some background knowledge about the ice age and global warming by having students brainstorm what they know about the topics, showing them a brief video clip, and introducing some of the text's academic vocabulary. Next, teachers could reread the text, pointing out the way in which the informational text is organized as well as the dependent clauses. Finally, students could read the text in pairs and summarize the information in their own words

Table 6.8. Analysis of Ice Age Text's Academic Language

Sociocultural Context	Discourse Complexity
• Assumes background knowledge related to the ice age • Presupposes understanding of scientific journals and why the word "nature" is capitalized and italicized (i.e., *Nature*) • Assumes background knowledge related to geography of the areas presented • Students whose first language is Spanish or another romance language could use cognates to unlock the meaning of unknown vocabulary words	• Informational text • Uses hyphens frequently; students may be unfamiliar with their use • The information is provided sequentially but without obvious markers such as "first," "next," and so on
Grammar and Syntax	**Academic Vocabulary**
• Mix of verb tenses (simple past—*filled, warmed,* past perfect—*had risen,* gerund—*melting*) • Dependent (*contrary to some popular findings*) and independent clauses (*This freshwater flood filled the North Atlantic*)	• Sea level • Greenhouse gases • The research suggests • Contrary to • For reasons that remain unexplained today • As a result • Ice sheet • Sediment cores • Millennia

What are your thoughts on having ELs read a text translation in their first language? In which cases might this strategy be effective?

as they read (either in their L1 or English). Another way to provide some ELs support so that they can access the complex grade level text is to provide a translated version of it in their home language.

Preteaching Content-Specific and Academic Vocabulary

The analysis of the ice age text yielded valuable information regarding the vast amount of vocabulary that ELs, especially those who are at lower levels of English language proficiency, might not be familiar with. Previewing this vocabulary with ELs will provide them support to comprehend the text as well as the lesson surrounding it. One way to preteach the vocabulary could be by presenting ELs with the terms on index cards and having them group the terms into the three categories provided in Table 6.9.

In Figure 6.4, another way to preteach academic vocabulary is exemplified. In this scenario, visuals are presented for many of the terms, which have been organized into the three categories. Other words and concepts are defined through explanations and synonyms. Students can match the terms with their visuals and/or definitions in English and/or their first language(s). They can then use the terms when discussing and writing about factors that may cause global warming as evidenced by the information in the text.

Instructing ELs in Vocabulary Learning Strategies: Use of Cognates

Teachers will need to instruct ELs in strategies to learn new vocabulary and make educated guesses at unknown words. One way is to teach them how to use cognates, or words that are have the same origin as another word. Even though there are not cognates across all languages, many students can benefit from honing their cognate skills. Table 6.10 shows examples from the ice age text of Spanish/English cognates that have the same meaning.

Sentence Frames as EL Support

Students can also write predictions, explanations, and cause-and-effect statements regarding the ice age, using evidence from the text to support

Table 6.9. Categorized Vocabulary

General Academic Vocabulary	Science Concepts/ Vocabulary	Time/Measurement Vocabulary
for reasons that remain unexplained today	ice sheet	millennia
as a result	carbon dioxide/CO_2	ancient
roughly equivalent to	sediment cores	today/modern
contrary to	ice cores	20,000 years ago to 10,000 years ago

Figure 6.4. Previewing Categorized Vocabulary With Visuals, Explanations, and Synonyms

Science Concepts	
Ice sheet	
Carbon dioxide CO_2	
Sediment cores	
Ice cores	

Time/Measurement	
Millennia	A millennium (plural millennia or millenniums) is a period of time equal to one thousand years 3rd millennium January 1, 2001 – December 31, 3000
Ancient	Aged, Antique, Bygone, Old-Fashioned, Outdated
Today/modern	

Social Studies Concepts	
Antarctica	
Greenland	
The Globe	

Academic vocabulary/Idiomatic Expressions	
For reasons that remain unexplained today	For reasons that we still dont' know now
As a result	Because of (effect comes next)
Roughly equivalent to	About the same as
Contary to	Something that is the opposite

Table 6.10. Use of Cognates to Access Text

English Word	Spanish Word
published	publicado
April	Abril
reconstructs	reconstruye
examined	examinaron
sediment	sedimento
air	aire
Antarctica	La Antártida
Greenland	Groenlandia
suggests	sugiere
carbon dixiode—CO_2	dióxido de carbono
round	ronda
global	global
vice versa	viceversa
continues	continúa
emissions	las emisiones de
gases	gases

their answers.[7] Depending on their level of proficiency in English, English learners may require extra support with the academic language and discourse of prediction, explanation, and cause and effect. Sentence frames for each of these three linguistic functions can give ELs the extra support they need to produce this type of oral and written discourse.

Sentence frames for predicting:

I anticipate that _____ causes global warming to occur.

I think _____ will happen because _____.

---

7. One of the major elements of the Common Core State Standards is citing evidence using text.

I think _____ might _____, because I know that _____.

Sentence frames for explaining:

One reason global warming may occur is because _____.

Another reason global warming may occur is because _____.

A third reason global warming may occur is because _____.

Sentence frames for cause and effect:

_____ is the most likely cause for global warming to occur. When _____happened, then _____ took place as a result. I know this because _____.

Which EL strategies have been most effective for your students? Why?

Ice Age Lesson Formative Assessment

A sample performance-based assessment is provided in Table 6.11 in the form of a holistic rubric that describes three levels of student performance. The rubric should be designed before

Table 6.11. Ice Age Sample Rubric

Element	5 Points	10 Points	15 Points
Demonstration of understanding of cause and effect of global warming	Student does not adequately demonstrate understanding of the basic tenets of global warming orally and/ or in writing	Student demonstrates sufficient understanding of the causes and effects of global warming orally and in writing	Student demonstrates deep understanding of the causes and effects of global warming orally and in writing
Use of academic language of cause and effect	Student does not use language of cause and effect as it relates to global warming	Student adequately uses language of cause and effect as it relates to global warming	Student effectively uses language of cause and effect as it relates to global warming
Use of content-specific vocabulary	Student uses basic, general vocabulary in speaking and writing about global warming	Student uses some content-specific technical vocabulary related to global warming	Student uses a wide variety of content-specific technical vocabulary related to global warming

the lesson is implemented with students, and it should also be shared with students, so they are aware of the teacher's expectations for how they will be assessed.

LESSON DESIGN AND IMPLEMENTATION REFLECTIVE TOOLS

The EL lesson design planning tool shown in Figure 6.5 can be used as a framework to plan scaffolded lessons for ELs. It can be used to frame collaboration with an ESL specialist as well as other teachers from the same content area or grade level.

Figure 6.5. EL Lesson Design Planning Tool

Element of EL Lesson Design	Yes	No	Comments
Have I created content and language objective(s) for the lesson?			
Have I analyzed the language demands of the text?			
Have I determined ELs' background knowledge of the topic?			
Have I provided scaffolds for ELs to access the text?			
Have I incorporated instruction of each language domain (speaking, listening, reading, and writing) in the lesson?			
Have I provided frequent opportunities for ELs to interact with each other and the teacher around the content?			
Have I provided support for ELs to use academic language with each other and the teacher?			
Have I determined which language domain(s) I would like to assess in this lesson?			
Have I determined the purpose for the assessment(s)?			
Have I designed at least one formative assessment?			
Are there any other concerns I have as I design and prepare to implement this lesson?			

Source: Adapted from Staehr Fenner & Kuhlman, 2012.

CONCLUSION

One important facet of advocacy for ELs involves ensuring that they are instructed effectively so that they can meaningfully participate in content-rich lessons along with their non-EL peers. The purpose of this chapter was to raise educators' awareness and provide concrete examples of how teaching ELs may differ from teaching non-ELs. Recommended resources found at the end of this chapter provide sources for more information on the topics described. Since effectively teaching ELs is a complex endeavor, all the approaches, considerations, and expertise that are required could not possibly be included in one chapter. Chapter 7 focuses on the many facets of assessment for ELs through an advocacy lens.

REFERENCES

August, D., Garcia-Belina, R., Bridgforth, M., King, A. S., & Haynes, E. F. (2013, March). *Helping teachers implement the Common Core State Standards with ELLs.* Presentation at TESOL annual convention, Dallas, TX.

August, D., & Shanahan, T. (2006). *Developing literacy in second-language learners: Report of the National Literacy Panel on Language-Minority Children and Youth.* Executive summary. Mahwah, NJ: Lawrence Erlbaum.

Bailey, A. L. (Ed.). (2007). *The language demands of school: Putting academic English to the test.* New Haven, CT: Yale University Press.

Bailey, A., Butler, F., & Sato, E. (2007). Standards-to-standards linkage under Title III: Exploring common language demands in ELD and science standards. *Applied Measurement in Education, 20*(1), 53–78.

Bailey, A., Butler, F., Stevens, R., & Lord, C. (2007). Further specifying the language demands of school. In A. Bailey (Ed.), *The language demands of school: Putting academic English to the test* (pp. 103–156). New Haven, CT: Yale University Press.

Ballantyne, K. G., Sanderman, A. R., & Levy, J. (2008). *Educating English language learners: Building teacher capacity.* Washington, DC: National Clearinghouse for English Language Acquisition.

Belcher, D. (2006). English for specific purposes: Teaching to perceived needs and imagined futures in worlds of work, study, and everyday life. *TESOL Quarterly, 40*(1), 133–156.

Common Core State Standards Initiative. (2012). Key ideas and details. *English language arts standards: Science & technical subjects: Grade 6–8.* Retrieved from http://www.corestandards.org/ELA-Literacy/RST/6–8

Cummins, J. (1979). *Cognitive/academic language proficiency, linguistic interdependence, the optimum age question, and some other matters* (Working Paper 19, Working Papers on Bilingualism). Toronto: Bilingual Education Project, The Ontario Institute for Studies in Education.

Cummins, J. (1980). The construct of proficiency in bilingual education. In J. E. Alatis (Ed.), *Georgetown University Round Table on Languages and*

Linguistics: Current issues in bilingual education, 1980 (pp. 81–103). Washington, DC: Georgetown University.

D'Angiulli, A., Siegel, L., & Maggi, S. (2004). Literacy instruction, SES, and word-reading achievement in English-language learners and children with English as a first language: A longitudinal study. *Learning Disabilities Research & Practice, 19*(4), 202–213.

de Jong, E. J., & Harper, C. A. (2007). ESL is good teaching "plus": Preparing standard curriculum teachers for all learners. In M. E. Brisk (Ed.), *Language, culture, and community in teacher education* (pp. 127–148). Mahwah, NJ: Lawrence Erlbaum.

Echevarria, J., Powers, K., & Short, D. (2006). School reform and standards-based education: A model for English language learners. *The Journal of Educational Research, 99*(4),195–210.

Featured profiles. (2009). *Education Week.* Retrieved from http://www.edweek.org/ew/qc/2009/17profiles.h28.html?intc=ml

Goldenberg, C. (2008). Teaching English language learners: What the research does—and does not—say. *American Educator, 33*(2), 8–23, 42–44.

Gonzalez, J., & Darling-Hammond, L. (1997). *New concepts for new challenges: Professional development for teachers of immigrant youth.* McHenry, IL: Center for Applied Linguistics, Delta Systems.

Graves, A., Gersten, R., & Haager, D. (2004). Literacy instruction in multiple-language first-grade classrooms: Linking student outcomes to observed instructional practice. *Learning Disabilities Research & Practice, 19*(4), 262–272.

Harper, C., & Staehr Fenner, D. (2010, March). *Comparing the revised TESOL/ NCATE and National Board Teaching Standards.* Paper presented at the 44th Annual TESOL Convention and Exhibit, Boston, MA.

Lee, O., Maerten-Rivera, J., Penfield, R., LeRoy, K., & Secada, W. (2008). Science achievement of ELLs in urban elementary schools: Results of a first-year professional development intervention. *Journal of Research in Science Teaching, 45*(1), 31–52.

Linan-Thompson, S., Vaughn, S., Hickman-Davis, P., & Kouzekanani, K. (2003). Effectiveness of supplemental reading instruction for second-grade English language learners with reading difficulties. *The Elementary School Journal, 103*(3), 221–238.

Linquanti, R. (2011). Strengthening assessment for English learner success: How can the promise of the Common Core Standards and innovative assessment systems be realized? In Policy Analysis for California Education and Rennie Center for Education Research & Policy (Ed). *The road ahead for state assessments* (pp. 13–25). Cambridge, MA: Rennie Center for Education Research & Policy. Retrieved from http://www.edpolicyinca.org/sites/default/files/2011_PACE_RENNIE_ASSESSMENT_REPORT.pdf

McLaughlin, B. (1992). Myths and misconceptions about second language learning. *CAL Digest.* Retrieved from http://www.cal.org/resources/digest/digest_pdfs/myths.pdf

Minaya-Rowe, L. (2004). Training teachers of English language learners using their students' first language. *Journal of Latinos and Education, 3*(1), 3–24.

Ochoa, A., & Cadiero-Kaplan, K. (2004). Towards promoting biliteracy and academic achievement: Educational programs for high school Latino English language learners. *The High School Journal, 87*(3), 27–43.

Ray, J. (2009). A template analysis of teacher agency at an academically successful dual language school. *Journal of Advanced Academics, 21*(1), 110–141.

Scarcella, R. (2003). *Academic English: A conceptual framework* (Technical Report 2003–1). Irvine: University of California Linguistic Minority Research Institute.

Short, D., & Echevarria, J. (1999). *The Sheltered Instruction Observation Protocol: A tool for teacher researcher collaboration and professional development.* Washington, DC: Center for Research on Education, Diversity & Excellence.

Staehr Fenner, D., & Snyder, S. (n.d.). *How can districts incorporate national teaching standards in designing professional development to benefit English language learners?* Boston, MA: Association of Latino Administrators and Superintendents. Retrieved from http://www.alasedu.net/resources/1/newsletters/Summer%20Newsletter/Building%20on%20the%20Standards.pdf

Thomas, W., & Collier, V. (1997). *School effectiveness for language minority students.* Washington, DC: National Clearinghouse for Bilingual Education.

Understanding Language. (2012). *Persuasion across time and space: Analyzing and producing persuasive texts.* Retrieved from http://ell.stanford.edu/sites/default/files/ela_archives/understanding_language_materials_Jan2013.pdf

Vaughn, S., Linan-Thompson, S., Mathes, P. G., Cirino, P., Carlson, C. D., Pollard-Durodola, S., . . . Francis, D. J. (2006). Effectiveness of Spanish intervention for first-grade English language learners at risk for reading difficulties. *Journal of Learning Disabilities, 39*(1), 56–73.

Williams, T., Hakuta, K., & Haertel, E. (2007). *Similar English learner students, different results: Why do some schools do better? A follow-up analysis based on a large-scale survey of California elementary schools serving low-income and EL students.* Mountain View, CA: EdSource.

World-Class Instructional Design and Assessment. (2012). *WIDA 2012 amplified ELD standards.* Retrieved from http://www.wida.us/downloadLibrary.aspx

Zetlin, A., MacLeod, E., & Michener, D. (1998). Professional development of teachers of language minority students through university-school partnership. *Teacher Education and Special Education, 21*(2), 109–120.

7 Advocating for ELs in Assessment

One of the most controversial topics that has a large potential impact on the education of ELs today is the role assessment plays in their educational experience. When the Elementary and Secondary Education Act (commonly referred to as No Child Left Behind or NCLB) was implemented in 2001, ELs began gaining more visibility in high-stakes assessment. With that legislation, the challenges inherent in assessing ELs fairly and equitably also began coming to the forefront. Educators of ELs must advocate for students by assessing them as equitably as possible and using their assessment data thoughtfully to improve their instruction.

Catherine Collier, expert on the assessment of ELs for special education, describes her views on advocating for ELs' assessment:

> Our voices should always be heard during full individual evaluations for special education placement as well as during the diagnostic stages of Response to Intervention (RTI). EL personnel are frequently the only members of the identification and assessment team who can speak to the cultural and linguistic responsiveness of the assessment procedures being used during RTI and special education evaluations. It is challenging for education personnel to assure fair and equitable assessment during intervention and evaluation of EL students as it is not possible to obtain a nationally standardized test that is completely culturally/linguistically non-biased. Only education personnel knowledgeable of EL student culture, language and transition/adaptation issues can determine

if an assessment process is fair and equitable for particular EL students and make the necessary modifications to assure this happens for ALL students.

In addition to the tools and procedures I have advocated, EL teachers and administrators can also work to develop locally normed, culturally and linguistically appropriate evaluation tools and authentic, dynamic assessment procedures. The research exists, the tools exist, the knowledge exists; we just need EL personnel to speak up and advocate for the use of these procedures to achieve fair and equitable assessment for EL students. (personal communication, 2012)

INTRODUCTION

Because there is so much room for error that can have absolutely detrimental ramifications for an EL's academic, personal, and professional lives, educators must arm themselves with research and best practice when it comes to the fair and equitable assessment of ELs. Educators who share the responsibility for ELs' academic success must be knowledgeable, vocal, and active advocates so that ELs are included fairly in the assessment process, which has historically put them at a distinct disadvantage when compared to non-ELs.

This chapter will shed light on several different high-stakes aspects of assessment for ELs and will provide educators some tools to help them advocate for ELs' equitable participation in different types of assessment. Topics included in this chapter are advocacy for collaborating with colleagues around the assessment of ELs, accommodations for ELs on end-of-year tests, English language proficiency/development assessment, assessing ELs for special education, and assessing ELs for gifted and talented programs.

> How would you define "high-stakes" assessment for ELs? In what ways does assessment of ELs differ from assessment of non-ELs?

WHAT THE RESEARCH TELLS US

O'Malley and Valdez Pierce (1996) note that assessment serves six basic purposes for ELs. The first three purposes have to do with language support services and include (1) screening to determine which students are ELs and subsequent identification of ELs, (2) placement in language support programs, and (3) reclassification as former ELs or exit from language support programs. The final three purposes are (4) monitoring for student progress, (5) program evaluation, and (6) accountability.

ELs are a heterogeneous mix of students with different literacies, knowledge bases, school experiences, and levels of English proficiency. An EL's achievement and solid background in the first language is the strongest predictor of future success in English (Thomas & Collier, 2002). Yet, many education policies include a one-size-fits-all, snapshot approach to assessing ELs that does not take ELs' multiple background variables into consideration. For example, NCLB (2001) mandates that most ELs take part in annual content and language assessments.[1] However, there are often limited ways for ELs to effectively demonstrate what they know and can do on multiple choice content tests in a language in which they are not yet proficient, and these limitations affect the validity of the test results.

English Language Proficiency or Development Assessments

Compared to non-ELs, ELs are held accountable on more measures of assessment and spend more time being assessed. Title III accountability requires ELs to make progress in learning English, to attain English language proficiency (ELP), and to learn academic content (NCLB, 2001). Unlike non-ELs, English learners must take part in annual English language proficiency or English language development assessments for each year that they are considered ELs. In addition, NCLB mandates that they also be tested on English language arts and reading yearly in Grades 3 through 8 and once in high school.[2]

Despite ELs' yearly participation in ELP assessments, few states have been able to validate their current English language proficiency assessment or accountability system because of validity issues in assessing ELs' English language proficiency (Wolf, Farnsworth, & Herman, 2008). Generally, students' receptive language is more advanced than their productive language (Gottlieb & Hamayan, 2002). For this reason, educators sometimes see students developing skills in listening and reading before their speaking and writing develop. Educators must therefore be aware of how ELs typically develop English when interpreting their English

---

1. There are some special circumstances in which ELs may be exempt from one English language arts content assessment if they have been in school in the United States for less than 12 months.

2. States also have regulations on when all students must be tested in social studies and science.

language proficiency test results and making decisions based on ELP assessment data. According to Tim Boals, executive director of World-Class Instructional Design and Assessment (WIDA, 2012),

> Equitable assessment of English language development is crucial for at least two overarching reasons: More effective instruction and clearer accountability. Teachers need accurate information about ELs' language development across all domains of listening, speaking, reading, and writing so they can plan instruction and support their students. This language information should also connect to content classes, or the specific language needed to succeed in school. In other words, it should be anchored to environments like the science class or mathematics class so teachers have specific guidance to differentiate language instruction while keeping content expectations high.
>
> English language proficiency assessments are part of school, district, and state accountability systems. So this is the second reason they must be equitable—meaning fair, valid, and reliable. If the assessments do not accurately portray where ELs are in their English language development, then EL programs and schools will be unfairly judged. While ELP assessments cannot be used for student-level accountability the way academic assessments are, the data do contribute to understanding language development in relation to achievement.
>
> School teachers and administrators need a shared understanding of the language development process and the role of sociocultural context in instruction and assessment if they are to have high but reasonable expectations of ELs' linguistic and academic progress. Assessments in and of themselves are not valid per se; rather, the data are valid for particular students in particular ways or contexts that require us as educators to understand our students before we begin interpreting score results. Only then can we be sure that our assessments are not misrepresenting what our students know and can do. (personal communication, 2012)

How well do you understand and use the results of your state's ELP test to inform instruction and reclassification of ELs?

Content Area Assessments for ELs

Even though most ELs are required to take part in summative content assessments, research suggests that ELs' scores on summative academic content assessments in English are not always representative of these students' content skills and knowledge. Research has clearly demonstrated that assessments designed mainly for native English speakers may not be as reliable and valid for ELs (Abedi, 2006). Due to this lack of reliability and validity, many experts caution that practitioners and policymakers interpret ELs' content assessment scores carefully, especially when using these content scores to make language support placement or EL redesignation/ exit decisions (Linquanti, 2001; Ragan & Lesaux, 2006). For these reasons, Abedi and Dietel (2004) posit that the use of multiple assessment measures is the only way to combat issues that surround accountability of ELs. We cannot use one sole assessment measure to make high-stakes decisions that impact the instruction of ELs. According to Lorraine Valdez Pierce of George Mason University,

> Testing is only one kind of assessment, and standardized testing in English is always a test of English language proficiency. Validity comes from inferences that are accurate, unbiased, and based on objective and predictive or observable criteria. But results cannot be accurate for ELs if they are based on assumptions that test-takers are native speakers of English, if they assume that test-takers are familiar with American history and culture, and/or if they use subjective language or have not been shown to be predictive of success for ELs.
>
> Teachers can ask administrators to allow ELs to stop taking any type of assessment, but especially timed, state standardized tests, when these students display clear signs of distress or anxiety, the most obvious of which is crying. Teachers can also obtain and/or provide professional development on valid and reliable assessment approaches for ELs for their school-based professional or collaborative learning communities. (personal communication, 2012)

Accommodations for ELs on Content and ELP Assessments

One way to provide ELs more access to demonstrating what they know and can do on content tests is through the use of testing accommodations. Thompson, Johnstone, and Thurlow (2002) define accommodations as student-focused options to level the playing field on large-scale tests. Willner, Rivera, and Acosta (2008) further describe two types of accommodations for ELs. The first type is direct linguistic support accommodations, which are adjustments to the text of the assessment with the intent of reducing the linguistic load necessary for ELs to access the content of the test. Direct linguistic support accommodations can be delivered in English or the EL's native language. Some examples of direct linguistic support include simplified text (or "plain English"), bilingual glossaries, and translated test questions. Indirect linguistic support accommodations involve adjustments to the conditions under which a test is taken to allow ELs to more efficiently use their linguistic resources. Indirect linguistic support accommodations do not focus on the language of the test. Instead, their focus is on adjustments to the test environment and test schedule. For example, allowing ELs extended time and a separate location to take their tests are indirect linguistic support accommodations.

While accommodation options for ELs may be plentiful, more does not equal better. Research on accommodations for ELs suggests that, at best, many commonly used accommodations may be minimally effective for ELs. In fact, assigning inappropriate accommodations for ELs may even hinder their performance on assessments (Rivera & Collum, 2004; Willner et al., 2008). Underscoring that accommodations must be carefully selected for ELs, Kieffer, Lesaux, Rivera, and Francis (2009) studied accommodations for ELs on large-scale assessments. Of the seven accommodations used, only using an English dictionary or glossary had a statistically significant effect on these ELs' performance. However, these results are particular to the ELs studied. Since all ELs bring different background experiences and strengths to the assessment arena, each EL's accommodations must be assigned on a case-by-case basis.

> How does your school or district determine which accommodations are used for ELs' instruction and assessment?

While all ELs are allowed accommodations on content assessments, ELs with disabilities are allowed accommodations on ELP assessments as well. The results of a study showed that 31 states provided some form of documentation for participation or accommodation of ELs with disabilities on state ELP assessments. The most common decision-making criteria for ELP assessment participation or accommodations used by approximately half of the states was the individualized education program (IEP), the 504 plan, or a decision by the ELP team (Albus & Thurlow, 2008).

Demographics of ELs in Special Education

There is wide variance among ELs who have been identified as needing—or not needing—special education services; in some schools and districts, ELs are overrepresented in special education; in others, they are underrepresented. According to data from the National Center for Education Statistics (http://nces.ed.gov/programs/coe/indicator_cgg.asp), approximately 13% of all students ages 3 to 21 (both ELs and non-ELs) are receiving some type of special education services (2012).

As of 2003, approximately 9% of ELs were receiving special education services across the nation, suggesting possible underrepresentation. However, within that number, great variations exist depending on the demographics of school districts in terms of the number of dually identified ELs as well as the ethnic origin of the students.

For example, in 2003, in districts that educated more than 100 ELs, an average of 9% of students were dually identified. However, in districts with fewer than 99 ELs, nearly 16% of ELs were dually identified (Zehler et al., 2003). Three decades of national surveys reveal evidence of persistent overrepresentation of minorities in special education (Artiles, Trent, & Palmer, 2004; Losen & Orfield, 2002). The most recent survey conducted by the National Research Council Panel (Donovan & Cross, 2002) found that schooling has an impact on the incidence of students in different racial or ethnic groups' special needs or giftedness due to the presence or lack of quality teachers, challenging classes, and adequate funding. Analyses of placement and opportunity-to-learn data also reveal that minority students who are in special education receive more exclusive and lower quality services than do White students (Losen & Orfield, 2002).

Artiles, Rueda, Salazar, and Higareda (2005) found that, compared to English proficient students, Latino English language learners are overrepresented in special education beginning in Grade 6 and that placement of these students in special education increases through Grade 12. Their analysis also found that placement in special education programs (mentally retarded [MR], language and speech [LAS], and learning disabled [LD]) increased for students who were in English immersion programs. According to the United Nations Educational, Scientific and Cultural Organization (UNESCO), 90% of children with disabilities in developing countries have no access to school (Council for Exceptional Children, 2012). This recently revealed statistic has huge implications on ELs with disabilities who immigrate to the United States and struggle academically, as these students may have had limited formal schooling in their first language.

Special Education Misclassifications of ELs

Of potential EL special education misclassifications, learning disabilities are the most common. Misclassification of a learning disability particular to reading levels can occur for ELs with low ELP because of linguistic features that impact comprehension, especially due to unfamiliar words, long phrases in questions, complex sentences, conditional/adverbial clauses, long noun phrases, relative clauses, prepositional phrases, passive voice, and negation (Abedi, 2006). Some misidentification of ELs with learning disabilities can occur due to similarities between the expected second language

When do you refer ELs for special education consideration? What triggers these referrals?

acquisition process and linguistic difficulties experienced by students with learning disabilities. Case and Taylor (2005) state that common characteristics in language development of ELs and students with learning disabilities occur in pronunciation (omissions, substitutions, and additions), syntax (negation, word order, and mood), and semantics (forms of figurative language such as proverbs, metaphors, and similes).

Assessment of ELs for Special Education Identification

One consideration of assessments used to determine ELs' eligibility for special education services is the potential for cultural bias of test items and the language of the test(s) used. Although cultural sensitivity is often part of the test item review process, cultural bias of test items can prohibit students' understanding of or access to test items. Also, depending on how the test was translated (e.g., direct translation, translation by a native speaker), the language of the test may be of concern (Abedi, 2006).

Overall, researchers have found clear patterns of difficulty assessing ELs for special education, including the following: difficulty differentiating between English language acquisition and learning disabilities, confusion about district rules with regard to when to refer an EL for special education evaluation, misunderstanding a student's low ELP as low IQ or a learning disability, overemphasis on test scores throughout the evaluation, limited use of prereferral strategies, uncertainty about which test(s) to use, heavy reliance on untrained bilingual assessors, negativity toward families, inadequate translation services, and overrepresentation of ELs in special education prevailing out of uncertainty of assessment results (Klingner & Harry, 2006).

Assessment of ELs for Gifted and Talented Programs

While ELs may be overrepresented in special education in some contexts, these students are vastly underrepresented in gifted and talented programs (Donovan & Cross, 2002; Zehler et al., 2003). For example, a study by the National Educational Longitudinal Study found that 17.6% of Asian students, 6.7% of Hispanic students, and only 2.1% of Native American students were identified as gifted, as compared to 9% of White students (Resnick & Goodman, 1997). Often, due to language barriers, ELs have fewer opportunities than native English speakers to be noticed by teachers for behaviors traditionally characteristic of gifted students (Aguirre, 2003).

In addition, ELs' giftedness may manifest itself in ways that are often not framed within the White, middle class school construct (Frasier & Passow,

1994; Montgomery, 2001). That is, ELs' gifts may occur within the cultural construct of learning English as an additional language. Educators must understand that behaviors that signal giftedness in the U.S. culture may signal disrespect in another (Iowa

> What does gifted and talented education look like for ELs in your context? Could ELs' participation in this program be increased?

Department of Education, 2008). A lack of communication between gifted and talented teachers and ESL teachers reduces opportunities to observe and know ELs in multiple educational settings (Gallagher & Coleman, 1994). The opportunity for ELs to be identified as gifted increases when educators collaborate around information leading to that identification (Harris, Plucker, Rapp, & Martinez, 2009).

Response to Intervention

One promising initiative in equitable assessment for ELs for special programs such as special education and gifted and talented is Response to Intervention (RTI). Echevarria and Vogt (2011) describe the two key understandings of RTI: (1) All children can learn when provided with appropriate, effective instruction, and (2) most academic difficulties can be prevented with early identification of need followed by immediate intervention. Thus, the RTI framework shifts the focus away from the intrinsic issue of the child being seen as having a problem and onto the extrinsic learning conditions of the classroom and school.

Echevarria and Vogt describe the three tiers of RTI for all students, including ELs. Tier 1 involves using research-based strategies that are effective for ELs. The key components of Tier 2 are using data to identify students in need of Tier 2 interventions, grouping students in small groups for interventions, conducting interventions, monitoring student progress, reflecting on data, and making decisions. Tier 3 involves intensive support in addition to core instruction, an increase in the duration and frequency of interventions, and a specific duration of time using frequent progress monitoring. The RTI process is recursive, and students may move in and out of tiers as appropriate.

EL COMMITTEES AS AN AVENUE TO ADVOCACY IN ASSESSMENT

One important step a school or district can take in designing a system where advocacy for ELs in assessment becomes a central focus is to form an EL committee. The purpose of an EL committee is to bring various stakeholders together to collaborate by sharing their strengths in making assessment decisions for ELs. Some suggested guidelines for who should make up the EL committee and what the purposes can be are below.

EL committee stakeholders may consist of the following members:

- Teacher of record and/or content teacher
- ESL or bilingual teacher
- Special education teacher (if the EL has an IEP or is being considered for special education referral)
- Test administrator
- Guidance counselor
- Assistant principal, principal, or designee
- Social worker
- School psychologist
- Speech/language pathologist
- Other educator(s) as appropriate
- Parent liaison
- EL parent or designated family member
- Interpreter

The functions performed by the EL committee may include the following:

- Discussing concerns/decisions regarding placement of ELs into an English language support program
- Reclassifying/exiting ELs from EL status
- Reviewing instructional programs or EL academic progress
- Discussing parental concerns
- Deciding which ELs qualify for exemption from state assessments
- Reviewing instructional program of reclassified/exited ELs during the postreclassification period
- Determining appropriate classroom and assessment accommodations for ELs
- Considering special education referral and placement decisions
- Considering gifted and talented identification and placement decisions

One of the most important functions of the EL committee is to bring a multifaceted set of perspectives to important assessment decisions that will affect ELs. For example, if an EL is being referred for special education consideration in the area of speech and language, a speech/language pathologist should be included in the school's EL committee to discuss typical behaviors students with speech and language issues may exhibit.

In addition, an ESL teacher should also be present to offer the perspective of how that EL's first language and culture may exhibit itself in that student's speech and language patterns. The student's content teacher can provide insight into typical expectations for all students at the EL's

> Does your school have an EL committee in place? If so, who participates in it? What works well, and what could be improved to equitably advocate for ELs' assessment?

grade level, and the EL's parent can share when the student learned to speak and if that student's speech in the L1 and/or English is comprehensible and comparable to that of his or her siblings. An interpreter can help ensure that the EL parents are able to express themselves and take part in the conversation. The school's administrator and guidance counselor will ensure that proper school policies are being followed. In this way, educators representing multiple perspectives can collaborate to inform the decision-making process for this student and lessen the chance for error.

USING ACCOMMODATIONS APPROPRIATELY FOR ELS' INSTRUCTION AND ASSESSMENT

As advocates for ELs, educators must have a deeper understanding of what accommodations are and also which accommodations to use for ELs in order for the accommodations to be effective. It is also important that teachers use the same direct linguistic support accommodations for ELs during instruction as they will use for assessment, to the degree this is possible, so that ELs are used to the linguistic support. That is, if an EL will use a bilingual word-to-word dictionary as an accommodation on content assessments, that EL should also be allowed to use that same bilingual word-to-word dictionary during classroom instruction. It also goes without saying that the same EL should be literate in his or her first language to use this accommodation.

In order for teachers to know which accommodations ELs will need in the classroom, their content assessment accommodations will need to be determined in the beginning of the school year and communicated to teachers early on. While using the same accommodations for instruction as assessment is the overarching guideline by which educators should operate, it may be impossible to include all allowed test accommodations in instruction. For example, even if the state allows test directions to be translated into the students' native languages, all teachers cannot translate all classroom instructions into those languages.

Since ELs are a heterogeneous population, teachers must carefully assign accommodations to them on a case-by-case basis. The tool below will help guide teachers and EL committees through the process. Teachers can adapt Dalton and Shafer Willner's (2012) teacher observation checklist, shown in Figure 7.1, to help them determine which accommodations should be used for ELs in classroom instruction and during assessments. States might allow different accommodations than the ones listed on the tool, so teachers need to adapt the possible accommodations accordingly.

Assigning Accommodations to ELs

Decisions for assigning accommodations should be, at minimum, aligned with the EL's ELP level, literacy in English, and literacy in the native language. It is not appropriate to assign every EL the same accommodation(s). These recommendations for the assignment of accommodations are derived from the EL accommodation research base (e.g., Abedi, Mirocha, Leon, & Goldberg, 2005; Acosta, Rivera, & Shafer Willner, 2008; Kopriva, Emick, Hipolito-Delgado, & Cameron, 2007; Pennock-Roman & Rivera, 2011). Recommended procedures for using EL-responsive criteria to assign accommodations have evolved during the past five years. An example of the most recent procedures can be found in the 2012–2013 *Iowa Guidelines for K–12 ELL Participation in Districtwide Assessments* (http:// educateiowa.gov). The EL accommodation assignment procedures found in the Iowa guidelines are derived from the state guideline exemplars noted in the 2008 *Descriptive Study of State Assessment Policies for Accommodating English Language Learners* (Shafer Willner, Rivera, & Acosta, 2008) and recommendations found in the related *Guide for the Refinement of State Assessment Policies for Accommodating English Language Learners* (Rivera, Acosta, & Shafer Willner, 2008).

Figure 7.1. General Rules of Thumb for Matching Accommodations by ELP Levels

Considerations When Selecting Accommodations for ELs:

A. Level of English language proficiency (ELP) on state ELP test

☐ Beginning, intermediate, or advanced ELP

B. Literacy development in English and/or the native language

☐ Native language literacy
☐ Interrupted schooling/literacy background

C. Factors that impact effective usage of accommodations

☐ Grade/age
☐ Affective needs
☐ Time in U. S. schools

ELs With Beginning ELP

ELs at the lowest levels of English language proficiency tend to experience the greatest need of accommodations but are the least able to use them. In general, the use of oral supports **such as verbatim reading of the entire test or clarify directions in English or the native language** are recommended over written accommodations in English; however, most of these would not be expected to produce much of an effect for the lowest proficiency levels.

ELs With Intermediate ELP

ELs at the intermediate level of ELP have usually developed some literacy in English and are expected to benefit from a wider variety of both written and oral accommodation options. Decision makers should note that the need for accommodations at this level varies considerably depending upon the unique background characteristics of the student as well as the literacy demands of the test. Similar to ELs with beginning ELP levels, the existing research suggests that native language accommodations such as **bilingual word-to-word dictionary (and extra time to use it)** as well as English accommodation are useful at the intermediate level. It may be more useful for these students to **request selected portions of the text be read-aloud** rather than have to sit through a read-aloud of the entire test.

ELs With Advanced ELP

For students at advanced ELP the need for most kinds of accommodations is expected to decrease. English/native language support in the form of **a bilingual word-to-word dictionary (and extra time to use it)** can be helpful if the EL is literate in his/her native language and has received recent instruction in that language (whether in the U.S. or abroad).

Steps for Teachers in Preparing Accommodations

1. **Individualize the initial list of accommodations for each EL based on the student's literacy development in English and/or the native language**

   - Adjust the list of accommodations based on student background factors concerning the student's previous schooling experiences.

   a. Native Language Literacy

   If the student has developed literacy in his or her native language after receiving instruction in the specific content area being assessed either in their home country or the U.S., provide the student a **word-to-word bilingual dictionary** (along with **extended time** to use it).

   b. Interrupted Schooling/Literacy Background

   If the EL has experienced interrupted formal education during his/her schooling career and as a result, has weaker literacy skills in his/her native language and English, it is highly probably that the EL is more oral-dominant in his/her developing English language proficiency). In this case, provide the EL with **oral language support** accommodations that are generally offered to ELs with beginning ELP (such as **verbatim reading of the entire test** rather than selected sections of the test and **scribe** test.)

2. **Individualize the initial list of accommodations for each EL to increase the likelihood of effective use during assessment.**

   - Adjust the list of accommodations selected in #1 and #2 above based on student background factors which can help ensure accommodations are useful to the student.

(Continued)

Figure 7.1. (Continued)

Grade/Age, Time in U.S. Schools, and Affective needs may all impact student ability to use ELL accommodations. (For example, older student sometimes refuse accommodations due to the embarrassment of receiving additional support in front of classmates. Students who have just arrived in the U.S. need to gain familiarity with U.S. testing practices and expectations. Anxiety can raise an EL's affective filter and impact test performance.)

- **Include the student in the process of assigning accommodations** to ensure use of the accommodation and student understanding of its use.
- If the student is unfamiliar with standardized testing or computer-based testing, provide **test preparation activities** prior to the assessment.
- Offer opportunities to **use the accommodations prior to the assessment** during instruction and assessment.
- When appropriate, administer tests in **special settings, with specialized personnel, in small groups or individually**, while not accommodations, are test administration adjustments that might be helpful for increasing students' level of comfort, facilitating test administration, and ensuring more accurate test results.

Review your decision.

Source: Dalton & Shafer Willner, 2012.

Which multiple assessment measures does your school or district use in making high-stakes assessment decisions for the participation of ELs in special programs?

Using Multiple Assessment Measures to Identify ELs for Special Programs

Since the EL population is heterogeneous, each EL student presents a unique case when being considered for special programs such as special education or gifted and talented programs. Because of ELs' heterogeneity, educators should use multiple selection criteria for identifying ELs for special programs.[3] The EL identification process may involve any combination of the assessments and other data described in Table 7.1.

Acculturation Quick Screen

One source of assessment data for ELs suggested in Table 7.1 is an acculturation scale. Dr. Catherine Collier has developed the widely used Acculturation Quick Screen (Figure 7.2) to provide educators

---

3. ELs can be included in both special education and gifted and talented programs if appropriate.

Table 7.1. Factors in Assessing ELs for Special Programs

Measure	Description	Considerations for Use With ELs for Special Programs
English language proficiency/ development tests	All ELs must take an annual assessment of English language proficiency or development	Knowing students' English proficiency levels is vital when making decisions about their placement in special programs. Decision makers need to be aware of students' level of English proficiency—as well as what that level of proficiency means—in order to make decisions about assessing the students' other abilities. English proficiency information is not meant to be exclusionary; it should provide insight into ELs' educational profile and complement the other information used to determine eligibility for special programs.
Acculturation scales	An acculturation scale consists of multiple questions and aims to provide data on the degree to which learners have acculturated to the U.S. school system. ELs entering U.S. schools from another country as well as ELs born in the United States must learn the unwritten rules that accompany being a student of the English language. ELs must understand the hidden codes that are involved in learning English and the school and U.S. culture. It is easier for some students than others to acquire this code-breaking skill. Being able to integrate into the school and U.S. culture may influence how the EL will be perceived by their peers and teachers. Acculturation scales are appropriate for individuals who have to learn rules and norms of a cultural environment that are different from their heritage culture.	It is important to know a student's level of acculturation to inform the evaluation of classroom performance. Educators may perceive ELs who are not yet acculturated in U.S. school settings as not bright, regardless of their academic ability. Since teachers may regard less acculturated ELs may as less bright, acculturation scale results can help educators make less biased judgments about ELs. Acculturation information should serve as one of multiple measures for the purpose of identifying ELs for special programs.

(Continued)

Table 7.1. (Continued)

Measure	Description	Considerations for Use With ELs for Special Programs
Assessment data	Multiple measures of assessment should be used to determine ELs' eligibility for special programs.	Educators should measure all students in verbal, quantitative, and nonverbal reasoning, and then pay particular attention to the highest scores within each ethnic and/or EL group as defined by local norms. Appropriate accommodations should be provided to ELs for all three of these types of assessment. Local norms should be established and used to compare ELs' assessment scores to other ELs from comparable linguistic and cultural groups with similar levels of schooling and English language proficiency.
Dynamic and performance-based assessments	In dynamic assessments, students are initially tested on material, receive an intervention, and then are retested to see what improvements resulted from the intervention. In this way, they are tested on their ability to use cognitive strategies to master new materials. Performance-based assessments are a series of tasks a student completes in specific cognitive ability areas in which they produce an authentic response.	These assessments focus on high-level thinking and problem-solving skills. They allow for ELs to more accurately demonstrate what they know and can do in a language other than their home language. Appropriate accommodations should be provided to ELs with both these types of assessment.
Portfolio assessments	Portfolio assessments contain a collection of student work culled from a variety of assignments to paint a more holistic picture of the student's academic ability and potential. Students or their teachers can compile work samples in various academic domains specific to the program in which the student will be identified.	Material in the portfolio can be completed in the student's home language as well as in English.

Measure	Description	Considerations for Use With ELs for Special Programs
Nonverbal assessments	Nonverbal assessments do not rely on language to be completed. Some researchers believe these tests provide a more equitable method of identifying gifted/talented students from historically underrepresented populations.	In order for nonverbal assessments to be suitable for ELs, their written directions should be comprehensible. Nonverbal assessment results should be used in conjunction with other assessment measures when determining EL eligibility for special programs.
Other EL Special Program Identification Data		
Student observations	Classroom observations can provide insight into the way the EL participates in the classroom and interacts with peers as well as teachers.	The educators observing ELs must be aware of the students' individual backgrounds, including each student's cultural norms, level of acculturation, and level of English language proficiency. An ESL teacher should also observe the EL.
Input from the student's cultural group	An educated adult who represents the EL's cultural group can provide input on the academic expectations and norms of the student's culture.	Knowing what is expected in school and how students relate to peers and adults can help educators make more informed decisions about inclusion in special programs.
Prior academic performance in previous schools	Prior academic performance information can provide insight into the EL's performance prior to the current U.S. school. This data source will help educators be aware of trends in that EL's academic performance in the home language and culture as applicable.	If the EL was schooled outside the United States, academic records may not always be available. If they are, they will need to be translated and interpreted. Academic achievement in the home country or previous school inside the United States should be noted.
Teacher-, parent-, peer-, and self-referral	Anyone in the EL's environment who believes that the particular student might be included in a special program should be eligible to nominate that child, including the EL's parents, peers, or even the EL him- or herself.	Educators should ensure that all stakeholders are aware of who may recommend ELs for special programs. EL parents may not feel comfortable nominating their own children due to their country's cultural norms. Rather than relying purely on parent or teacher nominations to screen for special program consideration, educators should use the nominations as a complement to other data gathered through the multiple-measure approach.

Source: Adapted from Iowa Department of Education, 2008.

Figure 7.2. Acculturation Quick Screen (AQS) Scoring Form

Student Name:		
Cultural/Environmental Factors	*Information*	*Scores*
1. Number of years in United States/Canada		
2. Number of years in School/District		
3. Number of years in ESL/Bilingual Education		
4. Native Language Proficiency		
5. English Language Proficiency		
6. Bilingual Proficiency		
7. Ethnicity/Nation of Origin		
8. % in School Speaking Student's Language/dialect		
	AQS Score Total	

1. Number Of Years in United States

Under one year = 1	Between four to five years = 4
Between one to two years = 2	Between five to six years = 5
Between two to four years = 3	Over six years = 6

2. Number of Years in School/District

Under two years = 1	Between four to five years = 4
Between one to two years = 2	Between five to six years = 5
Between two to four years = 3	Over six years = 6

3. Years in ESL/Bilingual Program

Up to one year in directed instruction = 1	Between two and two and a half years = 4
Between one and one and a half years = 2	Between two and a half to four years = 5
Between one and a half to two years = 3	Over four years = 6

4. Native Language Proficiency

Does not speak language, pre-production = 1	Advanced speech emergence, intermediate social fluency, limited academic fluency = 4
Pre-production to early production = 2	Advanced intermediate social and academic fluency = 5
Early production, limited social fluency = 3	Advanced social & academic fluency = 6

5. English Language Proficiency

Does not speak language, pre-production = 1	Advanced speech emergence, intermediate social fluency, limited academic fluency = 4
Pre-production to early production = 2	Advanced intermediate social & academic fluency = 5
Early production, limited social fluency = 3	Advanced social & academic fluency = 6

6. Bilingual Proficiency

Essentially monolingual = 1	Basic academic one, intermediate academic other = 4
Primarily one, some social in other = 2	Most academic in one, intermediate academic in other = 5
Limited academic either language, social both = 3	Bilingual in social and academic language = 6

7. Ethnicity/National Origin

American Indian, Native American, AK Native, Indigenous Populations, or First People = 1	West Asian or Middle Eastern = 4
Hispanic/Latino/Chicano or Caribbean = 2	Eastern European = 5
AfroAmer., African, East Asian, or Pacific Islander = 3	Western European = 6

8. Percent In School Speaking Student's Language Or Dialect

81% - 100% of enrollment = 1	30% -49% of enrollment = 4
66% - 80% of enrollment = 2	11% - 29% of enrollment = 5
50% - 65% of enrollment = 3	0% - 10% of enrollment = 6

Significantly Less Acculturated	Less Acculturated	In Transition	More Acculturated	Significantly More Acculturated
0-14	15-22	23-31	32-39	40-48

Source: Collier, 2013.

insight into the level of acculturation of individual ELs who are being considered for special programs, such as special education or gifted and talented programs.

Interpreting the Acculturation Quick Screen (AQS)

Level of Acculturation

Significantly Less Acculturated: 8–14

This student is at the beginning stage of adjustment to this environment and is probably experiencing severe culture shock and several symptoms of acculturative stress, such as distractibility, response fatigue, withdrawal, silence or not responding, code switching, and confusion in locus of control.

Less Acculturated: 15–22

The student is at critical phase in his or her cross-cultural adaptation and may exhibit high levels of anxiety followed by periods of depression due to the intensity of the adjustment he or she is facing. Care should be used at this stage, since it can be accompanied by a variety of unexpected emotional reactions. Signs of culture shock and symptoms of acculturative stress such as distractibility, response fatigue, withdrawal, silence or not responding, code switching, and confusion in locus of control can accompany these emotional reactions.

In Transition: 23–31

This student is in transition and is in the midst of cross-cultural adaptation and second language acquisition. He or she is probably still experiencing some culture shock and acculturative stress. Assistance with the acculturative process in the form of conventional bilingual and cross-cultural instructional techniques and assessment procedures should work well with these transition students.

More Acculturated: 32–39

Although students at this stage are fairly well acculturated, they will still have some cross-cultural education needs. They may be as well acculturated as many of their classmates. Their cross-cultural education needs can be met with conventional mainstream instruction, assessment and diagnostic procedures with sheltered instruction, and minor adjustments for differences in cognitive learning style.

Significantly More Acculturated: 40–48

This student may have some cross-cultural education needs, but conventional mainstream instruction, assessment, and diagnostic procedures should be possible without adaptation. Differences in cognitive learning style should be addressed. (Collier, 2013)

Dual Language Assessments

One way to provide a measure of an ELs' skills in both English and the native language as part of the special program eligibility process is by using dual language assessments. Dual language assessments can provide valuable information on an EL's acquisition of language in both English and the native language, which can be used to inform decisions regarding special education referral or placement in gifted and talented programs. Dual language assessments can provide another assessment data point to build a system of multiple measures that supports the equitable assessment of ELs.

The multiple components of dual language assessments can include formal, standardized evaluations of language in English and the first language, alternative and performance-based assessments, classroom observations, and consultations with ELs' families. The purposes of dual language assessments are to determine the EL's home language proficiency and skills, establish the EL's English proficiency and skills relative to local norms, identify the EL's dominant language(s), if any, and establish procedures for further evaluations, if warranted. If the EL is being referred for special education, the dual language assessment process can address referral concerns and recommend effective strategies and interventions for the student.

> To what degree are your ELs' first and second language skills taken into consideration during their assessment for participation in special programs?

Using Local Norms in Assessment

When it is your school or district's policy to use academic assessments to inform ELs' placement in special education programs or gifted and talented programs, it does not mean that ELs' scores must be compared to non-ELs' scores. So that ELs' scores on such assessments are more meaningful, educators can advocate for their ELs by comparing their ELs' scores with those of other ELs in the same age group who have had similar language and acculturation experiences. Local norms are the range of test scores that represent the average or usual performance of a restricted sample. When using local norms, the population of students being analyzed is a smaller set than a national set. Many group-administered ability and achievement tests offer local norms that are specific to a school or a district. When using local norms, a student's test performance is compared to that for other students whose demographic and background factors are similar.

ADVOCATING FOR ENGLISH LEARNERS' APPROPRIATE IDENTIFICATION FOR SPECIAL EDUCATION

Standardized assessments tend to assume that all children have similar life experiences, exposure to the same concepts and vocabulary, similar socialization practices, comparable early literacy experiences, similar exposure to content/subject material, and fluency in English. Even when using translated standardized assessments to determine ELs' eligibility for special education, educators must exercise caution, as several linguistic bias and translation issues skew the validity and reliability of such assessments for ELs. For example, test items may be organized by the order of English difficulty instead of reflecting the developmental order of the translated language. Also, words may represent the same concept but have different levels of difficulty across languages. Some words are common in one language but may not appear as frequently in another language (Peña, Bedore, & Rappazzo, 2003).

Difference or Disability

Certain aspects of the EL second language acquisition process[4] may reflect difficulties that indicate the presence of a disability. Table 7.2 outlines common second language acquisition errors such as errors in pronunciation, syntax, or semantics and their considerations for ELs.

EL SPECIAL EDUCATION CASE STUDIES

Two case studies help bring to life the complexities of determining whether an EL has a linguistic difference or a disability. The following two case studies are designed as two-part exercises. The first part paints a picture of what teachers typically see at the surface when an EL is suspected of having a disability. Then, the second part exemplifies the necessity of collaborating and providing multiple sources of information when an EL is being considered for special education assessment. To obtain the most authentic two-part case study experience, read only the first part of the

> Think of an EL who is experiencing academic difficulties. What are your challenges in discriminating that EL's second language acquisition processes from a potential disability?

---

4. I use the term *second language acquisition* even if the EL is acquiring English as a third, fourth, or otherwise additional language.

Table 7.2. Definitions and Considerations of Pronunciation, Syntax, and Semantics

Term	Definition	Considerations for ELs
Pronunciation	Omissions from, substitutions for, additions to, and distortion of speech	• Development of native-like pronunciation is sensitive to a wide variety of factors such as age at which the learner begins learning English and can take years. Many ELs will always speak with an accent, which is expected. • The normal process of developing native-like pronunciation can resemble an articulation disorder.
Syntax	Principles by which sentences are constructed (e.g., negation, word order, and mood)	• Dependent upon the level of proficiency, ELs' syntactical errors may resemble the errors of a student with a learning disability. • ELs may have difficulty with word order, complex or long sentences, and/or negation in receptive and productive language.
Semantics	The meaning of language through words, phrases, signs, and symbols	• Figurative language may be especially difficult for ELs, since it is often culturally bound. • Some words have multiple meanings (e.g., *scale* the fish vs. weigh it on the *scale*). • Proverbs, metaphors, personification, and similes are often difficult for ELs to master.

study, and use the Part 1 guiding questions to shape your reflection or group discussion around these topics. Then, read the second part of the case study and reflect upon the Part 2 guiding questions or discuss them with colleagues.

EL Case Study: Marco, Part 1—Introduction

Marco is a 14-year-old Dominican student who arrived at your school five months ago and was placed in the eighth grade. According

to anecdotal records his mother provided, he attended school from kindergarten through the seventh grade in the Dominican Republic (DR). He repeated the seventh grade one time in the DR, attending it for two years. His mother said that he had a tutor to help him with his school-work in the DR. Marco says that he was sup-posed to repeat the seventh grade again but came to the United States before being retained a second time. His U. S. science teacher referred him for special education, with concerns that he often seems lost in the classroom and that he has not developed English literacy skills as expected. He is due to attend high school next year, and his sci-ence teacher is concerned that his academic needs will not be addressed in the large high school. You are the ESL teacher on Marco's EL committee.

- What additional information would you like to have about Marco?
- With whom would you collaborate to gather more information about him?
- What will you do at this point in the special education referral process?
- What interventions would you suggest Marco's teachers implement in the meantime?

EL Case Study: Marco, Part 2—Additional Information

Since you had so many questions about Marco, you decided to do some detective work. First, you talked to him with the help of an inter-preter. From this discussion, you found out that he had lived with his grandmother for the past six years while his parents were in the United States arranging for his arrival. Marco also told you about his classroom setting in the DR, explaining how there were over 50 students in his class-room. When too many students were in the class, some had to sit outside, because there was not enough room for them all. When you asked about his tutor, he told you that his tutor worked with him for only one day and then did not appear again. Marco's school was closed for six months after a massive hurricane hit his village. You asked Marco what he did when he did not understand something in school. He said he did he not approach his teacher after class for extra help, because only the poorly behaved stu-dents did that. You asked Marco to produce a writing sample in Spanish. This writing sample was filled with phonetically based representations of words. The text he produced in Spanish was 27 lines long, but did not contain any capitalization or punctuation.

- How does this additional information impact the special education referral process for Marco?

- What would you still like to know about him?
- With whom will you collaborate to ensure he is instructed effectively?
- What action will you take with Marco?
- How can you advocate for Marco during this process?

EL Case Study: Bao Yu, Part 1—Introduction

Bao Yu, a 10-year-old Chinese (Mandarin)-speaking student, was born in the United States to Chinese parents. She was educated from kindergarten through the third grade in an English-only academic environment in an affluent East Coast suburb. She transferred to your West Coast school at the beginning of the present academic year as a fourth grader and is in your general education fourth grade class. Although she sounds like a native speaker in English, Bao Yu has been in an ESL program since kindergarten. She sounds as if she is orally fluent in social English, but her comprehension of complex informational texts places her at a first grade reading level. Bao Yu's writing is generally not cohesive, lacks appropriate punctuation, and does not use academic vocabulary, and she frequently spells common words incorrectly. Her notebooks are disorganized. She is not literate in Mandarin, as she has never received academic instruction in that language. However, she does speak some Mandarin at home. She has recently begun acting out in class. You are her fourth grade teacher.

- What additional information would you like to have about Bao Yu?
- With whom would you collaborate to gather more information about her?
- What will you do at this point in the special education referral process? Why?
- What classroom interventions would you implement with Bao Yu?

EL Case Study: Bao Yu, Part 2—Additional Information

Upon further investigation, you discover a few additional pieces of information about Bao Yu. You learn that she remained in the same school on the East Coast until her move to your school. You speak with Bao Yu's mother, who is fluent and literate in English and who helps Bao Yu with her homework nightly. You contact Bao Yu's former ESL teacher and learn that Bao Yu was given both pull-out ESL instruction and in-class language support. Her former ESL teacher expressed concern about her academic progress but did not refer her for special education because Bao Yu was very polite and did not act out in class. In the meantime, you consult with Bao Yu's current ESL and reading teachers to brainstorm interventions and strategies to support her. You implement these strategies and save samples of Bao Yu's work to document the outcomes of the interventions. To help Bao Yu become more confident with her writing, you teach her how to use a voice recorder to first capture what she'd like to write about and then transcribe her recording. Her level of frustration with writing does decrease slightly. However, after two months in your classroom with extra support, her level of writing in your fourth grade class has not improved significantly. Bao Yu also receives additional reading instruction through the support of the reading teacher but still reads at the same level in English.

- How does this additional information impact Bao Yu's special education prereferral process?
- What would you still like to know about Bao Yu?
- What action will you take with Bao Yu? Why?
- With whom will you collaborate so that Bao Yu can succeed?
- How can you advocate for Bao Yu during this process?

ADVOCATING FOR THE APPROPRIATE ASSESSMENT OF ENGLISH LEARNERS FOR INCLUSION IN GIFTED AND TALENTED PROGRAMS

While ELs may be over- or underrepresented in special education, ELs tend to be underrepresented across the nation in gifted and talented programs at the K–12 level. Before educators can begin to advocate for ELs' inclusion in gifted and talented programs in their school or district, they should first review the current EL demographics and inclusion processes in their context.

> Think of an EL who might be gifted and talented. What behaviors does this student exhibit that lead you to believe the student might be gifted and talented? How do these behaviors differ from those of non-EL gifted and talented students?

What an EL Gifted and Talented Student Might Look Like

In order for ELs to be appropriately included in gifted and talented programs, many educators will need to become aware that giftedness may display itself differently for ELs than non-ELs. Educators of ELs will need to ensure that they are aware of the complexities involved with the inclusion of ELs in gifted and talented programs and advocate for their consideration. In addition, educators with EL expertise must be part of the referral, assessment, and decision-making process whenever an EL is considered for inclusion in gifted and talented programs. Once ELs are placed in gifted and talented programs, ESL teachers should collaborate with gifted and talented teachers to help ensure instruction is accessible to ELs at different levels of English language proficiency.

The Galaxies of Thinking and Creative Heights of Achievement (GOTCHA) project defined characteristics that gifted and talented ELs demonstrate, which are divided into the realms of school, language, and culture. While the characteristics below are not set in stone, they may help illustrate the variety of ways a gifted and talented EL might exhibit his or her exceptional abilities. Each EL presents a unique case when being considered for gifted and talented programs. Because of this heterogeneity, educators should use multiple selection criteria for identifying ELs as gifted and talented students.

- School Based[5]

1. Is able to read in the native language two grade levels above the current grade level

2. Shows high ability in mathematics

3. Is advanced in creative domains (fluency, elaboration, originality, and flexibility)

4. Is a leader in multiple settings (e.g., playground, home, clubs, etc.)

- Language Based

1. Demonstrates language proficiency levels that are above those of nongifted students who are also English learners

2. Learns multiple languages at an accelerated pace

3. Shows the ability to code switch

4. Wants to teach others words from the home language

5. Is willing to translate for others

6. Has superior knowledge of heritage phrases and dialects along with the ability to translate meanings into English

7. Has a grasp of jokes related to cultural differences

---

5. Many of these abilities would be dependent upon the type, length, and quality of instruction in a student's native language as well. (For example, an EL who has not been instructed in his or her native language may not be able to read in his or her native language.)

- Culture Based

1. Balances behaviors between those expected in the heritage culture and those in the new culture

2. Is willing to share the heritage culture

3. Shows pride in heritage culture and ethnic background

4. Demonstrates a global sense of community and respect for cultural differences

Source: Diaz & Menendez, 1989.

CONCLUSION

This chapter focused on several areas of assessment in which advocacy is urgently needed for ELs, such as in accommodations, assessment for special education, and assessment for EL inclusion in gifted and talented programs. Because many types of assessments are inherently flawed for use with ELs, multiple measures of assessment are suggested when assessing ELs for high-stakes purposes. In addition to using multiple measures of assessment, collaboration with educators who represent multiple perspectives is a way to support the equitable assessment of ELs. One of the more challenging tasks is for educators to decide how to prioritize their EL assessment advocacy, with whom to collaborate, and which steps to take next. Chapter 8, the final chapter, explores ways to advocate for ELs so that they can be properly placed in courses that will lead to their graduation and successful continuation to college or career.

REFERENCES

Abedi, J. (2006). Psychometric issues in the ELL assessment and special education eligibility. *Teachers College Record, 108*(11), 2282–2303.

Abedi, J., Courtney, M., Mirocha, J., Leon, S., & Goldberg, J. (2005). *Language accommodations for English language learners in large-scale assessments: Bilingual dictionaries and linguistic modification* (CSE Report 666). Los Angeles: National Center for Research on Evaluation, Standards, and Student Testing, University of California.

Abedi, J., & Dietel, R. (2004, Winter). *Challenges in the No Child Left Behind Act for English Language Learners* (CRESST Policy Brief 7). Retrieved from http://www.cse.ucla.edu/products/newsletters/policybrief7.pdf

Acosta, B., Rivera, C., & Shafer Willner, L. (2008). *Best practices in the accommodation of English language learners: A Delphi study.* Prepared for the LEP Partnership, U.S. Department of Education. Arlington, VA: The George Washington University Center for Equity and Excellence in Education.

Aguirre, N. (2003). ESL students in gifted education. In I. A. Castellano (Ed.), *Special populations in gifted education: Working with diverse gifted learners* (pp. 17–27). Boston, MA: Allyn & Bacon.

Albus, D., & Thurlow, M. (2008). Accommodating students with disabilities on state English language proficiency assessments. *Assessment for Effective Intervention, 33*(3), 156–166.

Artiles, A. J., Rueda, R., Salazar, J., & Higareda, I. (2005). Within-group diversity in minority disproportionate representation: English Language Learners in urban school districts. *Exceptional Children, 71,* 283–300.

Artiles, A. J., Trent, S. C., & Palmer, J. (2004). Culturally diverse students in special education: Legacies and prospects. In J. A. Banks & C. M. Banks (Eds.), *Handbook of research on multicultural education* (2nd ed., pp. 716–735). San Francisco, CA: Jossey-Bass.

Case, R. E., & Taylor, S. S. (2005). Language difference or learning disability? Answers from a linguistic perspective. *The Clearing House, 78*(3), 127–130.

Collier, C. (2013). *Acculturation & culture shock activity set.* Retrieved from crosscultured.com/documents/CedarRapidsIA010313/Accultur%20act.pdf

Council for Exceptional Children. (2012). *Issue brief: United Nations Convention on the Rights of Persons with Disabilities.* Arlington, VA: Author.

Dalton, G., & Shafer Willner, L. (2012). *ELL accommodation assignment protocol created for the 2012 DC OSSE testing accommodations manual.* Washington, DC: District of Columbia Office of the State Superintendent. Retrieved from http://osse.dc.gov/publication/testing-accommodations-manual-and-policyaccommodations-manual-training

Diaz, V. T., & Menendez, M. L. (1989, March). *Galaxies of thinking and creative heights of achievement (GOTCHA).* Paper presented at the annual conference of the Massachusetts Association for Bilingual Education, Boston, MA.

Donovan, S., & Cross, C. (2002). *Minority students in gifted and special education.* Washington, DC: National Academy Press.

Echevarria, J., & Vogt, M. (2011). *RTI and English learners: Making it happen.* Boston, MA: Allyn & Bacon.

Frasier M. M., & Passow A. H. (1994). *Toward a new paradigm for identifying talent potential.* Storrs: The National Research Center on the Gifted and Talented, University of Connecticut.

Gallagher, J., & Coleman, M. R. (1994). *A Javits project: Gifted Education Policy Studies Program final report.* Chapel Hill: University of North Carolina, Gifted Education Policy Studies Program. (ERIC Document Reproduction Service No. ED371499)

Gottlieb, M., & Hamayan, E. (2002). Assessing oral and written language proficiency: A guide for psychologists and teachers. In R. B. Vega (Ed.), *Serving English language learners with disabilities* (pp. 13–17). Springfield: Illinois State Board of Education.

Harris, B., Plucker, J. A., Rapp, K. E., & Martinez, R. S. (2009). Identifying gifted and talented English language learners: A case study. *Journal for the Education of the Gifted, 32*(3), 368–393. Retrieved from http://www.eric.ed.gov/PDFS/EJ835865.pdf

Iowa Department of Education. (2008). *Identifying gifted and talented English language learners.* Des Moines, IA: The Connie Belin and Jacqueline N. Blank International Center for Gifted Education and Talent Development.

Kieffer, M. J., Lesaux, N. K., Rivera, M., & Francis, D. (2009). Accommodations for English language learners taking large-scale assessments: A meta-analysis on effectiveness and validity. *Review of Educational Research, 79*(3), 1168–1201.

Klingner, J. K., & Harry, B. (2006). The special education referral and decision-making process for English language learners: Child study team meetings and placement conferences. *Teachers College Record, 108*(11), 2247–2281.

Kopriva, R. J., Emick, J. E., Hipolito-Delgado, C. P., & Cameron, C. A. (2007). Do proper accommodation assignments make a difference? Examining the impact of improved decision making on scores for English language learners. *Educational Measurement: Issues and Practice, 26*(3), 11–20.

Linquanti, R. (2001). *The redesignation dilemma: Challenges and choices in fostering meaningful accountability for English learners* (Policy Report 2001–1). Santa Barbara: University of California Linguistic Minority Research Institute.

Losen, D., & Orfield, G. (Eds.). (2002). *Racial inequity in special education.* Cambridge, MA: Harvard Education Press.

Montgomery, D. (2001). Increasing Native American Indian involvement in gifted programs in rural schools. *Psychology in the Schools, 38*, 467–475.

No Child Left Behind (NCLB) Pub. L. No. 107–110 (2001).

O'Malley, J. M., & Valdez Pierce, L. (1996). *Authentic assessment for English language learners: Practical approaches for teachers.* Reading, MA: Addison-Wesley.

Peña, E., Bedore, L., & Rappazzo, C. (2003). Comparison of Spanish, English, and bilingual children's performance across semantic tasks. *Language, Speech, and Hearing Services in Schools, 34*, 5–16.

Pennock-Roman, M., & Rivera, C. (2011). Mean effects of test accommodations for ELLs and non-ELLs: A meta-analysis of experimental studies. *Educational Measurement: Issues and Practice, 30*(3), 10–28.

Ragan, A., & Lesaux, N. (2006). Federal, state, and district level English language learner program entry and exit requirements: Effects on the education of language minority learners. *Education Policy Analysis Archives, 14*, 20.

Resnick, D., & Goodman, M. (Fall, 1997). Research review. *Northwest Education Magazine, 3*(1), 33–37. Retrieved from http://educationnorthwest.org/webfm_send/1226

Rivera, C., Acosta, B., & Shafer Willner, L. (2008). *Guide for the refinement of state assessment policies for accommodating English language learners.* Prepared for the LEP Partnership, U.S. Department of Education. Arlington, VA: The George Washington University Center for Equity and Excellence in Education.

Rivera, C., & Collum, E. (2004, January.). *An analysis of state assessment policies addressing the accommodation of English language learners.* Issue paper prepared for the National Assessment Governing Board, Washington, DC.

Shafer Willner, L., Rivera, C., & Acosta, B. (2008). *Descriptive analysis of state 2006–2007 content area accommodations policies for English language learners.* Arlington, VA: The George Washington University Center for Equity and Excellence in Education.

Thomas, W. P., & Collier, V. P. (2002). *A national study of school effectiveness for language minority students' long-term academic achievement.* Santa Cruz: University of California, Center for Research on Education, Diversity & Excellence.

Thompson, S. J., Johnstone, C. J., & Thurlow, M. L. (2002). *Universal design applied to large scale assessments* (Synthesis Report 44). Minneapolis: University of Minnesota, National Center on Educational Outcomes.

Willner, L. S., Rivera, C., & Acosta, B. D. (2008). *Descriptive study of state assessment policies for accommodating English language learners.* Arlington, VA: George Washington University Center for Equity and Excellence in Education.

Wolf, M. K., Farnsworth, T., & Herman, J. (2008). Validity issues in assessing English language learners' language proficiency. *Educational Assessment, 13,* 80–107.

Zehler, A., Fleischman, H., Hopstock, P., Stephenson, T., Pendzick, M., & Sapru, S. (2003). *Descriptive study of services to LEP students and LEP students with disabilities* (vol. I Research Report). Arlington, VA: Development Associates.

8 Advocacy for ELs' Success Beyond Grade 12

INTRODUCTION

The focus of this final chapter is on advocating to support ELs as they develop their plans beyond high school. It concentrates on considerations as well as actions educators can take so that their ELs are on a path to graduating from high school and being positioned for meaningful employment or postsecondary education. Topics in this chapter include advocating for ELs' inclusion in credit-bearing coursework, collaboration to ensure ELs' smooth transitions, gaining access to college, and making informed career choices. With educators' support and innovation, ELs will have a better chance at successfully completing high school and attending college or finding employment.

WHAT THE RESEARCH TELLS US

ELs do not tend to find themselves in successful careers or as college graduates through their own good fortune. Quite often, these students require extra support from caring, informed adults to help them navigate the system in order to achieve successful futures. The research cited in this chapter defines the challenges ELs may face. It describes the impact of coursework choices on EL graduation, the role of the school counselor, the extra challenges for undocumented ELs, EL college enrollment and completion, EL graduation rates, and ELs' career choices.

EL Graduation Rate

As the U.S. population ages, immigrants and their children will compose much of the U.S. labor force growth during the next few decades. According to Lowell, Gelatt, and Batalova (2006), nearly one in five U.S. workers will be an immigrant by the year 2030. In order for the United States to be a player in such a global economy, the country will need highly skilled workers. Creating highly skilled workers begins with providing all of the nation's students—including ELs—a solid educational foundation in grades K–12.

However, according to several researchers, graduation rates for ELs are low due to these students' poor academic achievement, most often in the area of reading. Some researchers contend ELs' low graduation rates and low rates of academic achievement are in place because the U.S. educational system was designed for the mainstream, middle-class student, and education policies have not been appropriately adapted (Bowman-Perrott, Herrera, & Murry, 2010; Houseman & Martinez, 2002).

Among eighth graders across the United States who reported to the 2000 U.S. Census that they spoke English with difficulty, only 49% went on to earn a high school diploma four years later (National Center for Education Statistics, 2004). There is great variation within those numbers, especially when the EL graduation rate is compared to the non-EL graduation rate. For example, in New York City, the EL graduation rate was 35.8% for the class of 2008 compared to 56.4% for all students (Zehr, 2009). Zehr also notes that it is often difficult to track EL graduation rates, because many states and school districts do not specifically disaggregate the EL graduation rate from that of all students, and some states and districts do not accurately report their numbers.

> What is the EL graduation rate in your school, district, and state? What will you do with this information?

Data from the 2010–2011 academic year paint a stark disparity between states' graduation rates of ELs and those of non-ELs. Preliminary data released by the U.S. Department of Education (2012) showed that 58% of ELs and 86% of non-ELs graduated in Texas. California's ELs graduated at a rate of 60%, compared with 76% of non-ELs. In Florida, 53% of ELs graduated as compared to 71% of all students. In New York State, 46% of ELs graduate while 77% of all students do. Finally, Arizona reported the lowest EL graduation rate of all the states, with 25% of ELs in Arizona graduating from high school in four years as compared with 78% of all students (http://www2.ed.gov/documents/press-releases/state-2010–11-graduation-rate-data.pdf).

Content Courses as a Roadblock to EL Graduation

When ELs enroll in U.S. schools at the secondary level with low levels of English language proficiency, they are placed in a very challenging position. They need to earn enough credits to graduate from high school, but they also need to develop enough academic English to fully participate in and achieve in these credit-bearing courses. Short and Fitzsimmons (2007) coined the phrase "double the work" to describe how adolescent ELs must learn core content through a language in which they are not yet proficient and be held to the same accountability measures as their native-English-speaking peers. ELs do not always get scheduled into middle school and high school courses that will lead to graduation (including algebra and Advanced Placement (AP) and International Baccalaureate (IB) courses) or receive the support they need to succeed in these courses.

The Connection Between ELs' Coursework and High School Graduation

The classes into which an EL is placed are a greater predictor of the student's academic outcomes than that student's level of English language proficiency (Callahan, 2005). This finding underscores the need to challenge ELs academically while supporting them linguistically. Although the type of classes they take tends to predict ELs' academic outcome, high schools tend to track ELs into remedial literacy and mathematics courses and lower-level core academic courses (Gándara Rumberger, Maxwell-Jolly, & Callahan, 2003; Parrish et al., 2006). This tracking of ELs takes place despite numerous research findings that attest to the deleterious effects of such practices for this population of students (Callahan, 2005; Swail, Cabrera, Lee, & Williams, 2005).

Despite the tendency for ELs to be tracked into remedial courses, all students (including ELs) who are exposed to higher level math and science pathways in high school tend to score higher on college entrance exams such as the American College Test (ACT). These students who study mathematics and science are also more likely to be successful in college due to greater competence in mathematics (Conley, 2006). Also, successful completion of Algebra I in middle school allows students to enroll in more varied and high-level mathematics courses throughout their high school careers (Achieve, 2008; Ketterlin-Geller, Jungjohann, Chard, & Baker, 2007; Loveless, 2008).

What kind of mathematics courses do your school's ELs typically take? Are there any English language proficiency requirements for ELs to take certain content courses? What kind of linguistic support do they receive in mathematics?

These findings suggest that educators need to focus more of their efforts on appropriately placing ELs in high-level mathematics courses as well as providing ELs linguistic support in these courses so that these students can be positioned to achieve.

The Role of the School Counselor in EL Graduation

Research has found that the role of the school counselor is essential in contexts with immigrant students (Pederson & Carey, 2003). In fact, guidance counselors can be a strong force in sharing the responsibility to educate ELs. For example, Roysircar-Sodowsky and Frey (2003) found that the school counselors' role can extend beyond that of merely scheduling courses and putting ELs on a pathway toward graduation. Counselors can positively impact ELs by supporting ELs emotionally and helping them mitigate stressors that interfere with their academic achievement, thus helping pave the way for their academic success.

Researchers have suggested several ways in which guidance counselors can support ELs' academic achievement. For example, guidance counselors who speak ELs' home languages can provide individual and group interventions with ELs. These sessions conducted in ELs' home languages can facilitate communication and enable students to express and deal with any emotional issues more effectively (Thorn & Contreras, 2005). To that end, Toffoli and Allan (1992) found that creating a school counseling curriculum that addresses the unique emotional realities ELs often face will promote greater self-understanding and better coping skills for these students.

> What kind of support do your school's guidance counselor(s) provide to ELs and their families?

EL College Enrollment Versus Graduation

There is very limited information about the rates at which ELs attend and graduate from college, because college participation is not monitored or included in federal policy (Short & Fitzsimmons, 2007). In fact, states have only recently been required to monitor EL high school graduation rates (Zehr, 2009). However, it is known that ELs are frequently the first in their family to attend college (American Youth Policy Forum, 2009). A report by the Pew Research Center (Fry & Taylor, 2013) shows that, in 2012, 69% of Latino high school graduates pursued higher education in comparison with 67% of White graduates. However, Latinos are still less likely than Whites to complete a bachelor's degree.

The American Association of Community Colleges' *Fact Sheet* (2012) notes that community colleges serve nearly half the undergraduate students in the United States. Among these community college students, approximately one quarter nationwide come from immigrant backgrounds (National Center for Education Statistics, 2006). Further, there are community colleges located in immigrant communities that serve a higher percentage of students from immigrant backgrounds.

These statistics mean that many ELs are in need of access to rigorous coursework and academic support throughout their K–12 careers, guidance in the college application process, support with academic assessments, information about college financial aid opportunities, and testing and application fee waivers (Robertson & Lafond, 2008). These extra supports are necessary to help level the playing field for ELs who are first generation college applicants, and for their families, who are most likely unfamiliar with the U.S. college application process.

> What does the college acceptance and graduation rate look like for ELs in your district? What kind of programs or initiatives are in place to provide ELs support during the college enrollment and graduation process?

Career Choices for ELs

There is very limited research on the career choices of racial and ethnic minorities (Flores et. al, 2006). One study stands out on this topic. For example, Fouad and Byars-Winston (2005) conducted a meta-analysis of literature linking career aspirations to differences in race and ethnicity and found that race/ethnicity did not influence career goals but did have an impact on students' perceptions of career opportunities and barriers. Language ability, education, and socioeconomic factors are all possible barriers that can prevent ELs from reaching their career aspirations.

One area in which there is emerging research is on the topic of Latino career choice. Such research has shown that, for Latinos who do attend college, the most popular majors for undergraduate students are in the social sciences, business, psychology, and education. At the master's and doctoral level, Latino students more commonly earn degrees in education, public administration, and psychology than such fields as healthcare, engineering, computer information science, and business (Llagas & Snyder, 2003).

Currently, there has been a significant push in supporting Latino student interest in science, technology, engineering, and mathematics (STEM) professions because of the growing number of Latino students entering the workplace as well as an increase in the number of STEM jobs available (Crisp & Nora, 2012). While there has been an uptick in the number of

Latino students pursuing STEM degrees at the postsecondary level, these students are much less likely to actually earn a STEM degree or certificate than their non-Latino peers (Chen & Weko, 2009). This disparity indicates a need for ongoing academic support throughout Latinos' educational careers as well as financial support at the postsecondary level (Crisp & Nora, 2012).

> What kinds of careers do your ELs aspire to? How knowledgeable are your ELs and their families about the kind of education, training, and English language skills their chosen careers will require?

Undocumented ELs and College

The roadblocks to college and career are much more pronounced for undocumented ELs who would like to enroll in college. There are numerous ELs who fall into the category of students who were not born in the United States but were brought to the United States at a young age and do not possess immigration documentation. Not all undocumented youth are ELs, but many are. There are an estimated 700,000 undocumented young adults aged 18 to 34 who have completed high school. Of these undocumented youth, less than half (49%) are in college or have attended college compared with 71% of U.S.-born residents (Passel & Cohn, 2011).

These undocumented students need access to strong mentors, information about postsecondary education, financial support, and lower levels of family obligations in order to even begin to think about postsecondary education (Gonzales, 2010). Because they are unable to apply for federal loans and financial aid and in many states are required to pay out-of-state-tuition fees at state schools, they must deal with financial challenges beyond those of their documented peers. In addition, the belief that they have to keep their family's immigration status a secret often prevents them from sharing their status with school personnel. If undocumented students or their families do share this information, many teachers and counselors are untrained in how to meet the needs of these students. These factors cause many undocumented high school graduates to give up on the possibility of continuing their education when they realize the obstacles that they face (Abrego & Gonzales, 2010).

Rodriguez and Cruz (2009) note that English is as much a gatekeeping factor as it is a facilitative factor for ELs and undocumented immigrant students in their successful transition to college. Due to the lower socioeconomic status level of these two groups of students, the financial constraints of transitioning to

> Are you aware of any undocumented immigrants in your context who have college aspirations? What can you do to help them achieve their goals?

college tend to further compound their challenges. While the community college system can be a helpful option to both of these groups of students, this system tends to be overburdened with multiple demands and shrinking resources.

ADVOCATING FOR ENGLISH LEARNERS' SUCCESSFUL FUTURES

Despite the numerous challenges ELs face in being admitted to and completing college or entering a successful career, there is much that informed educators can do to advocate for these students. The equity audit shown in Table 8.1 details considerations, questions, and implications for educators to use to reflect upon advocacy for ELs' futures and to prioritize next steps for them.

Table 8.1. EL Graduation, College, and Career Equity Audit

Consideration	Questions to Ask	Implications
Course enrollment	Are ELs enrolled in advanced courses, mainstream courses, or remedial courses? How does course enrollment vary depending on ELs' level of English language development?	If ELs at low levels of English language development tend to be placed in remedial courses, they may never gain enough credits to graduate. If ELs are enrolled in advanced courses without enough linguistic support, they may also not receive credit for these courses, which will have a bearing on their graduation and chances at postsecondary education.
Alternative programs	Are there alternatives for ELs that will lead to their graduation?	ELs are allowed to attend high school until the age of 22. If they don't earn enough credits to graduate on time, they cannot be enrolled in a traditional school model. Alternatives such as newcomer schools, GED programs, or schools for older ELs that lead to graduation can provide these ELs a path to a high school diploma.
Preventing long-term ELs	Are there checks in place to ensure ELs gain academic English language proficiency in an expected time frame?	ELs may fall through the cracks and remain in ESL programs for several years even if born in the United States, which may lead to them not receiving enough credits to graduate. Ensuring that ELs' progress is checked each year will help determine which ELs need extra language support.

(Continued)

Table 8.1. (Continued)

Consideration	Questions to Ask	Implications
Class makeup	Are ELs isolated from non-ELs, or are they grouped heterogeneously? Are ELs' teachers models of academic English speakers?	If ELs don't have authentic academic English modeled for them, they will be less likely to acquire the academic English necessary for success in school.
Guidance counselors	Are guidance counselors empathetic, bilingual, and bicultural? Are counselors familiar with the unique challenges ELs face in graduating and attending college or finding meaningful employment?	Guidance counselors should recognize the unique linguistic and cultural contexts in which ELs attend school. They should work collaboratively with ESL teachers and the community to provide ELs support in graduation, career, and/or college.
Pathways to college	Are there special supports in place for ELs and their families to provide them information and assistance in attending college?	ELs and their families will need extra guidance to navigate the U.S. college system. They will need support in meeting high school course requirements for college, preparing for tests, applying for college, and requesting financial aid.
Support in college	Is there any support available from local colleges to help ELs be successful in that context?	ELs may require extra assistance with the language required to be successful in college courses, meet academic and cultural expectations, and select college courses.
Pathways to career	What kind of career support is in place for ELs who do not wish to enroll in college?	ELs will benefit from assistance in choosing careers that are meaningful to them. They may need help applying for jobs, practicing for interviews, and learning about the culture of employment.
Other	Are there any other issues that are related to ELs' success during and after their K–12 education that may impact their path to college and/or career?	

Source: Adapted from Alford & Nino, 2011, p. 67.

EL Coursework

Since one thing that may stand in the way of ELs' futures is their lack of coursework that leads to high school graduation credits, educators must be proactive in closely examining all ELs' coursework. Educators should focus on each EL in a case-by-case basis to collaboratively determine whether each EL is taking courses that will lead to high school graduation as well as whether each EL is receiving enough linguistic support to be successful. The EL coursework checklist in Figure 8.1 is a tool to help

Figure 8.1   Ripple Effect of EL Advocacy

For Each EL	Yes	No	Action to Take
Does the student have an understanding of the different types of high school diplomas available?			
Is the student aware of the courses that must be taken to lead to the type of diploma desired?			
Is the student's level of English language proficiency prohibiting him or her from taking challenging courses that lead to graduation?			
Does/did the student have access to algebra in the eighth grade as a gateway to calculus in high school?			
Are credit-bearing content classes challenging but not frustrating for this student?			
Do this student's classes lead to high school graduation?			
Has the proper course sequence been followed for all courses?			
Does (do) the student's ESL course(s) count as English language arts credit-bearing course(s)?			
Has the student been tested in the home language to determine whether proficiency in the home language can count toward foreign language credits?			
Does the student have access to afterschool tutoring in subjects that lead to graduation?			
Does the student have a mentor to help him or her navigate through the school year?			
Has the student expressed a desire to attend college?			
Have multiple educators encouraged the EL to attend college and shared information about college with the family in the home language?			
Are the student's family members aware of the college application process and/or the steps needed for their child to obtain gainful employment?			

teachers, counselors, and administrators at the middle and high school levels determine whether ELs are taking courses that will lead to graduation and postsecondary education if desired by the EL.[1]

---

1. Part of ELs' desire to attend college will stem from educators setting high expectations for them and encouraging them and their families that college is possible.

At Valley High School in Sacramento, California, ELs, their parents, and counselors have a meeting upon the students' enrollment in school to determine which classes the students need to meet graduation requirements and to avoid classes that they might already have taken in their home country. The school's goal is to avoid repetition and support language acquisition.

The Calexico High School in Calexico, California, is located in a bilingual, bicultural community on the southern border of the United States. Ninety-eight percent of Calexico's students are Latino, and 80% are English learners. The school has eliminated the tracking system and has high expectations for all students. Groups of students are organized into academies and supervised by teams of teachers to help all students feel connected academically as well as socially. Three language options are available for required courses. Courses may be taught through Spanish, English, or sheltered English. The same number of credits is granted for all three options, and all options provide academically challenging study for students that leads to postsecondary education and other opportunities. Through their commitment to providing all students with more opportunities to succeed, the staff at Calexico High School has created a highly effective secondary school program for immigrant students.

Source: Walqui, 2000.

Collaboration to Ensure ELs' Smooth Transitions

As ELs transition from elementary school to middle school and from middle school to high school, it is possible for them to slip through the cracks. Even if they have made progress in elementary school, once ELs arrive in a larger middle school, where their teachers do not know their academic and personal stories, they may struggle on an academic and/or personal level and not know where to turn for support. The same is true for middle school ELs who transition to a different high school, where they might not know any teachers or guidance counselors well enough to ask for help.

To help create a safety net for ELs and encourage a smoother transition for them as they progress from elementary to middle school and from middle school to high school, one day can be set aside to hold a meeting at the end of the academic year. For ELs transitioning from an elementary to a middle school context, the meeting should involve the elementary and middle school ESL teachers, guidance counselors, and one administrator from each school at the very least. For ELs transitioning from a middle to a high school context, the middle and high school ESL teachers, guidance counselors, and one administrator from each school should meet. Middle school personnel will need to meet with both the elementary school and the high school and will have to allow for two meeting days.

The school with the younger students should supply a list of their ELs and have their ELs' academic records on hand. For each EL on the list, staff should discuss the following:

- The EL's home language and background experiences
- How long the EL has been in an ESL program
- The EL's level of English language proficiency or development in each of the four domains (speaking, listening, reading, and writing)
- The courses the EL has previously taken and grades in course-work
- The courses the EL will need to take to graduate
- The kind of language support available at the old and new schools
- The student's academic strengths and areas of need
- The student's personal strengths and areas of need
- Any pertinent information about the EL that might affect his or her learning (e.g., learning style, refugee status, long-term EL status, IEP)
- What kind of personal support the EL had in the old setting and will have in the new setting
- Two "buddies" at the new school—one peer and one educator

Bringing together various stakeholders in each EL's education helps foster a sense of shared responsibility to educate each EL at each school level. Collaborating in this way helps weave together a safety net of informed educators who will be better positioned to look out for these ELs so that they don't get lost in the system. Also, the ELs and their families should know that their educators are taking this extra step to advocate for their success in school. Ideally, these same groups of educators should check in quarterly to monitor their ELs' progress in the new setting.

Seal of Biliteracy

California and New York have recently adopted a State Seal of Biliteracy that celebrates students' proficiency in the four domains of language. California's State Seal of Biliteracy provides recognition to high school students—both EL and non-EL—who have attained a high level of proficiency in speaking, listening, reading, and writing in one or more languages in addition to English. Maxwell (2012) reported that more than 10,000 graduates in the class of 2012 had earned the special distinction.

212 Advocating for English Learners

In New York State, students who have demonstrated attainment of the criteria for the award receive a State Seal of Biliteracy on their diploma or transcript. Educators can advocate for this policy at the district level to recognize their ELs' home language literacy skills and to also promote an environment that places value on proficiency in more than one language. California's eligibility requirements for this endorsement are shown in Figure 8.2, and a checklist for meeting them is shown in Figure 8.3, with the first line filled in for a single sample student. (Additional sheets can be attached to this checklist for more names.)

Figure 8.2.   Eligibility Requirements for California State Seal of Bilteracy

Eligibility Criteria for a Student Whose Primary Language is English

Each of these three academic requirements shall be fulfilled.

1. Students must have completed all English–language arts (ELA) requirements for graduation with an overall grade point average (GPA) of 2.0 or above in those classes.

2. Students must have passed the California Standards Test (CST) in ELA (administered in Grade 11) at the "proficient" level.

3. Students must demonstrate proficiency in one or more languages other than English through **one** of the following methods:

   a) Pass a foreign language Advanced Placement (AP) exam, including American Sign Language, with a score of three or higher.

   b) Pass an International Baccalaureate examination with a score of four or higher.

   c) Successfully complete a four-year high school course of study in a foreign language and attain an overall grade point average of 3.0 or above in that course of study.

   d) If no AP examination or off-the-shelf language test exists and the district uses its own language examination, the school district must certify to the State Superintendent of Public Instruction (SSPI) that the test meets the rigor of a four-year high school course of study in that foreign language.

   e) If a district offers a language examination in a language in which an AP examination or off-the-shelf examination exists, the district language examination must be approved by the SSPI.

   f) Pass the Scholastic Assessment Test (SAT) II foreign language exam with a score of 600 or higher.

Eligibility Criteria for a Student Whose Primary Language Is Not English

If the primary language of a student in grades nine to twelve, inclusive, is other than English, the student shall also meet the following two academic requirements:

1. Achieve Early Advanced proficiency level on the California English Language Development Test (CELDT), which may be administered an additional time, as necessary.

2. Meet the requirements above as stated in 1, 2, and 3.

Figure 8.3. California State Seal of Biliteracy Requirements Checklist

Last Name	First Name	(1) ELA Requirements	(2) Passage of CST Proficient Level with GPA of 2.0 or above	(3) Method of Demonstrating Proficiency	If primary language is other than English, student attained required CELDT score and met all other requirements
(Name)	(Name)	Passed	Passed	(c) Foreign language 4 years	Passed

Source: http://www.cde.ca.gov/sp/el/er/sealofbiliteracy.asp

GRANTING HIGH SCHOOL CREDITS TO ENGLISH LEARNERS

Although ELs may face several potential roadblocks to high school gradua-tion, some educators have already tapped their own resources to advocate for their ELs to succeed in high school and graduate. One example of this type of advocacy that supports ELs' high school graduation focuses on the school enrollment process, and the second example describes a successful summer school program that leads to ELs' acquisition of high school credits.

ESOL Entry Assessment

Kate Montgomery, ESOL entry assessment teacher, writes,

In Fairfax County Public Schools (VA), the education of ELs begins with obtaining initial placement information for each student at the ESOL Assessment Center. This information provides teachers with a starting point so that they can begin identifying and meeting a new ESOL student's needs.

The ESOL Entry Assessment Team assesses new students to FCPS who speak a language other than or in addition to English. This team of ESOL Assessment Teachers works hand-in-hand with Multilingual Services/Student Registration to assess and register students centrally, the goal being to obtain a student's English language proficiency level for placement purposes and information about the student's prior schooling. In addition, the ESOL Assessment Center offers credit testing in high school mathematics and English Language Arts to secondary students coming from a foreign country. If students are able to pass the mathematics and English Language Arts assessments, they are immediately awarded high school credits for those courses. This is an excellent opportunity for eligible students to earn high school credits before they enroll in the school system. It is crucial that a student's prior educational experience in their home country be recognized and honored whenever possible. A multilingual registrar reviews a student's transcript from his/her previous school(s) to determine eligibility for the following assessments:

- Algebra I, Algebra II, and Geometry for high school mathematics credit(s) (offered in a number of languages)
- English 9, for students who have completed 9th grade, and English 9 and 10, for students who have completed 10th grade, for high school English Language Arts credit(s)
- World Language Credit Exam for high school world language credit(s) (offered in 20 languages[2])

This entire assessment process speaks to the high level of advocacy that FCPS demonstrates for ELs. The teachers take time to speak to parents/guardians about their child's assessment results and answer questions, for example. (personal correspondence, 2012)

---

2. Fairfax County Public Schools offers high school world language credit for ELs who can prove proficiency in speaking, listening, reading, and writing in their home language(s).

Mentoring

Informal mentoring can make a huge difference in an EL's experience at the elementary, middle, and high school levels. Short and Fitzsimmons (2007) describe a mentoring program in Hoover High School in San Diego, California. The school has established strong systems of communication about students among teachers, other faculty, administration, parents, and community members. All teachers are asked to take 10 students "under their wing" and to mentor, monitor, and follow up with them as they progress through the school year. For many ELs, this mentorship is vital to their acclimation to school and life in the United States. Teachers are strongly encouraged to communicate with parents as much as possible, to the point of scheduling occasional check-in phone calls to discuss students' successes.

CAREER SUPPORT FOR ENGLISH LEARNERS

Schools should also consider providing career support that takes ELs' unique characteristics into consideration. Schools do not always pay enough attention to the end goal of college, which is to prepare students for fulfilling careers.

Summer Scholars Program: The English for Speakers of Other Languages (ESOL) Summer Scholars program, coordinated by the ESOL Program Office for Prince William County Public Schools (Virginia), was created to help motivate ELs to stay in school and graduate. Unlike traditional summer school remediation programs, the Summer Scholars program offers core content classes as a first-time enrollment opportunity, allowing students to take a year-long course in just six weeks, earn credit, and accelerate progress toward graduation. ELs in Grades 9 through 12 are selected for this free opportunity based on teacher recommendation, and priority is given to older ELs. Program components include academics, American cultural experiences, community-based connections, and home partnerships.

Newcomer ELs receive a mini high school experience by rotating among classes in English, computer technology, social studies, mathematics, science, and orientation to an American high school. ELs more proficient in English enroll in content classes needed for graduation that are taught by trained master teachers. These teachers deliver their content lessons in English with the appropriate linguistic supports to aid these students' comprehension of content in English.

Further support is provided through ESL student graduates currently on a career path who are assigned as Summer Scholars' role models and tutors. ELs' parents receive guidance on high school graduation requirements and future planning. ELs in the Summer Scholars program boast a course pass rate of an astonishing 99%. In 2010, ELs in the Summer Scholars program passed their end-of-year state content assessment at a rate of 95% and outperformed non-ELs on similar assessment measures. The program has achieved its goal of increasing the number of ELs graduating immediately following their participation in the Summer Scholars program. More than 2,000 high school students have earned graduation credit as a result of the program.

What kind of mentoring program—if any—does your school have in place for ELs? Is it formal or informal?

Having students spend some time thinking about careers might help them have a better idea about the role of college in reaching their career goals. In some cases, students may decide that college is not immediately necessary for them to obtain their career goals. One suggestion for helping ELs think about and make long-term plans for careers is by inviting former ELs to come to school and speak about which career they have chosen, what kind of education or training they needed for their career, and how they use their first language skills and cultural competence in their career.

The EL Career Self-Assessment Tool shown in Figure 8.4 can help ELs consider different career options that are of interest to them. ELs' teachers can use the tool as a needs assessment that identifies gaps for ELs and can use the results of this tool to plan future lessons and advocacy efforts. Local businesses can be brought to the school to expose ELs to different careers and options.

Figure 8.4. EL Career Self-Assessment Tool

1. A career that I am interested in is _____.
2. I am interested in this career because _____.
3. I know someone who works in this career: YES NO
4. The education I will need for this career is _____.
5. The training I will need for this career is _____.
6. I will need to speak English (a little, somewhat, a lot) for this career.

Improving ELs' Participation in School-to-Career Programs

What kind of careers do your ELs wish to enter? To what degree are they aware of the type of education, training, and English language skills they will need to realize their dreams?

Many schools and districts may already have some type of career coaching program in place. However, when providing career services to ELs, some programs will require additional support so that ELs can participate. Table 8.2 outlines some potential barriers to participation in successful school-to-career programs for ELs and offers suggestions for EL advocacy in this area.

Table 8.2. Barriers to ELs' Participation in School-to-Career Programs, and Suggested Strategies

Potential Barrier to ELs	Suggested Strategy for Advocacy
School-to-career staff may be inadequately prepared.	Collaborate with community organizations that support English learners by inviting them to provide training or school-to-career services.
There may be a lack of home language materials related to careers. School staff and others may not be aware of the best channels or methods by which to disseminate these materials. Parents of English learners may not speak English.	Find resources to translate and prepare culturally appropriate materials. Identify appropriate outlets, such as community organizations, to ensure widespread access and dissemination to the targeted audiences. Hold meetings with EL families to provide information on careers orally.
Concerns could arise over placing English learners in the workplace.	Provide extensive job, language, and culture preparation for interns who are English learners. Provide training for supervisors who will closely manage interns' work.
Lack of documentation in some cases means that students cannot be paid wages.	Involve undocumented students in community service learning as appropriate.
Prohibitive graduation requirements sometimes limit English learners' access to wide course offerings.	Provide professional development to teachers on how to use school-to-career pedagogies to meet graduation requirements.

Source: Adapted from Allen, DiBona, & Reilly, 1998.

INNOVATIVE SECONDARY SCHOOL MODELS FOR ELS

Example of an Exemplary Career Program: Some career education programs exist that go out of their way to draw upon ELs' strengths and provide them the support to be successful. One such exemplary program is called FACES for the Future (facesforthefuture.org).

There are many ELs who are in a situation in which time may be working against them when it comes to high school graduation. For example, newcomer as well as long-term ELs may have not developed enough academic English to support their acquisition of content. Both

FACES for the Future supports high school students from across the state of California in finding a pathway to college and a career in the healthcare industry. Often this support extends to undocumented students, which is not surprising, since California is home to 25% of the undocumented immigrants in the nation. FACES contends that, "Despite misrepresentations in the media, most undocumented students are hardworking and show tremendous resiliency in achieving high school graduation and preparation for college." The FACES for the Future founding belief is that youth are a source of profound assets and strength, and that diversity among healthcare professionals can contribute to improved healthcare practice and outcomes. FACES for the Future is widely considered as a best-practice model for healthcare workforce development for youth, particularly those who are considered at risk.

In what ways do you involve local businesses in partnerships supporting ELs' career choices?

types of ELs may not earn enough high school graduation credits to put them on a clear path to graduation while they are still eligible for schooling. Yet, there are some innovative middle school and high school models that have become examples of advocacy for ELs by shaping their schools around ELs' unique needs. Columbus Global Academy and The Internationals Network for Public Schools are examples of schools that work successfully with ELs to support them to achieve high school graduation.

Columbus Global Academy

The Columbus Global Academy (CGA) (http://www.columbus.k12.oh.us/website.nsf/(ccs_pages)/Columbus_Global_Academy_FAQ?opendocument?OpenForm&parented=yes) in Ohio is a school designed to meet the academic, social, and language-learning needs of students who have recently arrived in the United States and who have little or no literacy skills in English or in their native language. The school serves approximately 500 students in the sixth through twelfth grades. Students entering the school have lived in the United States for less than one year and have little or no formal education and/or little or no literacy in their native language or in English. In order to enter the school, students must score at the beginning level on the English placement test and must have been in the United States for less than one year. Approximately 60% of CGA's students have had their formal education interrupted, and the most common first languages spoken are Somali, Spanish, and Mai Mai.

Middle school students usually attend CGA for one or two years before being placed at a traditional middle or high school with an ESL program. Some high school–aged students transfer to a traditional high school after one or two years at CGA, but many choose to remain until they are eligible to graduate or until they reach the age of 22. At CGA, English language instruction is integrated into content instruction. Students are also taught culturally bound social skills and the U.S. school routine. In addition, instructional assistants, fluent in another language, assist teachers and work one-on-one and with small groups of students.

The Internationals Network for Public Schools

The Internationals Network for Public Schools (http://www.intern ationalsnps.org/index.html) is a network of 17 schools—including thirteen schools in the New York City area, two schools in California, and one school in Virginia—that enroll ELs who live in the neighboring communities and have been in the country for four years or less. Among this network's reasons for success with ELs is the strengths perspective through which they view ELs. The schools' approach is described in the following way: "A badge of prestige replaces the 'stigma' of immigrant status for students, families, and faculty." The network's self-described greatest accomplishment has been that the New York schools graduate students at rates that more than double the rate for ELs in the established regional

> Which features of these schools could you replicate in your context? How?

network of New York City schools. Additionally, 90% of the network's New York City area graduates go on to college. The California and Virginia network schools are also on track to achieve similar outcomes.

SUPPORTING ENGLISH LEARNERS' ENTRANCE TO COLLEGE

While ELs work on a clear path toward high school graduation, they and their parents should consider college as within their reach. The college application process is usually daunting enough for native English speaking parents. Students interested in attending college and their parents must know how to work the system to eventually attend the college of their choice. Navigating the system includes choosing—and excelling—in multiple endeavors, such as academics, extracurricular activities, community service, and/or athletics. In addition, students must write convincing college applications, shine on college admissions assessments such as the SAT or ACT, and apply for financial aid when necessary. They must also choose colleges that will best serve them in attaining their well-articulated professional goals.

ELs will require more information about and support for applying to college than non-ELs. Table 8.3, adapted from an article written by Colorín

Colorado (2008), outlines multiple suggestions for how educators can support ELs as they consider and apply for college and also leaves room for educators to write down their reactions to each suggestion individually or in a collaborative group.

Table 8.3. EL College Suggestions, Explanations, and Reactions

Suggestion	Explanation	Educator's Reaction
Start early.	The earlier educators start to talk about higher education with ELs, the more time ELs have to mentally prepare for the possibility of college. Some ELs, especially potential first generation college students, may not get the message that college is possible from anyone else. ELs should begin hearing about college in the preschool and early elementary years. Also, families of ELs (especially families of migrant students) may move often and may not stay in the same school or district until graduation. Therefore, teachers and schools need to take advantage of opportunities to talk about college with ELs as often as possible.	
Get EL families involved as soon as possible.	Talking about college with EL families from the time their children are young gives families a chance to plan ahead and to save some money. Knowing that college is a possibility also provides them with another reason to support their children's academic success throughout their education. EL parent liaisons and ESL teachers or coordinators can help determine the most effective ways to communicate with EL students' parents.[3]	
Host college information sessions with EL families.	Educators can break up the broad college information topic into different sessions so as not to be too overwhelming for EL families. Suggested sessions include an overview of college, sequence of college preparatory middle and high school coursework, choosing a college major, choosing a college, writing college applications, taking college entrance exams, and applying for financial aid. Interpreters should be present at these sessions, and all written information should be provided in the parents' home language.[4]	
Create a resource center for students and parents.	ELs and their families must have access to the information they need in their home language. Invite students and parents in for formal and informal workshops and advising sessions in which they can ask questions and talk with other families who are going through the same steps. Families can support each other through the process. Make sure information is available about	

---

3. For more information on communicating with EL families, please see Chapter 5.

4. For more information on how to increase family involvement at school events, please see Chapter 5.

Suggestion	Explanation	Educator's Reaction
	the different kinds of admissions processes, such as early admissions and early decision, and the benefits of and rules for each. Educators can post the information online and create binders of information in families' languages. Make sure to disseminate this resource to community organizations that work with EL families.	
Tour local college campuses.	Visiting a local college campus can tell EL students a great deal about what their experience might be like. ELs may not know what to ask about or look for in a college. Educators can prepare them for the experience and also debrief about their impressions afterward. Educators can take them to two-year and four-year campuses to compare the benefits of each type of institution. ELs' families should be invited as well.	
Meet with college admissions counselors.	Meeting with college admissions counselors as a group will provide ELs better information about which college courses will best meet their needs and which kinds of support are available on campus. Admissions counselors can share with students what they need to do to have a strong application, such as ensuring they have the proper coursework on their transcripts and experiences that make them stand out from other applicants. Holding a college admissions meeting exclusively with ELs will help ELs feel comfortable asking questions.	
Develop relationships with colleges that will be a good fit for EL students.	As educators work with colleges, they may note which ones are more receptive to nonnative speakers of English. Also, former ELs may share which colleges were more supportive of their unique cultural and linguistic qualities. One way to develop a relationship with colleges is by hosting an annual college fair for ELs at the school and preparing ELs for the fair beforehand.	
Help ELs establish goals.	Helping ELs to set academic and career goals will get them thinking about what is needed to achieve those goals. Teachers can have students research careers, salaries, and educational programs so that they have realistic ideas about what to expect. Teachers should share their own experiences establishing goals and choosing a college with ELs.	
Create an EL college bulletin board or webpage.	Posting information about other former ELs who are successful in college will allow students to see where their friends have gone to college and will motivate them to achieve what their peers have accomplished. Teachers can post photos of EL high school graduates who have gone on to college, as well as the name of the college and/or program they are attending. Such a display sends the message to ELs, their parents, other students, and school staff that the school values ELs' success.	

(Continued)

Table 8.3. (Continued)

Suggestion	Explanation	Educator's Reaction
Keep in touch with ELs who have graduated.	Educators can have EL graduates come back to the school to talk about their college experiences, including what worked, what didn't work, and what they would recommend to their peers. Such students can also be a tremendous resource in terms of recommending programs and financial aid opportunities. In addition, ELs are more likely to connect on a more personal level with college students who represent their cultures and are closer to them in age.	
Encourage and support ELs while talking honestly with them about the college application process.	College may not be an option for some ELs for a number of reasons, and educators can help those students decide what steps they will take after high school by talking with them about their goals and the obstacles they face. For example, undocumented ELs may face additional challenges applying for college. Educators can connect with community organizations to help provide more support to ELs for whom college may not be an immediate option.	
Discuss these initiatives with colleagues throughout the district, and collaborate.	When a college-going culture is part of all of the schools in a district, ELs and their families will receive the message that college is indeed within their grasp and that their schools and teachers believe in them. Creating a supportive culture will also allow school officials to become more aware of the kinds of opportunities they present for their EL students, families, and community.	

Source: Adapted from Colorín Colorado, 2008.

Susan Lafond, former ESOL teacher in New York State, shares that she focused a great deal on supporting ELs who were college bound. She arranged to have speakers come in, including former ELs who went to college. She helped ELs apply to colleges, fill out applications, understand terminology, and fill out the FAFSA form. She made SAT prep CDs available to her students and wrote recommendation letters. For one student who got waitlisted at a college, she called the college personally and helped persuade the college to accept him.

At Sunnyside High School in Fresno, California, teachers discussed the significant number of Latino students enrolled in their Spanish for Native Speakers class who had ambitions of attending college but were not enrolled in college preparatory classes. The school decided to incorporate components of the Advancement Via

Individual Determination (AVID) program into the Spanish for Native Speakers and Advanced Placement Spanish courses, presenting the information in students' first language. AVID materials were translated into Spanish, and a four-year plan was developed. Student progress was monitored by both the Spanish teacher and the AVID coordinator. Discussions about financial aid, college application, and immigration concerns were all incorporated into the classes. As a result of this multifaceted initiative involving multiple stakeholders, the school saw an increase in the number of Latino students in AP classes and greater Latino student involvement in school activities over time. These students were also able to pass the California High School Exit Exam the first time they took it (Martinez, 2008).

Advocating for Migrant ELs' Access to College

For ELs who are part of migrant families, entering college can become even more of a daunting task than for nonmigrant ELs. These students may have missed the opportunity to earn high school credits while moving from state to state. Advocating for migrant students' access to college will require some additional efforts that extend beyond those for nonmigrant ELs. In addition, some migrant ELs may also be undocumented, so educators will need to take extra steps for those ELs who are both migrant and undocumented.

Alicia Sanchez, head of the migrant program at Quincy High School in Quincy, Washington, has set and voiced high expectations for seniors in the program. Sanchez aims to help migrant students envision college life as a reality. To that end, she takes them on college tours and helps them to apply for scholarships and other financial support. The biggest challenge for Sanchez is emphasizing the importance of the high school credit system. Quincy High School operates on a trimester system, and if students miss school due to moving as part of the agricultural migration stream, they lose credit. Sanchez communicates with migrant parents that these credits represent whole classes, and if students lose credit, they get a "0." Sanchez holds parent meetings for seniors in the program to focus on this credit issue as she figures out where each student is on his or her particular road to college (Green, 2011).

Supporting ELs in College

Once ELs have been accepted to college, many may think the difficult part is already behind these students. On the contrary, ELs—especially first generation college students—will often require an extra layer of support to succeed in college. Like many college students, ELs may require remedial coursework in reading and mathematics. Also, an issue that may not be as obvious is that ELs may be different from many of their classmates due to their language, culture, and former educational experiences. ELs will likely benefit from making personal connections with mentors and peers who can relate to their particular circumstances and can provide them support so they can fit in and succeed in the unfamiliar college context.

In Northfield, Minnesota, a program called Tackling Obstacles and Raising College Hopes (TORCH) is committed to helping the district's growing Latino student population graduate from high school and experience success at college. TORCH currently serves about 350 students, including 50 in college. In 2012 all of Northfield High School's Latino students graduated. In all, 49 TORCH alumni have gone on to a two-year certificate program or college degree. The program keeps tabs on students throughout high school and during their college years. TORCH offers afterschool tutoring, home visits, and financial aid in some cases. It also takes families on college tours each spring. Northfield is home to two liberal arts colleges, St. Olaf College and Carleton College. Both colleges support TORCH students by offering college student volunteers who mentor and tutor many of these first generation, low-income students. Through the project, TORCH students feel connected to college campuses and college students as they transition to their next phase of education with a support system already in place (Baier, 2012).

Many ELs will not choose to attend a four-year college and will opt for a community college, which is often a more affordable choice. In addition, community colleges offer ESL training, academic and vocational programs, job skills training, and a range of academic, employment, and social support services. While community colleges often are a popular choice for ELs, these students will still require some extra support to succeed in this context. The Community College Consortium for Immigrant Education (CCCIE) is a national network of 23 community colleges and other professional and research organizations that have joined forces in order to increase educational and workforce opportunities for immigrant students. CCCIE's mission is to (1) increase national awareness of the role of community colleges in immigrant education and (2) support the work of community colleges to strengthen and expand services for immigrant students, including ESL instruction, college readiness, college completion, career readiness, and employment and advancement. CCCIE believes that ensuring educational access and success for immigrants and children of immigrants is critical to increasing U.S. college completion and workforce readiness (Casner-Lotto, 2011).

CONCLUSION

This chapter shone a light on the challenges ELs face in planning for bright futures in postsecondary education or a career track. It highlighted several potential roadblocks that could prevent ELs from graduating from high school, attending college, and finding meaningful employment. The chapter suggested several ways in which educators can advocate for ELs as they plan their next steps, and provided several examples of schools, districts, and organizations that have created innovative programs to support ELs as they move into college and the U.S. workforce.

REFERENCES

Abrego, L. J., & Gonzales, R. G. (2010). Blocked paths, uncertain futures: The postsecondary education and labor market prospects of undocumented Latino youth. *Journal of Education for Students Placed at Risk, 15*(1–2), 144–157.

Achieve, Inc. (2008, May). *The building blocks of success: Higher-level math for all students* (Policy brief). Washington, DC: Author.

Alford, B., & Nino, M. C. (2011). *Leading academic achievement for English language learners: A guide for principals.* Thousand Oaks, CA: Corwin.

Allen, L., DiBona, N., & Reilly, M. C. (1998). *A guide to involving English language learners in school to career initiatives.* Providence, RI: Northeast and Islands Regional Educational Laboratory at Brown University. Retrieved from http://www.alliance.brown.edu/pubs/ell/ell.pdf

American Association of Community Colleges. (2012). *Community college fact sheet.* Retrieved from http://www.aacc.nche.edu/AboutCC/Documents/FactSheet2012.pdf

American Youth Policy Forum. (2009). *Moving English language learners to college- and career-readiness* (ELL issue brief). Washington, DC: Author.

Baier, E. (2012, December 12). Northfield program shrinks Latino achievement gap [Radio program episode]. In *All things considered.* St. Paul: Minnesota Public Radio. Retrieved from http://minnesota.publicradio.org/display/web/2012/12/13/ground-level-latino-connections-torch

Bowman-Perrott, L. J., Herrera, S., & Murry, K. (2010). Reading difficulties and grade retention: What's the connection for English language learners? *Reading & Writing Quarterly, 26*(1), 91–107.

Callahan, R. (2005). Tracking and high school English learners: Limiting opportunity to learn. *American Educational Research Journal, 42*(2), 305–328.

Casner-Lotto, J. (2011). *Increasing opportunities for immigrant students: Community college strategies for success.* Valhalla, NY: Community College Consortium for Immigrant Education. Retrieved from http://www.cccie.org/images/stories/Increasing_Opportunities_for_Immigrant_Students_2011.pdf)

Chen, X., & T. Weko. (2009). *Students who study science, technology, engineering, and mathematics (STEM) in postsecondary education* (NCES 2009–161). Washington, DC: Institute of Education Sciences, National Center for Education Statistics, U.S. Department of Education.

Colorin Colorado. (2008). *Creating a college-going culture for English language learners.* http://www.colorincolorado.org/article/28915/

Conley, D. (2006). *What we must do to create a system that prepares students for college success.* San Francisco, CA: West Ed.

Crisp, G., & Nora, A. (2012). *Overview of Hispanics in science, mathematics, engineering and technology (STEM): K–16 representation, preparation and participation* (White paper). Retrieved from www.hacu.net/images/hacu/ . . . /Hispanics_in_STEM_Crisp_Nora.pdf

Flores, L. Y., Berkel, L. A., Nilsson, J. E., Ojeda, L., Jordan, S. E., Lynn, G. L., & Leal, V. M. (2006). Racial/ethnic minority vocational research: A content and trend analysis across 36 years. *Career Development Quarterly, 55,* 2–21.

Fouad, N. A., & Byars-Winston, A. M. (2005). Cultural context of career choice: Meta-analysis of race/ethnicity differences. *The Career Development Quarterly, 53,* 223–233.

Fry, R., & Taylor, P. (2013). *Hispanic high school graduates pass whites in rate of college enrollment.* Washington, DC: Pew Hispanic Center. Retrieved from http://www.pewhispanic.org/files/2013/05/PHC_college_enrollment_2013–05.pdf

Gándara, R., Rumberger, R., Maxwell-Jolly, J., & Callahan, R. (2003). English learners in California schools: Unequal resources, unequal outcomes. *Education Policy Analysis Archives, 11*(36), 1–54.

Gonzales, R. G. (2010). On the wrong side of the tracks: Understanding the effects of school structure and social capital in the educational pursuits of undocumented immigrant students. *Peabody Journal of Education, 85,* 469–485.

Green, T. (2011, January 27). Helping students migrate to success. *Quincy Valley Post-Register.* Retrieved from http://www.qvpr.com/articles/helping-students-migrate-success

Houseman, N. G., & Martinez, M. R. (2002). *Preventing school dropout and ensuring success for English language learners and native American students* (Report no. ED-99-CO-0137). Washington, DC: Office of Educational Research and Improvement.

Ketterlin-Geller, L., Jungjohann, K., Chard, D., & Baker, S. (2007, November). Making math count: From arithmetic to algebra. *Educational Leadership, 65,* 66–71.

Llagas, C., & Snyder, T. D. (2003). *Status and trends in the education of Hispanics* (NCES 2003–008). Washington, DC: U.S. Department of Education, National Center for Education Statistics.

Loveless, T. (2008, September). *The misplaced math student: Lost in eighth–grade algebra.* The Brown Center report on American education. Washington, DC: Brookings Institution.

Lowell, B. L., Gelatt, J., & Batalova, J. (2006). *Immigrants and labor force trends: The future, past and present.* Washington, DC: Migration Policy Institute. Retrieved from http://www.migrationpolicy.org/ITFIAF/TF17_Lowell.pdf

Martínez, V. R. (2008). How one school is helping Latino ELL students through AVID. *ACCESS, 14*(1), 8.

Maxwell, L. (2012, August 1). New York becomes second state to recognize biliteracy. *Education Week.* Retrieved from http://blogs.edweek.org/edweek/learning-the-language/2012/08/new_law_makes_new_york_second_.html

National Center for Education Statistics. (2004). *The condition of education, 2004.* Washington, DC: Author. Retrieved from http://nces.ed.gov/ programs/coe

National Center for Education Statistics. (2006). *Profile of undergraduates in U.S. postsecondary education institutions 2003–04 with a special analysis of community college students.* Washington, DC: U.S. Department of Education.

Parrish, T. B., Merickel, A., Perez, M., Linquanti, R., Socias, M., & Spain, A. (2006, January). *Effects of the implementation of Proposition 227 on the education of English learners, K–12: Findings from a five-year evaluation* (Final Report for AB 56 and AB 1116). Washington, DC: American Institutes for Research, and San Francisco, CA: WestEd.

Passel, J. S., & Cohn, D. (2011). *Unauthorized immigrant population: National and state trends.* Washington, DC: Pew Hispanic Center. Retrieved from http://pewhispanic.org/reports/report.php?ReportID=133

Pederson, P. B., & Carey, J. C. (2003). *Multicultural counseling in schools: A practical handbook.* Boston, MA: Allyn & Bacon.

Robertson, K., & Lafond, S. (2008). *Getting ready for college: What ELL students need to know.* Retrieved from http://www.colorincolorado.org/article/28377/

Rodriguez, G. M., & Cruz, L. (2009). The transition to college of English learner and undocumented immigrant students: Resource and policy implications. *The Teachers College Record, 11*(10), 2385–2418.

Roysircar-Sodowsky, G., & Frey, L. L. (2003). Children of immigrants: Their worldviews value conflicts. In P. Pederson & J. C. Carey (Eds.), *Multicultural counseling in schools: A practical handbook* (pp. 61–83). Boston, MA: Allyn & Bacon.

Short, D., & Fitzsimmons, S. (2007). *Double the work: Challenges and solutions to acquiring language and academic literacy for adolescent English language learners.* A report to Carnegie Corporation of New York. Washington, DC: Alliance for Excellent Education.

Swail, W. S., Cabrera, A., Lee, C., & Williams, A. (2005). *Latino students and the educational pipeline: Pathways to the bachelor's degree for Latino students.* Bethesda, MD: Educational Policy Institute.

Thorn, A. R., & Contreras, S. (2005). Counseling Latino immigrants in middle school. *Professional School Counseling, 9*(2), 167–173.

Toffoli, G., & Allan, J. (1992). Group guidance for English as a second language students. *School Counselor, 40*(2), 136–146.

Walqui, A. (2000, June). *Strategies for success: Engaging immigrant students in secondary schools.* Washington, DC: Center for Applied Linguistics. Retrieved from http://www.cal.org/resources/digest/0003strategies.html

Zehr, M. A. (2009). Graduation rates on ELLs a mystery. *Education Week, 29*(3), 20–21. Retrieved from http://www.edweek.org/ew/articles/2009/09/04/03ellgrads.h29.html

Index